THE STORY OF THE NATIONS

BUDDHIST INDIA

THE STORY OF THE NATIONS

BUDDHIST INDIA

BY

T. W. RHYS DAVIDS, LL.D., PH.D.

PROFESSOR OF PALI AND BUDDHIST LITERATURE AT
UNIVERSITY COLLEGE LONDON
AUTHOR OF "BUDDHISM : ITS HISTORY AND
LITERATURE," ETC.

GYAN

Published by

GYAN

Gyan Publishing House
5, Ansari Road
Daryaganj, New Delhi-110002
Phone: 011-47034999, 9811692060
E-mail: books@gyanbooks.com

Distribution Network
gyanbooks.com
India, USA, Canada, UK, Australia, France

ISBN : 978-81-212-2456-7 (HB)
First Published, 1903

2nd Impression 2021

Printed at: Gyan Press, Delhi.

Buddhist India
Author: T. W. Rhys Davids

THE STORY OF THE NATIONS

BUDDHIST INDIA

BY

T. W. RHYS DAVIDS, LL.D., PH.D.

PROFESSOR OF PALI AND BUDDHIST LITERATURE AT UNIVERSITY COLLEGE
LONDON

AUTHOR OF "BUDDHISM: ITS HISTORY AND LITERATURE," ETC.

NEW YORK
G. P. PUTNAM'S SONS
LONDON: T. FISHER UNWIN
1903

FIG. 50.—THE GREAT BUDDHIST TOPE AT SĀNCHI BEFORE RESTORATION.

PREFACE

IN the following work a first attempt has been made to describe ancient India, during the period of Buddhist ascendancy, from the point of view, not so much of the brahmin, as of the rajput. The two points of view naturally differ very much. Priest and noble in India have always worked very well together so long as the question at issue did not touch their own rival claims as against one another. When it did—and it did so especially during the period referred to—the harmony, as will be evident from the following pages, was not so great.

Even to make this attempt at all may be regarded by some as a kind of *lèse majesté*. The brahmin view, in possession of the field when Europeans entered India, has been regarded so long with reverence among us that it seems almost an impertinence now, to put forward the other. "Why not leave well alone? Why resuscitate from the well-deserved oblivion in which, for so many centuries, they have happily lain, the pestilent views of these tiresome people? The puzzles of Indian history have been solved by respectable men in Manu and the Great Bhárata, which have the advantage of being equally true for five centuries before Christ and five centuries after. Shade of Kumárila! what are we coming to when the writings of these fellows—renegade brahmins among them too—are actually taken seriously, and mentioned without a sneer? If by chance they say anything well, that is only because it was better said, before they said it, by the orthodox brahmins, who form, and have always formed, the key-stone of the arch of social life in India. They are the only proper authorities. Why trouble about these miserable heretics?"

Well, I would plead, in extenuation, that I am not the first guilty one. People who found coins and inscriptions have not been deterred from considering them seriously because they fitted very badly with the brahmin theories of caste and history. The matter has gone too far, those theories have been already too much shaken, for any one to hesitate before using every available evidence. The evidence here collected, a good deal of it for the first time, is necessarily imperfect; but it seems often to be so suggestive, to throw so much light on points hitherto dark, or even unsuspected, that the trouble of collecting it is, so far at least, fairly justified. Any words, however, are, I am afraid, of little avail against such sentiments. Wherever they exist the inevitable tendency is to dispute the evidence, and to turn a deaf ear to the conclusions. And there is, perhaps, after all, but one course open, and that is to declare war, always with the deepest respect for those who hold them, against such views. The views are wrong. They are not compatible with historical methods, and the next generation will see them, and the writings that are, unconsciously, perhaps, animated by them, forgotten.

Another point of a similar kind, which ought not in this connection to be left unnoticed, is the prevalent pessimistic idea with regard to historical research in India. There are not only wanting in India such books giving consecutive accounts of the history as we are accustomed to in Europe, but even the names and dates of the principal kings, and battles, and authors, have not been preserved in the literature—that is, of course, in the brahmin literature which is all that has hitherto been available to the student. That is unfortunately true, and some of the special causes which gave rise to this state of things are pointed out below. But the other side of the question should not be ignored. If we compare the materials available for the history, say, of England in the eighth or ninth century A.D. with the materials available for the history of India at the same period the difference is not so very marked. The more proper comparison, moreover, would be made with Europe; for India is a continent of many diverse nations. And in the earlier periods, though we have inherited a connected history of one corner in the south-east of the continent, the records handed down for the rest of Europe are perhaps as slight and as imperfect as those handed down in India. What is of more importance, in Europe, for the earlier periods, all the inherited materials have been made available for the historical student by properly edited and annotated editions, and also by dictionaries, monographs, and helps of all sorts. In India much of the inherited material is still buried in MS., and even so much as is accessible in printed texts has been by no means thoroughly exploited. Scarcely anything, also, has yet been done for the excavation of the ancient historical sites. We might do well to recollect, when we read these complaints of the absence of materials, that the remedy lies, to a very large extent, in our own hands. We might so easily have more. We do not even utilise the materials we have.[1]

To speak out quite plainly, it is not so much the historical data that are lacking, as the men. There are plenty of men able and willing to do the work. But it is accepted tradition in England that all higher education may safely be left to muddle along as it best can, without system, under the not always very wise restrictions of private beneficence. One consequence is that the funds have to be administered in accord with the wishes of benefactors in mediæval times. The old studies, theology, classics, and mathematics, have a superabundance of endowment. The new studies have to struggle on under great poverty and difficulty. There is no chair of Assyriology, for instance, in England. And whereas in Paris and Berlin, in St. Petersburg and Vienna, there are great seminaries of Oriental learning, we see in London the amazing absurdity of unpaid professors obliged to devote to the earning otherwise, of their living,

[1] See on this question the very apposite remarks of Professor Geiger in his monograph *Dīpavaṃsa und Mahāvaṃsa*' (Erlangen, 1901).

the time they ought to give to teaching or research. And throughout England the state of things is nearly as bad. In all England, for instance, there are two chairs of Sanskrit. In Germany the Governments provide more than twenty—just as if Germany's interests in India were more than ten times as great as ours. Meanwhile our Government is supine and placid, confident that, somehow or other, we shall muddle through; and that this is no business of theirs.

This work has been long delayed, and has suffered much from the necessity laid upon me of trying to write it in scraps of time rescued, with difficulty, from the calls of a busy life. I can only hope that other scholars, more able and less hampered than myself, will be able to give to the problems of entrancing interest I have ventured to raise a consideration more worthy of them, in every way, than I have been able to give.

T. W. RHYS-DAVIDS.

October, 1902.

CONTENTS

CHAPTER		PAGE
I.	THE KINGS	1
II.	THE CLANS AND NATIONS	17
III.	THE VILLAGE	42
IV.	SOCIAL GRADES	52
V.	IN THE TOWN	63
VI.	ECONOMIC CONDITIONS	87
VII.	WRITING—THE BEGINNINGS	107
VIII.	WRITING—ITS DEVELOPMENT	121
IX.	LANGUAGE AND LITERATURE.	
	I. GENERAL VIEW	140
X.	LITERATURE.	
	II. THE PĀLI BOOKS	161
XI.	THE JĀTAKA BOOK	189
XII.	RELIGION—ANIMISM	210
XIII.	RELIGION—THE BRAHMIN POSITION	238
XIV.	CHANDRAGUPTA	259

CHAPTER		PAGE
XV.	ASOKA	272
XVI.	KANISHKA	308
	APPENDIX	321
	INDEX	323

ILLUSTRATIONS

PAGE

THE GREAT BUDDHIST TOPE AT SĀNCHI BEFORE RESTORATION . . . . *Frontispiece*

KING PASENADI IN HIS CHARIOT. ABOVE IS THE WHEEL OF THE LAW 9
From the Bharahat Tope. Pl. xiii.

AJĀKASATTU STARTING OUT TO VISIT THE BUDDHA 14

KINGS AND QUEENS WATCHING A PROCESSION AS IT LEAVES A FORT 64
From the Sanchi Tope.

FAÇADE OF MANSION 65
From the Bharahat Tope. Pl. xxxi.

SUDHAMMO, THE MOTE-HALL OF THE GODS . . . 67
From the Bharahat Tope. Pl. xvi.

ANCIENT OPEN-AIR BATH AT ANURĀDHAPURA (NO. 1) 69

ANCIENT OPEN-AIR BATH AT ANURĀDHAPURA (NO. 2) 71

OLD INDIAN SCROLLWORK 72

A ZIGGARAT 73
From Ragozin's "Story of Chaldea."

THE THOUSAND PILLARS. RUINS OF THE FOUNDATION OF THE SEVEN-STORIED GREAT BRAZEN PALACE AT ANURĀDHAPURA 75
From Cave's "Ruined Cities of Ceylon."

PAGE

THE SPLIT ROCK. GAMBLING SCENE FROM THE BHARAHAT TOPE 77

SCROLLWORK ORNAMENT AS USED OUTSIDE HOUSES AND ON TOPES IN BUDDHIST INDIA . . . 79
From the Bharahat Tope. Pl. xliii.

GROUND PLAN AND RESTORATION OF THE BHARAHAT STŪPA 81
From Cunningham's "Stūpa of Bharhut." Pl. iii.

RESTORATION (BY W. SIMPSON) OF THE AHIN POSH TOPE 83
From the Proceedings of the R. I. B. A.

A STŪPA AS CARVED ON THE BAS-RELIEFS . . . 84
From Cunningham's "Stūpa of Bharhut." Pl. xxxi.

THE JETAVANA DĀGABA 85

SPECIMENS OF ANCIENT JEWELRY FOUND IN THE SĀKIYA TOPE 89
From J. R. A. S., 1898.

OLD INDIAN GIRDLE OF JEWELS 91
From the figure of Sirimā Devatā on the Bharahat Tope. Pl. li.

OLD INDIAN NECKLACES 92

OLD INDIAN LOCKET. OLD INDIAN EARRING. OLD INDIAN LOCKET 93
Size of original.

MEDALLION ON THE BHARAHAT TOPE 95
Pl. xxiv. Fig. 3.

ANCIENT INDIAN HEAD-DRESS 97
From a medallion on the Bharahat Tope. Pl. xxiv. Fig. 2.

ANĀTHA PIṆḌIKA'S GIFT OF THE JETAVANA PARK . 99
From the Bharahat Tope. Pl. lxvii.

ANCIENT INDIAN COINS 106

ERAN COINS 115

PAGE

LEAF OF MS. FROM THE GOSINGA VIHĀRA OF AN OLD BUDDHIST ANTHOLOGY 122

DR. HOEY'S BRICK TABLET, WITH BUDDHIST SUTTA INSCRIBED ON IT 123

THE COPPER PLATE FROM TAKKA-SILĀ . . . 125
"Epigraphia Indica," vol. iv.

THE MAUNG-GON GOLD PLATE 126
From "Epigraphia Indica," vol. v., p. 101.

LEAF FROM THE BOWER MS. BIRCH BARK CUT TO IMITATE PALM LEAVES, WITH HOLES FOR STRINGS TO TIE THEM UP WITH 127

THE INSCRIBED VASE FROM THE SĀKIYA TOPE . 129

THE PEPPÉ VASES 131
Found by Mr. Peppé in the Sākiya Tope.

RUINS OF THE SĀKIYA TOPE, PUT UP BY HIS RELATIVES OVER THEIR PORTION OF THE ASHES FROM THE FUNERAL PYRE OF THE BUDDHA . 133

FRAGMENT OF THE THIRTEENTH ROCK EDICT OF ASOKA, DISCOVERED BY PROFESSOR RHYS-DAVIDS AT GIRNAR 135

THE BANYAN DEER JĀTAKA STORY 193
Three episodes on one bas-relief.

SIRIMĀ DEVATĀ 216
From the Bharahat Tope. Pl. xxiii.

MODERN IMAGE OF ŚRĪ AS CONSORT VISHṆU . 218
From Burgess's "Cave Temples of India," p. 524.

HINDOO GODDESS OF LUCK 221

VESSAVAṆA KUVERA, KING OF THE YAKSHAS, AND REGENT OF THE NORTH 222
From the Bharahat Tope. Pl. xxii.

PAGE

CHAKAVĀKA, KING OF THE NĀGAS 222
From Cunningham's "Stūpa of Bharhut." Pl. xxi. Fig. 3.

NĀGA MERMAIDS IN WATER 223
From Burgess and Grünwedel's "Buddhist Art in India."

SEATED NĀGA; BACK VIEW 225
From a fresco in Cave 11 at Ajanta.

ELEPHANTS BEFORE THE WISDOM TREE . . . 228
From Cunningham's "Stūpa of Bharhut." Pl. xxx.

THE WISDOM TREE OF KASSAPA, THE BUDDHA . 229
From Cunningham's "Stūpa of Bharhut." Pl. xxx.

THE BUDDHA PREACHING TO NĀGAS DWELLING IN A SACRED TREE 233
From a Buddhist carving at Takt-i-bahi. J. R. A. S., 1899.

DETAILS OF THE SCULPTURES ON THE GATES OF SĀNCHI TOPE 279

DETAILS ON THE SCULPTURES ON THE GATES OF SĀNCHI TOPE 281

REAR VIEW OF THE NORTHERN GATE OF SĀNCHI TOPE 283

JAIN TEMPLE AT KHUJARAO 285

THE GREAT BUDDHIST TOPE AT SĀNCHI BEFORE RESTORATION 287

SĀNCHI TOPE. A GENERAL VIEW FROM THE SOUTH. 289

EASTERN GATE OF SĀNCHI TOPE 291

REAR VIEW OF THE EASTERN GATE OF SĀNCHI TOPE 293

PAGE

DETAILS FROM EASTERN GATE OF SĀNCHI TOPE . 301

DETAILS FROM EASTERN GATE OF SĀNCHI TOPE . 303

MAP OF THE KIṄGDOM OF ASOKA AS DESCRIBED IN THE INSCRIPTIONS AND IN THE ENGRAVED EDICTS 320

BUDDHIST INDIA

CHAPTER I

THE KINGS

WHEN Buddhism arose there was no paramount sovereign in India. The kingly power was not, of course, unknown. There had been kings in the valley of the Ganges for centuries, long before Buddhism, and the time was fast approaching when the whole of India would be under the sway of monarchical governments. In those parts of India which came very early under the influence of Buddhism, we find, besides a still surviving number of small aristocratic republics, four kingdoms of considerable extent and power. Besides, there were a dozen or more of smaller kingdoms, like the German dutchies or the seven provinces into which England was divided in the time of the Heptarchy. No one of these was of much political importance. And the tendency towards the gradual absorption of these domains, and also of the republics, into the neighbouring kingdoms, was already in full force. The evidence at present available is not sufficient to give us an exact idea either of the extent of country, or of the number of the population, under the one or the other form of government; nor has any attempt been so far made to trace the history of political institutions in India before the rise of Buddhism. We can do no more, then, than state the fact — most interesting from the comparative point of view — that the earliest Buddhist records reveal the survival, side by side with more or less powerful monarchies, of republics with either complete or modified independence.

It is significant that this important factor in the social condition of India in the sixth and seventh centuries B. C. has remained hitherto unnoticed by scholars either in Europe or in India. They have relied for their information about the Indian peoples too exclusively on the brahmin[1] books. And these, partly because of the natural antipathy felt by the priests towards the free republics, partly because of the later date of most of the extant priestly literature, and especially of the law books, ignore the real facts. They convey the impression that the only recognised, and in fact universally prevalent, form of government was that of kings under the guidance and tutelage of priests. But the Buddhist records, amply confirmed in these respects by the somewhat later Jain ones, leave no doubt upon the point.

[1] This word, always pronounced, and till lately always spelt, in England, with an *i*, is spelt in both Sanskrit and Pali, *brāhmaṇa*. It seems to me a pity to attempt to introduce a spelling, *brahman*, which is neither English nor Indian.

As regards the monarchies, the four referred to above as then of importance are as follows:

1. The kingdom of Magadha, with its capital at Rājagaha (afterwards at Pāṭaliputta), reigned over at first by King Bimbisāra and afterwards by his son Ajātasattu.

2. To the north-west there was the kingdom of Kosala—the Northern Kosala—with its capital at Sāvatthi, ruled over at first by King Pasenadi and afterwards by his son Viḍūḍabha.

3. Southwards from Kosala was the kingdom of the Vamsas or Vatsas, with their capital at Kosambi on the Jumna, reigned over by King Udena, the son of Parantapa.

4. And still farther south lay the kingdom of Avanti, with its capital Ujjeni, reigned over by King Pajjota.

The royal families of these kingdoms were united by matrimonial alliances; and were also, not seldom in consequence of those very alliances, from time to time at war. Thus Pasenadi's sister, the Kosala Devī, was the wife of Bimbisāra, King of Magadha. When Ajātasattu, Bimbisāra's son by another wife (the Videha lady from Mithilā), put his father Bimbisāra to death, the Kosala Devī died of grief. Pasenadi then confiscated that township of Kāsi, the revenues of which had been granted to the Kosala Devī as pin money. Angered at this, Ajātasattu declared war against his aged uncle.[1] At first victory inclined to Ajātasattu. But in the fourth campaign he was taken prisoner, and not released until

[1] Properly "brother of his stepmother."

he had relinquished his claim. Thereupon Pasenadi not only gave him his daughter Vajirā in marriage, but actually conferred upon her, as a wedding gift, the very village in Kāsi in dispute. Three years afterwards Pasenadi's son Viḍūḍabha revolted against his father, who was then at Ulumba in the Sākiya country. The latter fled to Rājagaha to ask Ajātasattu for aid; but was taken ill and died outside the city gates.[1] We shall hear farther on how both Viḍūḍabha, and his brother-in-law Ajātasattu, were subsequently in conflict with the adjoining republican confederacies, the former with the Sākiyans, the latter with the Vajjians of Vesāli.

The royal families of Kosambi and Avanti were also united by marriage. The commentary on verses 21–23 of the Dhammapada gives a long and romantic story of the way in which Vāsula-dattā, the daughter of King Pajjota of Avanti, became the wife, or rather one of the three wives, of King Udena of Kosambi. The legend runs that Pajjota (whose fierce and unscrupulous character is there painted in terms confirmed by one of our oldest authorities[2]) inquired once of his courtiers whether there was any king whose glory was greater than his own. And when he was straightway told that Udena of Kosambi surpassed him, he at once determined to attack him. Being then advised that an open campaign would be certainly disastrous, but that an ambush—the more easy as Udena would go anywhere to capture a fine elephant—might

[1] S. 1. 83; Jāt. 2. 403, 4. 343; Avad. Śat. 51.

[2] *Mahā Vagga of the Vinaya*, viii. 1. 23, and following.

succeed, he had an elephant made of wood and deftly painted, concealed in it sixty warriors, set it up in a defile near the boundary, and had Udena informed by spies that a glorious elephant, the like of which had never been seen, was to be found in the frontier forest. Udena took the bait, plunged into the defile in pursuit of the prize, became separated from his retinue, and was taken prisoner.

Now Udena knew a charm of wonderful power over the hearts of elephants. Pajjota offered him his life and freedom if he would tell it.

"Very well," was the reply, "I will teach it you if you pay me the salutation due to a teacher."

"Pay salutation to you — never!"

"Then neither do I tell you my charm."

"In that case I must order you to execution."

"Do as you like! Of my body you are lord. But not of my mind."

Then Pajjota bethought him that after all no one else knew the charm, and he asked Udena if he would teach it to someone else who would salute him. And being answered yes, he told his daughter that there was a dwarf who knew a charm; that she was to learn it of that dwarf; and then tell it to him, the King. And to Udena he said that a hunchback woman would salute him from behind a curtain, and that he had to teach her the charm, standing the while himself outside the curtain. So cunning was the King to bar their friendship. But when the prisoner day after day rehearsed the charm, and his unseen pupil was slow to catch it up and to repeat it, Udena at last one day called out impatiently, "Say it so, you hunchback! How thick lipped you must be, and heavy jawed!"

Then she, angered, rejoined: "What do you mean, you wretched dwarf, to call such as I am hunchback?"

And he pulled the corner of the curtain to see, and asked her who she was, and the trick was discovered, and he went inside, and there was no more talk that day of learning charms, or of repeating lessons.

And they laid a counter-plot. And she told her father that a condition precedent to the right learning of the charm was the possession of a certain potent herb picked under a certain conjunction of the stars, and they must have the right of exit, and the use of his famous elephant. And her wish was granted. Then one day, when her father was away on a pleasure jaunt, Udena put her on the elephant, and taking also money, and gold-dust in bags of leather, set forth.

But men told Pajjota the King; and he, angry and suspecting, sent a force in rapid pursuit. Then Udena emptied the bag of coins. And the pursuers waiting to gather them up, the fugitives forged ahead. When the pursuers again gained on them, Udena let loose a bagful of gold-dust. Again the pursuers delayed. And as they once more gained on the fugitives, lo! the frontier fortress, and Udena's own troops coming out to meet their lord! Then the pursuers drew back; and Udena and Vāsula-dattā entered, in safety and in triumph, into the city; and with due pomp and ceremony she was anointed as his Queen.

So far the legend; and it has a familiar sound as if echoes of two of our classical tales had been confused in India. No one would take it for sober history. It is probably only a famous and popular story retold of well-known characters. And when a learned scholar summarises it thus: "Udena eloped with her on an elephant, leaving behind him a bag full of gold in order to prevent a prosecution"[1]—we see how easily a very slight change in expression may, in retelling, have altered the very gist of the tale. But it is sufficient evidence that, when the tradition arose, King Pajjota of Avanti and King Udena of Kosambi were believed to have been contemporary rulers of adjoining kingdoms, and to have been connected by marriage and engaged in war.

We hear a good deal else about this Udena, King of the Vacchas or Vaṃsas of Kosambi. Formerly, in a fit of drunken rage, at a picnic, because his women folk left him, when he was sleeping, to listen to a religious discourse by Piṇḍola (a highly respected and famous member of the Buddhist Order), he had had Piṇḍola tortured by having a nest of brown ants tied to him.[2] Long afterwards the King professed himself an adherent of the Buddha's in consequence of a conversation he had with this same man Piṇḍola, on the subject of self-restraint.[3] At another picnic the women's pavilion was burnt, with his Queen, Sāmavatī, and many of her attendants.[4] His father's name was Parantapa; and he had a son named Bodhi,

[1] *J. P. T. S.*, 1888, *sub voce.*

[2] Jāt. 4. 375.

[3] S. 4. 110.

[4] Ud. 7. 10 = Divy, 533.

after whom one of the Suttantas is named [1] and concerning whom other details are given.[2] But Udena survived the Buddha,[3] and we are not informed whether Bodhi did, or did not, succeed him on the throne.

Pasenadi, the King of Kosala, is described as a very different character. The whole of the Third Saṃyutta, consisting of twenty-five anecdotes, each with a moral bias, is devoted to him. And there are about an equal number of references to him in other parts of the literature. Educated at the celebrated seat of learning, Takkasilā, in the extreme north-west, he was placed, on his return, by his father, Mahā Kosala, upon the throne.[4] As a sovereign he showed himself zealous in his administrative duties, and addicted to the companionship of the good.[5] And he extended his favour, in full accord with the well-known Indian toleration, to the religious of all schools of thought alike.[6] This liberality of thought and conduct was only strengthened when, early in the new movement, he proclaimed himself an adherent, in a special sense, of the Buddha's.[7] This was in consequence of a talk he had had with the Buddha himself. The King had asked him how he, being so young, as compared with other already well-known teachers, could claim an insight beyond theirs. The reply simply was that no "religieux" should be despised because of his youth. Who would show disrespect to a prince, or to a venomous serpent, or to

[1] M. No. 85. [2] Vin. 2. 127, 4. 198, 199; Jāt. 3. 157.
[3] P. V. A. 141. [4] Dhp. A. 211. [5] S. 1. 83.
[6] D. 87; Ud. 2. 6; S. 1. 75. [7] S. 1. 70.

FIG. I—KING PASENADI IN HIS CHARIOT. ABOVE IS THE WHEEL OF THE LAW.

[From the Bharahat Tope. Pl. xiii.]

a fire, merely because it was young? It was the nature of the doctrine, not the personal pecularities of the teacher, that was the test.

Sumanā, the King's aunt, sister of his father, Mahā Kosala, was present at this conversation, and made up her mind to enter the Order, but delayed doing so in order to nurse an aged relative. The delay was long. But on the death of the old lady, Sumanā, then old herself, did enter the Order, and became an Arahat, and is one of the Buddhist ladies whose poems are preserved in the Therī Gāthā. The aged relative was Pasenadi's grandmother; so that we have four generations of this family brought before us.[1]

A comparison between Dīgha I. 87 and Divyāvadāna 620—where the same action is attributed in the older book to King Pasenadi and in the younger to King Agnidatta—makes it highly probable that Pasenadi (used as a designation for several kings) is in reality an official epithet, and that the King's real personal name was Agnidatta.

Among the subjects chosen for the bas-reliefs on the Bharahat tope, in the third century B.C., is one representing Pasenadi issuing forth on his chariot, drawn by four horses with their tails and manes elaborately plaited, and attended by three servants. Above him is figured the Wheel of the Law, the symbol of the new teaching of which the King of Kosala was so devoted a supporter.

It is stated that is was from the desire to associate himself by marriage with the Buddha's family that

[1] Thag. A. 22; comp. S. I. 97; Vin. 2. 169; Jāt. 4. 146.

Pasenadi asked for one of the daughters of the Sākiya chiefs as his wife. The Sākiyas discussed the proposition in their Mote Hall, and held it beneath the dignity of their clan. But they sent him a girl named Vāsabha Khattiyā, the daughter, by a slave girl, of one of their leading chiefs. By her Pasenadi had the son, Viḍūḍabha, mentioned above. And it was in consequence of the anger kindled in Viḍūḍabha's heart at the discovery of the fraud that, having determined to wreak his vengeance on the Sākiyas, he, on coming to the throne, invaded their country, took their city, and put to death a great number of the members of the clan, without distinction of age or sex. The details of the story have not been found as yet in our oldest records.[1] But the main circumstance of the war against the clan is very early alluded to, and is no doubt a historical fact. It is said to have preceded only by a year or two the death of the Buddha himself.

The beginning of this story, on the other hand, seems very forced. Would a family of patricians in one of the Greek republics have considered a marriage of one of their daughters to a neighbouring tyrant beneath their dignity? And in the present case the tyrant in question was the acknowledged suzerain of the clan.[2] The Sākiyas may have considered the royal family of Kosala of inferior birth to themselves. There is mention, in several passages, of the pride of the Sākiyas.[3] But, even so,

[1] But see Dhp. A. 216, foll.; Jāt. 4. 145, foll.

[2] Pabbajjā Sutta, verse 18 (S. N. 122).

[3] For instance, D. 1. 90, 91; Vin. 2. 183; J. 1. 889, 4. 145.

we cannot see, in the present state of our knowledge, why they should object. We know that the daughter of one of the chiefs of a neighbouring clan, equally free and equally proud, the Licchavis of Vesāli, was married to Bimbisāra, king of Magadha.[1] It is, furthermore, almost certain that the royal family at Sāvatthi was simply one of the patrician families who had managed to secure hereditary consulship in the Kosala clan. For the chiefs among the Kosalas, apart from the royal family, and even the ordinary clansmen (the *kula-puttā*), are designated by the very term (*rājāno*, kings), which is applied to the chiefs and clansmen of those tribes which had still remained aristocratic republics.[2] And it is precisely in a very natural tendency to exaggerate the importance of the families of their respective founders that the later records, both of the Jains and of the Buddhists, differ from the earlier ones. It is scarcely probable, therefore, that the actual originating cause of Viḍūḍabha's invasion of the Sākiya territory was exactly as set out above. He may have used the arrogance of the Sākiyas, perhaps, as a pretext. But the real reasons which induced Viḍūḍabha to attack and conquer his relatives, the Sākiyas, were, most likely, the same sort of political motives which later on induced his cousin, Ajātasattu of Magadha, to attack and conquer *his* relatives, the Licchavis of Vesāli.

We hear already of Ajātasattu's intention to attack them in the opening sections of the *Book of*

[1] See the genealogical table in Jacobi's *Jaina Sutras*, I, xv.

[2] Sum. 239.

the Great Decease,[1] and the Buddha is represented[2] as making the not very difficult forecast that eventually, when the Licchavis had been weakened by luxury, he would be able to carry out this intention. But it was not till more than three years afterwards that, having succeeded, by the treachery of the brahmin Vassakāra, in sowing dissension among the leading families of Vesāli, he swooped down upon the place with an overwhelming force, and completely destroyed it.

We are also told that Ajātasattu fortified his capital, Rājagaha, in expectation of an attack about to be made by King Pajjota of Ujjeni.[3] It would be most interesting to know whether the attack was ever made, and what measure of success it had. We know that afterwards, in the fourth century B.C., Ujjeni had become subject to Magadha, and that Asoka, when a young man, was appointed governor of Ujjeni. But we know nothing else of the intermediate stages which led to this result.

About nine or ten years before the Buddha's death, Devadatta, his first cousin, who had long previously joined the Order, created a schism in the community. We hear of Ajātasattu, then the Crown Prince, as the principal supporter of this Devadatta, the quondam disciple and bitter foe of the Buddha, who is the Judas Iscariot of the Buddhist story.[4]

[1] Translated in my *Buddhist Suttas*. The name there is Vajjians. But that the Licchavis were a sub-clan of the Vajjians is clear from A. 4. 16.

[2] S. 2. 268.

[3] M. 3. 7.

[4] S. 2. 242; *Vinaya Texts*, 3. 238–265; Sum. 138, etc.

About the same time Bimbisāra, the King, handed over the reins of government to the Prince. But it

FIG. 2.—AJĀTASATTU STARTING OUT TO VISIT THE BUDDHA.

was not long before Devadatta incited him, in order to make quite sure, to slay the King. And Ajātasattu carried out this idea in the eighth year before the Buddha's death, by starving his father slowly to death.

Once, subsequently, when remorse had fastened upon him, we hear of his going, with a great retinue, to the Buddha and inquiring of him what were the fruits, visible in this present life, of becoming a member of a religious order.[1] An illustration of the King saluting the Buddha on this occasion is the subject of one of the bas-reliefs on the Bharhut Tope.[2] As usual the Buddha himself is not delineated. Only his footprints are shown.

At the close of the discourse the King is stated to have openly taken the Buddha as his guide in future, and to have given expression to the remorse he felt at the murder of his father. But it is also distinctly stated that he was not converted. There is no evidence that he really, after the moment when his heart was touched, continued to follow the Buddha's teaching. He never, so far as we know, waited again either upon the Buddha, or upon any member of the Order, to discuss ethical matters. And we hear of no material support given by him to the Order during the Buddha's lifetime.

We are told, however, that, after the Buddha's death, he asked (on the ground that he, like the Buddha, was a Kshatriya) for a portion of the relics; that he obtained them; and built a *stupa* or burial-mound over them.[3] And though the oldest au-

[1] The famous Suttanta, in which this conversation is set out,—the Sāmañña Phala,—is translated in full in my *Dialogues of the Buddha*.

[2] Cunningham, *Stūpa of Bharhut*, Pl. xvi., Fig. 3.

[3] *Book of the Great Decease*, chap. vi.

thority says nothing about it, younger works state that on the convocation of the First Council at Rājagaha, shortly after the decease, it was the King who provided and prepared the hall at the entrance to the Sattapaṇṇi cave, where the rehearsal of the doctrine took place.[1] He may well have thus showed favour to the Buddhists without at all belonging to their party. He would only, in so doing, be following the usual habit so characteristic of Indian monarchs, of patronage towards all schools.

Mention is made occasionally and incidentally of other kings—such as Avanti-putta, King of the Sūrasenas;[2] and the Eleyya of A. 2. 188, who, together with his courtiers, was a follower and supporter of Uddaka, the son and pupil of Rāma, and the teacher of Gotama. But the above four are the only ones of whom we have accounts in any detail.

[1] See, for instance, M. B. V. 89.

[2] M. 2. 83.

CHAPTER II

THE CLANS AND NATIONS

IT is much the same with the clans. We have a good deal of information, which is, however, at the best only fragmentary, about three or four of them. Of the rest we have little more than the bare names.

More details are given, very naturally, of the Sākiya clan than of the others. The general position of their country is intimated by the distances given from other places.[1] It must have been just on the border of Nepalese and English territory, as is now finally settled by the recent discoveries of the tope or burial-mound put up by the Sākiyas over the portion they retained of the relics from the Buddha's funeral pyre, and of Asoka's inscription, *in situ*, recording his visit to the Lumbini garden in which the Buddha was born.[2] Which of the numerous ruins in the immediate vicinity

[1] 60 yojanas = 450 miles, from Rājagaha; 50 yojanas = 375 miles, from Vesāli; 6 or 7 yojanas = 50 or 60 miles, from Sāvatthi; and so on. Compare the passages quoted in Rh. D., *Ancient Coins and Measures of Ceylon*, p. 16.

[2] *J. R. A. S.* 1897, 618, and 1898, 588.

2

of these discoveries are those of Kapilavastu, the chief town of the clan, and which are the remains of the other townships belonging to them, will be one of the questions to be solved by future exploration.[1] Names of such townships mentioned in the most ancient texts are Cātumā, Sāmagāma, Khomadussa, Silāvatī, Metalupa, Ulumpa, Sakkara, and Devadaha.

It was at the last-mentioned place that the mother of the Buddha was born. And the name of her father is expressly given as Añjana the Sākiyan.[2] When, therefore, we find in much later records the statements that she was of Koliyan family; and that Prince Devadaha, after whom the town was so named, was a Koliyan chief, the explanation may well be that the Koliyans were a sort of subordinate subdivision of the Sākiya clan.

The existence of so considerable a number of market towns implies, in an agricultural community, a rather extensive territory. Buddhaghosa has preserved for us an old tradition that the Buddha had eighty thousand families of relatives on the father's side and the same on the mother's side.[3] Allowing six or seven to a family, including the dependents, this would make a total of about a million persons in the Sākiya territory. And though the figure is purely traditional, and at best a round

[1] The old Kapilavastu was probably at Tilaura Kot. But Mr. Peppé's important discoveries at the Sākiya Tope may be on the site of a new Kapilavastu, built after the old city was destroyed by Viḍūḍabha (see above, p. 11).

[2] Apadāna, quoted in Therig. Cy. p. 152.

[3] See *Dialogues of the Buddha*, i. 147, note.

number (and not uninfluenced by the mystic value attached to it), it is, perhaps, not so very far from what we might expect.

The administrative and judicial business of the clan was carried out in public assembly, at which young and old were alike present, in their common Mote Hall (*santhāgāra*) at Kapilavastu. It was at such a parliament, or palaver, that King Pasenadi's proposition (above, p. 11) was discussed. When Ambaṭṭha goes to Kapilavastu on business, he goes to the Mote Hall where the Sākiyas were then in session.[1] And it is to the Mote Hall of the Mallas that Ānanda goes to announce the death of the Buddha, they being then in session there to consider that very matter.[2]

A single chief—how, and for what period chosen, we do not know—was elected as office-holder, presiding over the sessions, and, if no sessions were sitting, over the State. He bore the title of *rāja*, which must have meant something like the Roman consul, or the Greek archōn. We hear nowhere of such a triumvirate as bore corresponding office among the Licchavis, nor of such acts of kingly sovereignty as are ascribed to the real kings mentioned above. But we hear at one time[3] that Bhaddiya, a young cousin of the Buddha's, was the rāja; and in another passage, Suddhodana, the Buddha's father (who is elsewhere spoken of as a simple citizen, Suddhodana the Sākiyan), is called the rāja.

A new Mote Hall, built at Kapilavastu, was

[1] Ambaṭṭha Suttanta, translated in my *Dialogues of the Buddha*, i. 113.

[2] M. P. S. 6. 23.

[3] Vin. 2. 181.

finished whilst the Buddha was staying at the Nigrodhārāma (the pleasaunce under the Banyan Grove) in the Great Wood (the Mahāvana) near by. There was a residence there, provided by the community, for recluses of all schools. Gotama was asked to inaugurate the new hall, and he did so by a series of ethical discourses, lasting through the night, delivered by himself, Ānanda, and Moggallana. They are preserved for us in full at M. 1. 353, foll., and S. 4. 182, foll.

Besides this Mote Hall at the principal town we hear of others at some of the other towns above referred to. And no doubt all the more important places had such a hall, or pavilion, covered with a roof, but with no walls, in which to conduct their business. And the local affairs of each village were carried on in open assembly of the householders, held in the groves which, then as now, formed so distinctive a feature of each village in the long and level alluvial plain. It was no doubt in this plain, stretching about fifty miles from east to west, and thirty or forty miles to the southward from the foot of Himalaya Hills, that the majority of the clan were resident.

The clan subsisted on the produce of their rice-fields and their cattle. The villages were grouped round the rice-fields, and the cattle wandered through the outlying forest, over which the peasantry, all Sākiyas by birth, had rights of common. There were artisans, probably not Sākiyas, in each village; and men of certain special trades of a higher standing; the carpenters, smiths, and potters for instance, had villages of their own. So also had the brahmins, whose services were in request at every domestic event. Khomadussa, for instance, was a brahmin settlement. There were a few shops in the bazaars, but we do not hear of any merchants and bankers such as are mentioned as dwelling at the great capitals of the adjoining kingdoms. The villages were separated one from another by forest jungle, the remains of the Great Wood (the Mahā Vana), portions of which are so frequently mentioned as still surviving throughout the clanships, and which must originally (not so very long, probably, before the time under discussion) have stretched over practically the whole level country between the foot of the mountains and the Great River, the Ganges. After the destruction of the clans by the neighbouring monarchies this jungle again spread over the country. From the fourth century onwards, down to our own days, the forest covered over the remains of the ancient civilisation.

This jungle was infested from time to time by robbers, sometimes runaway slaves.[1] But we hear of no crime, and there was not probably very much, in the villages themselves—each of them a tiny self-governed republic. The Koliyan central authorities were served by a special body of peons, or police, distinguished, as by a kind of uniform, from which they took their name, by a special headdress. These particular men had a bad reputation for extortion and violence.[2] The Mallas had similar officials,[3] and it is not improbable that each of the clans had a somewhat similar set of subordinate servants.

[1] Vin. 4. 81. [2] S. 4. 341. [3] D. 2. 159, 161.

A late tradition tells us how the criminal law was administered in the adjoining powerful confederate clan of the Vajjians, by a succession of regularly appointed officers,—"Justices, lawyers, rehearsers of the law-maxims, the council of representatives of the eight clans, the general, the vice-consul, and the consul himself." Each of these could acquit the accused. But if they considered him guilty, each had to refer the case to the next in order above them, the consul finally awarding the penalty according to the Book of Precedents. We hear of no such intermediate officials in the smaller clans; and even among the Vajjians (who, by the by, are *all* called "rājas" in this passage), it is not likely that so complicated a procedure was actually followed.[1] But a book of legal precedents is referred to elsewhere,[2] and tables of the law also.[3] It is therefore not improbable that written notes on the subject were actually in use.

The names of other clans, besides the Sākiyas, are:

2. The Bhaggas of Suṃsumāra Hill.
3. The Bulis of Allakappa.
4. Kālāmas of Kesaputta.
5. The Koliyas of Rāma-gāma.
6. The Mallas of Kusinārā.
7. The Mallas of Pāvā.
8. The Moriyas of Pipphalivana.
9. The Videhas of Mithilā. } = The Vajjians.
10. The Licchavis of Vesāli. }

[1] James Alwis, *Introduction to Pāli Grammar*, p. 99; and Geo. Turnour, *J.B.A.S.* vii. 991.

[2] Jāt. 3. 292.

[3] Jāt. 5. 125.

There are several other names of tribes of which it is not yet known whether they were clans or under monarchical government. We have only one instance of any tribe, once under a monarchy, reverting to the independent state. And whenever the supreme power in a clan became hereditary, the result seems always to have been an absolute monarchy, without legal limitations of any kind.

The political divisions of India at or shortly before the time when Buddhism arose are well exemplified by the stock list of the Sixteen Great Countries, the Sixteen Powers, which is found in several places in the books.[1] It is interesting to notice that the names are names, not of countries, but of peoples, as we might say Italians or Turks. This shows that the main idea in the minds of those who drew up, or used, this old list was still tribal and not geographical. The list is as follows:

1. Angā	9. Kurū
2. Magadhā	10. Pañcālā
3. Kāsī	11. Macchā
4. Kosalā	12. Sūrasenā
5. Vajjī	13. Assakā
6. Mallā	14. Avantī
7. Cetī	15. Gandhārā
8. Vaṃsā	16. Kambojā

1. The Aṇgas dwelt in the country to the east of Magadha, having their capital at Champā, near the

[1] *E.g.*, Aṅguttara, 1. 213; 4. 252, 256, 260; *Vinaya Texts*, 2. 146.

modern Bhagalpur. Its boundaries are unknown. In the Buddha's time it was subject to Magadha, and we never hear of its having regained independence. But in former times[1] it was independent, and there are traditions of wars between these neighbouring countries. The Anga rāja in the Buddha's time was simply a wealthy nobleman, and we only know of him as the grantor of a pension to a particular brahmin.[2]

2. The Magadhas, as is well known, occupied the district now called Behar. It was probably then bounded to the north by the Ganges, to the east by the river Champā, on the south by the Vindhya Mountains, and on the west by the river Soṇa. In the Buddha's time (that is, inclusive of Anga) it is said to have had eighty thousand villages[3] and to have been three hundred leagues (about twenty-three hundred miles) in circumference.[4]

3. The Kāsis are of course the people settled in the district round Benares. In the time of the Buddha this famous old kingdom of the Bhāratas had fallen to so low a political level that the revenues of the township had become a bone of contension between Kosala and Magadha, and the kingdom itself was incorporated into Kosala. Its mention in this list is historically important, as we must conclude that the memory of it as an independent state was still fresh in men's minds. This is confirmed by the very frequent mention of it as such in the Jātakas, where it is said to have been over two

[1] J. v. 316, vi. 271.
[2] M. 2. 163.
[3] Vin. i. 179.
[4] Sum. 148.

thousand miles in circuit.[1] But it never regained independence; and its boundaries are unknown.

4. The Kosalas were the ruling clan in the kingdom whose capital was Sāvatthi, in what is now Nepal, seventy miles north-west of the modern Gorakhpur. It included Benares and Sāketa; and probably had the Ganges for its southern boundary, the Gandhak for its eastern boundary, and the mountains for its northern boundary. The Sākiyas already acknowledged, in the seventh century B.C., the suzerainty of Kosala.

It was the rapid rise of this kingdom of Kosala, and the inevitable struggle in the immediate future between it and Magadha, which was the leading point in the politics of the Buddha's time. These hardy mountaineers had swept into their net all the tribes between the mountains and the Ganges. Their progress was arrested on the east by the free clans. And the struggle between Kosala and Magadha for the paramount power in all India was, in fact, probably decided when the powerful confederation of the Licchavis became arrayed on the side of Magadha. Several successful invasions of Kāsī by the Kosalans under their kings, Vanka, Dabbasena, and Kaṃsa, are referred to a date before the Buddha's time. And the final conquest would seem to be ascribed to Kaṃsa, as the epithet "Conqueror-of-Benares" is a standing addition to his name.[2]

5. The Vajjians included eight confederate clans,

[1] Jāt. 4. 442, 5. 41.

[2] Vin. 1. 342; Jāt. 1. 262, 2. 403, 3. 13, 168, 211, 5. 112.

of whom the Licchavis and the Videhans were the most important. It is very interesting to notice that while tradition makes Videha a kingdom in earlier times, it describes it in the Buddha's time as a republic. Its size, as a separate kingdom, is said to have been three hundred leagues (about twenty-three hundred miles) in circumference.[1] Its capital, Mithilā, was about thirty-five miles north-west from Vesāli, the capital of the Licchavis. There it was that the great King Janaka ruled a little while before the rise of Buddhism.[2] And it is probable that the modern town of Janak-pur preserves in its name a memory of this famous rajput scholar and philosopher of olden time.

6. The Mallas of Kusinārā and Pāvā were also independent clans, whose territory, if we may trust the Chinese pilgrims, was on the mountain slopes to the east of the Sākiya land, and to the north of the Vajjian confederation. But some would place it south of the Sākiyas and east of the Vajjians.

7. The Cetis were probably the same tribe as that called Ceḍi in older documents, and had two distinct settlements. One, probably the older, was in the mountains, in what is now called Nepal.[3] The other, probably a later colony, was near Kosambi to the east[4] and has been even confused with the land of the Vaṃsā, from which this list makes them distinct.[5]

[1] Jāt. 3. 365, 4. 316.

[2] Satap. Brāh. xi. 6. 2, 1, etc.; Jāt. 6. 30–68, etc.

[3] Jāt. 5. 514, 518.

[4] Vin. 1. 108; Jāt. 1. 360; Divy. 184–191.

[5] Baden-Powell in the *J. R. A. S.*, 1898, p. 321.

8. Vaṃsā is the country of the Vacchas, of which Kosambi, properly only the name of the capital, is the more familiar name. It lay immediately to the north of Avanti, and along the banks of the Jumna.

9. The Kurus occupied the country of which Indraprastha, close to the modern Delhi, was the capital; and had the Panchālas to the east, and the Matsyas to the south. Tradition gives the kingdom a circumference of two thousand miles.[1] They had very little political importance in the Buddha's time. It was at Kammāssa-dhamma in the Kuru country that several of the most important Suttantas—the Mahā Satipaṭṭhāna, for instance, and the Mahā Nidāna—were delivered. And Raṭṭhapāla was a Kuru noble.[2]

10. The two Pañcālas occupied the country to the east of the Kurus, between the mountains and the Ganges. Their capitals were Kampilla and Kanoj.

11. The Macchas, or Matsyas, were to the south of the Kurus and west of the Jumna, which separated them from the Southern Pañcālas.

12. The Sūrasenas, whose capital was Madhurā, were immediately south-west of the Macchas, and west of the Jumna.

13. The Assakas had, in the Buddha's time, a settlement on the banks of the Godhāvari.[3] Their capital was Potana, or Potali.[4] The country is mentioned with Avanti in the same way as Anga is with Magadha,[5] and its position on this list, between Sūrasena and Avanti, makes it probable that, when

[1] Jāt. 5. 57, 484. [2] M. 2. 55. [3] S. N. 977.
[4] Jāt. 3. 3; D. 2. 235. [5] Jāt. 5. 319.

the list was drawn up, its position was immediately north-west of Avanti. In that case the settlement on the Godhāvari was a later colony; and this is confirmed by the fact that there is no mention of Potana (or Potali) there. The name of the tribe is also ambiguous. Sanskrit authors speak both of Aśmakā and of Aśvakā. Each of these would be Assakā, both in the local vernacular and in Pāli. And either there were two distinct tribes so called, or the Sanskrit form Aśvakā is a wrong reading, or a blunder in the Sanskritisation of Assakā.

14. Avanti, the capital of which was Ujjeni, was ruled over by King Caṇḍa Pajjota (Pajjota the Fierce) referred to above. The country, much of which is rich land, had been colonised or conquered by Aryan tribes who came down the Indian valley, and turned west from the Gulf of Kach. It was called Avanti at least as late as the second century A.D.,[1] but from the seventh or eighth century onwards it was called Mālava.

15. Gandhārā, modern Kandahar, was the district of Eastern Afghanistan, and it probably included the north-west of the Panjab. Its capital was Takkasilā. The King of Gandhārā in the Buddha's time, Pukkusāti, is said to have sent an embassy and a letter to King Bimbisāra of Magadha.[2]

16. Kambojā was the adjoining country in the extreme north-west, with Dvāraka as its capital.

From the political point of view this list is curious. Some names we should expect to find—Sivi, for in-

[1] See Rudradāman's Inscription at Junagaḍh.

[2] Alwis, *Introduction*, etc., p. 78.

stance, and Madda and Sovīra, and Udyāna and Virāta—are not there. The Mallas and the Cetis occupy a position much more important than they actually held in the early years of Buddhism. Vesāli, soon to become a "Magadha town,"[1] is still independent. And Angā and Kāsī, then incorporated in neighbouring kingdoms, are apparently looked upon as of equal rank with the others. It is evident that this was an old list, corresponding to a state of things existent some time before, and handed on by tradition in the Buddhist schools. But this only adds to its interest and importance.

Geographically also the list is very suggestive. No place south of Avanti (about 23° N.) occurs in it; and it is only at one place that the list goes even so far to the south as that. Not only is the whole of South India and Ceylon ignored in it, but there is also no mention of Orissa, of Bengal east of the Ganges, or even of the Dekkan. The horizon of those who drew up the list is strictly bounded on the north by the Himālayas, and on the south (except at this one point) by the Vindhya range, on the west by the mountains beyond the Indus, and on the east by the Ganges as it turns to the south.

The books in which the list has been preserved have preserved also abundant evidence of a further stage of political movement. And in geographical knowledge they look at things from an advanced point of view. They know a very little farther south at the one point where the old list goes farthest in that direction.

[1] Sutta Nipāta, 1013.

The expression Dakkhiṇāpatha which occurs in an isolated passage in one of our oldest documents[1] cannot indeed possibly mean the whole country comprised in our modern phrase the Dekkan. But it is used, in the very passage in question, as descriptive of a remote settlement or colony on the banks of the upper Godhāvari.[2] The expression does not occur in any one of the Four Nikāyas. When it appears again, in a later stage,[3] it seems still to refer only, in a vague way, to the same limited district, on the banks of the Godhāvari. And it is coupled with Avanti, the Avanti of the ancient list.

The expression, in its form, is curious. It means "the Southern Road," a strange name to apply to any fixed locality. Already in a Vedic hymn[4] though it is one of the latest, we hear of a banished man going along the "path of the South." No doubt at different times different points on that path had been reached. In the Buddha's time the most southerly town is given (at S. N. 1011) as Patiṭṭhāna, the place afterwards called Paithana, and Baithana by the Greeks (73° 2′E. by 21° 42′ N.). And the extreme southerly point reached at all is the hermitage on the Godhāvari, about 20° N.[5]

[1] Sutta Nipāta, 976.

[2] The spelling of the word *Alakassa*, the name of this remote settlement, is doubtful. See verse 997. Spence Hardy's *Manual*, p. 334, confirms the various reading *Mulakassa*.

[3] Vin. 1. 195, 196; 2. 298.

[4] Rig Veda, x. 61. 8.

[5] There was an older and more famous Patiṭṭhāna, also a ferry, more generally known as Payāga, on the site of the Allahabad of to-day. Perhaps this more southern one was named after it.

One place still farther south may possibly be referred to incidentally as known in the Buddha's time. A teacher of olden time named Tagarasikhin, is several times mentioned.[1] Sikhin is otherwise known as a name, and the distinctive epithet Tagara may possibly be local, and mean "of Tagara," the modern Ter, 76° 12′ E. by 18°, 19′ N.[2] But the point is very doubtful, the place is not mentioned elsewhere, and I think another explanation of the name is more likely.

Besides this extension in the Dekkan, the Nikāyas speak also of sea voyages out of sight of land[3] and they mention the Kalinga forest,[4] and the settlement on the coast there, with its capital Dantapura.[5] The Vinaya has a probable reference to Bharukaccha,[6] and the Udāna one to Suppāraka.[7] These points, taken together (and no doubt others can be traced), show a marked advance in geographical knowledge. But it is suggestive to notice that the advance is limited, and that there is still no reference whatever either to South India or to Ceylon, which play so great a part in the story of the Rāmāyaṇa.[8]

These geographical considerations are of very considerable importance for the history of later

[1] M. 3. 69; S. 1. 92; Ud. 5. 3; Jāt. 3. 299.

[2] See Mr. Fleet's article in the *J. R. A. S.*, 1901, p. 542; and compare Burgess, *Cave Temples of India*, p. 248.

[3] D. 1. 222; A. 3. 368; compare Jāt. 3. 267.

[4] M. 1. 378.

[5] D. 19. 36.

[6] Vin. 3. 38.

[7] Ud. 1. 10.

[8] We must accept Professor Jacobi's happy suggestion as to the mythological basis of the latter part of the Rāmāyaṇa. Vālmīki, in transplanting the ancient myth of the atmospheric battles from the

Vedic and early Sanskrit literature. They go far to confirm Professor Bhandarkar's recent views as to the wholesale recasting of brahmin literature in the Gupta period. If Āpastamba, for instance, as Hofrath Dr. Bühler thought, and Hiranya-Keśin, wrote in the south, below the Godhāvarī, then they must be later than the books whose evidence we have been considering.

The consideration of this question has been hindered by a generally accepted hypothesis which does not fit the facts. It is supposed that the course of Aryan migration lay along the valleys of the Ganges and the Jumna. It cannot have been so simple. We must postulate at least two other lines of equal importance—one down the Indus, round the Gulf of Cutch, and so up to Avanti; and another along the foot of the mountains from Kashmir, by way of Kosala, to the Sākiya country, and so on through Tirhut to Magadha and Anga. There is a great deal more evidence available, both in literature and in the conclusions to be drawn from language, as to tribal migration in India than has yet been collected or analysed. Mr. Grierson, for instance, has only just recently pointed out the important fact that, even now, the dialects of Rājasthān have a close resemblance to the dialects spoken along the Himālayas not only in Nepal but as far west, at least, as Chambā. This would tend

heavens to the earth, in turning the deities of the ancient poetry into human heroes, in raising up to the level of those heroes the local deities of agriculture, naturally chose as the district where he localises so revolutionary a story a land, Lankā, with all the charm of mystery. Mystery involves knowledge, but not too much knowledge.

to show that their ancestors must have been living close together when they began their wanderings to the east and the south respectively. Both started from the Northern Panjab, and probably neither migration followed the Ganges route.[1]

These children of hillmen tended to cleave to the hills; and, like mountaineers all the world over, were generally distinguished by a sturdy independence, both in politics and religion. Widely separated, they were always sympathetic; and any forward movement, such as Buddhism, readily found supporters among them.

Another point on which this geographical evidence throws light is the date of the colonisation of Ceylon. That cannot have taken place in any considerable degree before the period in which the Nikāyas were composed. We know it had become a well-established fact at the time of Asoka. It must have happened, therefore, between these two dates; and no doubt nearer to the earlier of the two. The Ceylon chronicles, therefore, in dating the first colony in the very year of the Buddha's death (a wrong synchronism which is the cause of much confusion in their early chronology) must be in error.

It would be of great assistance on several questions if we could form some conclusion as to the number of inhabitants in Northern India in the seventh century, B.C.; though any such conclusion would necessarily be of the vaguest description. To judge from the small numbers of the great cities, and from the wide extent of forest and wilderness,

[1] *J. R. A. S.*, 1901, p. 808.

mentioned in the books, it cannot have been very large. Perhaps the whole territory may have contained fifteen to twenty millions. In the fourth century, B.C., the confederation formed to oppose Alexander was able to muster an army of four hundred thousand. And in the third century, B.C., Megasthenes describes the army of Magadha as then consisting, in peace time, of two hundred thousand foot, three hundred elephants, and ten thousand chariots.

The following is a list of the principal cities existing in India in the seventh century B.C.

Ayojjhā (from which the Anglo-Indian word Oudh is derived) was a town in Kosala on the river Sarayu. The city owes all its fame to the fact that the author of the Rāmāyaṇa makes it the capital at the date of the events in his story. It is not even mentioned in the Mahābhārata; and was quite unimportant in the Buddha's time. There is another Ayojjhā in the extreme west; and a third is said (wrongly, I think) to have been situate on the Ganges.[1]

Bārāṇasi (Benares) on the north bank of the Ganges, at the junction between it and the river Baraṇa. The city proper included the land between the Baraṇa and a stream called the Asi, as its name suggests. Its extent, including the suburbs, is often stated to have been, at the time when it was the capital of an independent kingdom (that is, some

[1] See Jāt. 4. 82: Saṃyutta 3. 140, 4, 179 (but the reading must be corrected).

time before the rise of Buddhism) twelve leagues, or about eighty-five miles. Seeing that Megasthenes gives the circuit of the walls of Pāṭaliputta, where he himself lived, as 220 stadia (or about twenty-five miles), this tradition as to the size of the city, or rather county, Benares at the height of its prosperity seems by no means devoid of credit. Its Town Hall was then no longer used as a parliament chamber for the transaction of public business. Public discussions on religious and philosophical questions were carried on in it.[1]

Champā, on the river of the same name, was the ancient capital of Angā. Its site has been identified by Cunningham with the modern villages of similar names twenty-four miles east of Bhagalpur; and is stated to have been sixty leagues from Mithilā[2] It was celebrated for its beautiful lake, named after Queen Gaggarā, who had had it excavated. On its banks was a grove of Champaka trees, well known for the fragrant odour of their beautiful white flowers. And there, in the Buddha's time, wandering teachers were wont to lodge.[3] The Indian colonists in Cochin China named one of the most important of their settlements after this famous old town.[4] And the Champā in Angā was again, in its turn, so named after the still older Champā in Kashmīr.

Kampilla, the capital of the Northern Pañcālas. It was on the northern bank of the Ganges, about long. 79° W., but its exact site has not yet been decided with certainty.

[1] Jāt. 4. 74.
[2] Jāt. 6. 32.
[3] *Dialogues of the Buddha*, I. 144.
[4] I-Tsing's Travels, p. 58.

Kosambi, the capital of the Vatsas or Vaṃsas. It was on the Jumna, and thirty leagues, say 230 miles, by river from Benares.[2] It was the most important *entrepôt* for both goods and passengers coming to Kosala and Magadha from the south and west.[3] In the Sutta Nipāta (1010–1013) the whole route is given from a place south of Ujjen, through Kosambi to Kusinārā, with the stopping-places on the way. The route from Kosambi to Rājagaha was down the river.[4] In the Buddha's time there were already four distinct establishments of his Order in the suburbs of Kosambi—the Badarika, Kukkuṭa, and Ghosita Parks, and the Mango Grove of Pāvāriya.[5] The Buddha was often there, at one or other of these residences; and many of his discourses there have been handed down in the books.

Madhurā, on the Jumna, the capital of the Sūrasenas. It is tempting to identify it with the site of the modern Mathura, in spite of the difference in spelling. Very ancient remains have been found there. The king of Madhurā in the Buddha's time bore the title of Avanti-putto,[6] and was therefore related to the royal family at Ujjeni. Madhurā was visited by the Buddha,[7] and was the residence of Mahā Kaccāna,[8] one of his most influential disciples, to whom tradition attributes the first grammatical treatment of the Pāli language, and after whom the oldest Pāli grammar is accordingly named. As Mad-

[1] Jāt. 4. 28; 6. 236.
[2] Com. on Aṅguttara, 1. 25.
[3] *Vinaya Texts*, 2. 189; 3. 67, 224, 233.
[4] *Vinaya Texts*, 3. 382.
[5] Vin. 4. 16; Sum. 319.
[6] M. 2. 83.
[7] A. 2. 57.
[8] M. 2. 83.

hurā is mentioned in the Milinda (331) as one of the most famous places in India, whereas in the Buddha's time it is barely mentioned, the time of its greatest growth must have been between these dates. It was sufficiently famous for the other Madhurā, in Tinnevelly, first mentioned in the Mahāvansa,[1] to be named after it. A third Madhurā, in the extreme north, is mentioned at Jāt. 4. 79, and Peta Vatthu Vaṇṇanā, 111.

Mithilā, the capital of Videha, and the capital therefore of the kings Janaka and Makhādeva, was in the district now called Tirhut. Its size is frequently given as seven leagues, about fifty miles, in circumference.[2]

Rājagaha, the capital of Magadha, the modern Rajgir. There were two distinct towns; the older one, a hill fortress, more properly Giribbaja, was very ancient, and is said to have been laid out by Mahā Govinda the architect.[3] The later town, at the foot of the hills, was built by Bimbisāra, the contemporary of the Buddha, and is Rājagaha proper. It was at the height of its prosperity during, and immediately after, the Buddha's time. But it was abandoned by Sisunāga, who transferred the capital to Vesāli; his son Kāḷāsoka transferring it to Pāṭaliputta, near the site of the modern Patna.[4] The fortifications of both Giribbaja and Rājagaha are still extant, 4½ and 3 miles respectively in circumference; the most southerly point of the walls of

[1] Turnour's edition, p. 51. [2] Jāt. 3. 365; 4. 315; 6. 246, etc.
[3] Vimāna Vatthu Commentary, p. 82. But compare Dīgha, xix. 36.
[4] Bigandet, 2. 115.

Giribbaja, the "Mountain Stronghold," being one mile north of the most northerly point of the walls of the new town of Rājagaha, the "King's House." The stone walls of Giribbaja are the oldest extant stone buildings in India.

Roruka, or in later times Roruva, the capital of Sovīra, from which the modern name Surat is derived, was an important centre of the coasting trade.[1] Caravans arrived there from all parts of India, even from Magadha.[2] As Ophir is spelt by Josephus and in the Septuagint Sophir, and the names of the ivory, apes, and peacocks imported thence into Palestine are Indian names, it is not improbable that Roruka was the seaport to which the authors of the Hebrew chronicles supposed that Solomon's vessels had traded. For though the more precise name of the port was Roruka, we know from such expressions as that used in the Milinda, p. 29, that the Indians talked about sailing to Sovīra. The exact site has not yet been rediscovered, but it was almost certainly on the Gulf of Kach, somewhere near the modern Kharragoa. When its prosperity declined, its place was taken by Bharukaccha, the modern Bharoch, or by Suppāraka, both on the opposite, the southern, side of the Kathiawad peninsula.

Sāgala. There were three cities of this name. But the two in the far East[3] were doubtless named (even if the readings in the MSS. are correct, and I doubt them in both cases) after the famous Sāgala

[1] Dīgha, xix. 36; Jāt. 3. 470.
[2] Vimāna, V. A. 370; Divy. 544.
[3] Jāt. 5. 337, and Com. on Therī Gāthā, p. 127.

in the extreme north-west, which offered so brave a resistance to Alexander, and where King Milanda afterwards reigned. It lay about 32° N. by 74° E., and was the capital of the Maddas. Cunningham thought he had found the ruins of it; but no excavations have been carried out, and the exact site is still therefore uncertain.

Sāketa, the site of which has been indentified with the ruins, as yet unexplored, at Sujān Kot, on the Sai River, in the Unao district of the modern province of Audh.[1] In ancient times it was an important city in Kosala, and sometimes the capital.[2] In the Buddha's time the capital was Sāvatthi. Sāketa is often supposed to be the same as Ayojjhā (Oudh),[3] but both cities are mentioned as existing in the Buddha's time. They were possibly adjoining, like London and Westminster. But it is Sāketa, and not Ayojjhā, that is called one of the six great cities of India.[4] The Añjana Wood near by Sāketa is the place at which many of the Buddhist Suttas are said to have been spoken. The distance from Sāketa northwards to Sāvatthi was six leagues, about forty-five miles,[5] and could be covered in one day with seven relays of horses.[6] But there was a broad river on the way, only to be crossed by ferry; and there are constant references to the dangers of the journey on foot.

[1] Führer, *Monumental Antiquities of N. W. Provinces and Oudh*, p. 275.

[2] Mahāvastu, 1. 348; Jāt. 3. 270.

[3] *E. g.* Cunningham's *Ancient Geography*, p. 405.

[4] Rh. D., *Buddhist Suttas*, p. 99.

[5] *Vinaya Texts*, 2. 147.

[6] Majjhima, 1. 149.

Sāvatthi, or Srāvasti, was the capital of Northern Kosala, the residence of King Pasenadi, and one of the six great cities in India during the lifetime of the Buddha. Archæologists differ as to its position; and the decision of this vexed point is one of the first importance for the early history of India, as there must be many inscriptions there. It was six leagues north of Sāketa,[1] forty-five leagues north-west of Rājagaha,[2] more than one hundred north-east of Suppāraka,[3] thirty leagues from Sankassa,[4] and on the bank of the Achiravatī.[5]

Ujjeni, the capital of Avanti, the Greek Ozēnē, about 77° E. and 23° N. There Kaccāna, one of the leading disciples of the Buddha, and also Asoka's son Mahinda, the famous apostle to Ceylon, were born. In later times there was a famous monastery there called the Southern Mount; and in earlier times the capital had been Māhissati.[6] Vedisa, where the famous Bhilsa Topes were lately found, and Erakaccha, another well-known site, were in the vicinity. Vedisa was fifty leagues from Pāṭaliputta.[7]

Vesāli. This was the capital of the Licchavi clan, already closely related by marriage to the kings of Magadha, and the ancestors of the kings of Nepal, of the Mauryas, and of the dynasty of the Guptas. It was the headquarters of the powerful Vajjian con-

[1] *Vinaya Texts*, 2. 147.
[2] Rh. D., *Buddhist Birth Stories*, p. 130.
[3] Divyāvadāna, 43.
[4] Jātaka, 4. 265.
[5] *Vinaya Texts*, 2. 24, 222.
[6] Dīgha, xix. 36.
[7] Maha Bodhi Vaṃsa, 98.

federacy, afterwards defeated, but not broken up, by Ajātasattu. It was the only great city in all the territories of the free clans who formed so important a factor in the social and political life of the sixth century B.C. It must have been a great and flourishing place. But though different guesses have been made as to its site, no one of them has yet been proved to be true by excavation. It was somewhere in Tirhut; and just three leagues, or, say, twenty-five miles, north of the Ganges, reckoned from a spot on the bank of that river, five leagues, say thirty-eight miles, from Rājagaha.[1] Behind it lay the Great Forest, the Mahāvana, which stretched northwards to the Himālayas. In that wood a hermitage had been built by the community for the Buddha, and there many of his discourses were delivered. And in an adjoining suburb, the founder of the Jains, who was closely related to some of the leading chiefs, was born. We hear of its three walls,[2] each of them a *gāvuta*, a cow's call, distant from the next[3]; and of the 7707 rājas, that is Licchavi chiefs, who dwelt there[4]; and of the sacred pool in which they received their consecration.[5] There were many shrines of pre-Buddhistic worship in and around the city, and the discovery and excavation of the site is most desirable.

The same may indeed be said of all these ancient cities. Not one of them has been properly excavated. The archæology of India is, at present, an almost unworked field.

[1] Dhammapāla on S. N., 2. 1. [2] Jātaka, 1. 389.
[3] *Ib.* 1. 504. [4] *Ib.* 1. 504, 3. 1. [5] *Ib.* 4. 148.

CHAPTER III

THE VILLAGE

IN the Buddha's time and in that portion of North India where the Buddhist influence was most early felt—that is to say in the districts including and adjoining those now called the United Provinces and Behar—the social conditions were, on the whole, simple. But there are several points of great interest on which they differed from those of the same districts now, and from those of related tribes in Europe then.

Divergent theories have been propounded to explain these differences. The influence of food and climate is assigned a paramount importance. Vegetarian diet is supposed to explain the physical and mental degeneracy proved by the presumed absence of political movements and ardent patriotism. Or the enervating and tropical heat of the sultry plains is supposed to explain at once the want of political vigour and the bad philosophy. Or the overwhelming mental effect of the mighty powers of nature —the vivid storms of thunder and lightning, the irresistible rays of the scorching sun, the depressing majesty of the great mountains—are called upon as a sufficient explanation of the inferiority of the Indian peoples. Or the contact with aboriginal tribes in a semi-savage state of development, the frequent intermarriages, and the consequent adoption of foolish and harmful superstitions, are put forward as the reasons for whatever we find strange in their life and thought.

It may be doubted whether our knowledge of the state of things in the seventh century B.C., either on the shores of the Mediterranean on the one hand, or in the Ganges Valley on the other, is sufficiently clear and precise to justify our taking for granted the then inferiority of the Indians. In some respects it would seem to be the other way. In intellectual vigour, at least, the Indians were not wanting. That Europeans should believe, as a matter of course, in the vast superiority of Europeans, not only now, but always, is psychologically interesting. It is so like the opinion of the ancient Greeks about barbarians, and of the modern Chinese about foreigners. But the reasons given are vague, and will scarcely bear examination. I recollect hearing Professor Bühler at the Oriental Congress in Paris, in 1897, when the argument of climate was adduced, entering an emphatic caution. As Inspector of Schools in India for many years, he knew the climate well; and observed that exaggerated estimates of its baneful influence had been most often advanced by those who had never been in India. Those who had lived there knew the great amount of energy and work, both physical and intellectual, that was not only possible, but habitual, to both Europeans and the natives of India. I can fully confirm this. The climate has its positive advantages. All the other most ancient civilisations (in Egypt for instance, in Mesopotamia, and in China) grew up, under somewhat similar outward conditions, in warm and fertile river valleys. And climate varies greatly even in India. We must not forget that the Sākiya country, at least, in which Buddhism arose, stretched up into the lower slopes of the Himālayas. And in the seventh century B.C. the most powerful kingdom was the Northern Kosala, whose capital lay under the hills, and whose power mainly depended on the mountaineers drawn from its vicinity.

It is probable that economic conditions and social institutions were a more important factor in Indian life than geographical position. Now the social structure of India was based upon the village. We do not as yet know all the details of its organisation; and no doubt different villages, in different districts, varied one from another in the customs of land-tenure and in the rights of individual householders as against the community.

It is a common error, vitiating all conclusions as to the early history of India, to suppose that the tribes with whom the Aryans, in their gradual conquest of India, came into contact, were savages. Some were so. There were hill tribes, gypsies, bands of hunters in the woods. But there were also settled communities with highly developed social organisation, wealthy enough to excite the cupidity of the invaders, and in many cases too much addicted to the activities of peace to be able to offer, whenever it came to a fight, a prolonged resistance. But they were strong enough to retain, in some cases, a qualified independence, and in others to impose upon the new nation that issued from the struggle many of their own ideas, many of the details of their own institutions.

And in many cases it never came to a struggle at all. The country was immense. Compared with its wide expanse the tribes and clans were few. Often separated one from the other by broad rivers and impenetrable forest, there must have been ample opportunity for independent growth, and for the interaction of peaceful contact.

These circumstances will explain the divergency in the village arrangements. But in some respects they were all similar. We nowhere hear of isolated houses. The houses were all together, in a group, separated only by narrow lanes. Immediately adjoining was the sacred grove of trees of the primeval forest, left standing when the forest clearing had been made. Beyond this was the wide expanse of cultivated field, usually rice-field. And each village had grazing ground for the cattle, and a considerable stretch of jungle, where the villagers had common rights of waste and wood.

The cattle belonged severally to the householders of the village. But no one had separate pasture. After the crop was cut the cattle roamed over the field. When the crops were growing they were sent all together, under the charge of a herdsman, hired by the village collectively, to the village grazing grounds beyond the field.[1] The herdsman was an important personage, and is described as

"knowing the general appearance of each one of his charge and the marks upon it, skilled to remove flies' eggs from their hide and to make sores heal over, accustomed to keep a good fire going with smoke to keep the gnats away, knowing where the fords are and the drinking places, clever in choosing pasture, leaving milk in the udders, and with a proper respect for the leaders of the herd."[2]

The fields were all cultivated at the same time, the irrigation channels being laid by the community, and the supply of water regulated by rule, under the supervision of the headman. No individual or corporate proprietor needed to fence his portion of the fields. There was a common fence; and the whole field, with its rows of boundaries, which were also the water channels, bore the appearance of the patched robe of a member of the Buddhist Order.[3]

As a general rule the great field was divided into plots corresponding in number to that of the heads of houses in the villages; and each family took the produce of its share. But there was no such proprietary right, as against the community, as we are accustomed to in England. We hear of no instance of a shareholder selling or mortgaging his share of the village field to an outsider; and it was impossible for him to do so, at least without the consent of the

[1] Jāt. i. 194.

[2] M. 1. 222; A. 5. 350. Comp. Jāt. 3. 401; and perhaps Rig Veda, x. 19.

[3] Vin. 1. 287; comp. 2. 185, Jāt. 4. 276.

village council. We have three instances of sales of land in the books.[1] But in one case it was forest land cleared by the proprietor or his ancestors. A very old text[2] apparently implies that a piece of ground was given as a sacrificial fee. But it is at once added that the earth itself said,—and Mother Earth was a most dread divinity,—"No mortal must give me away!"

Neither had any individual the right of bequest, even to the extent of deciding the shares of his own family. All such matters were settled by custom, by the general sense of the community as to what was right and proper. And the general sense did not recognise the right of primogeniture. Very often a family, on the death of a householder, would go on as before under the superintendence of the eldest son. If the property were divided, the land was equally divided among the sons. And though the eldest son received an extra share (differing in different places and times) in the personal property, that also was otherwise divided equally.[3] We find in the earliest law book, that of Gautama, a statement that the youngest son also, as in the analogous English law of gavelkind, received an extra share; but in the later law books this disappears. The women, too, had their personal property, chiefly jewelry and clothes; and the daughters inherited from the mother. They had no need of a separate share of the land, as they had the advantage of the produce falling to the share of their husbands and brothers.

[1] Vin. 2. 158, 159; Jāt. iv. 167.
[2] Śat. Br. xiii. 7, 15.
[3] Gaut. 18. 5–17; Baudh. 2. 2, 3; Āpast. 2. 6, 14.

No individual could acquire, either by purchase or inheritance, any exclusive right in any portion of the common grassland or woodland. Great importance was attached to these rights of pasture and forestry. The priests claimed to be able, as one result of performing a particular sacrifice (with six hundred victims!), to ensure that a wide tract of such land should be provided.[1] And it is often made a special point, in describing the grant of a village to a priest, that it contained such common.[2]

What happened in such a case was that the king granted, not the land (he had no property in the land), but the tithe due, by custom, to the government as yearly tax. The peasantry were ousted from no one of their rights. Their position was indeed improved. For, paying only the same tax as before, they thus acquired the protection of a strong influence, which would not fail, on occasion, to be exerted on their behalf.

Not that they were usually without some such protection. It was through the village headman that all government business was carried on, and he had both opportunity and power to represent their case to the higher officials. From the fact that the appointment of this officer is not claimed for the king until the later law books[3] it is almost certain that, in earlier times, the appointment was either hereditary, or conferred by the village council itself.

This village headman had, no doubt, to prepare

[1] Śat. Br. 13. 3, 7.

[2] *Dialogues of the Buddha*, I. 108, etc. Comp. M. 3. 133; Jāt. vi. 344.

[3] Manu, vii. 115; Vishnu, iii. 7–10.

the road, and provide food, on the occasion of a royal person or high official visiting his village. But we find no mention of *corvée*, forced labour (rāja-kāriya) at this period. And even in the law books which refer to a later date, this is mentioned as a service due from artisàns and mechanics, and not from villagers.[1]

On the other hand villagers are described as uniting, of their own accord, to build Mote-halls and Rest-houses and reservoirs, to mend the roads between their own and adjacent villages, and even to lay out parks. And it is interesting to find that women are proud to bear a part in such works of public utility.[2]

The economic conditions in such villages were simple. None of the householders could have been what would now be called rich. On the other hand there was a sufficiency for their simple needs, there was security, there was independence. There were no landlords, and no paupers. There was little if any crime. What crime there was in the country (of which later) was nearly all outside the villages. When the central power was strong enough, as it usually was, to put down dacoity, the people, to quote the quaint words of an old Suttanta, "pleased one with another and happy, dancing their children in their hands, dwelt with open doors."[3]

The only serious inroad upon that happiness seems to have been famine resulting from drought. It is true that Megasthenes, long ambassador at the court of Magadha, says that, owing to irrigation, famines

[1] Gaut. x. 31; Vas. xix. 28; Manu, vii. 138.

[2] Jāt. I. 199.

[3] *Dialogues of the Buddha*, I. 176.

were quite unknown. But we have too many references to times of scarcity, and that, too, in the very districts adjacent to Patna where Megasthenes lived,[1] to accept his statement as accurate for the time we are discussing. As those references refer, however, to a date two centuries earlier, it is possible (but not, I think, very probable) that things, in this respect, had improved in the interval between the times referred to in our records, and that of Megasthenes. We shall see below, in the chapter on Chandragupta, that his statements often require correction. And this is, more probably, merely another instance of a similar kind.

It was under some such economic conditions as these that the great bulk—say at least 70–80 per cent.—of the people lived. In the books, ancient and modern, a few of the remaining few are so much more constantly mentioned (precisely because they differ from the mass, and the mass is taken for granted as understood) that the impression given to the reader is apt to be entirely misleading. These others—priests and kings, outcasts and jugglers, soldiers, citizens, and mendicant thinkers—played their part, and an important part. But the peoples of India, then much more even than now, were, first and foremost, village folk. In the whole vast territory from Kandahar nearly to Calcutta, and from the Himālayas southwards to the Run of Kach, we find mentioned barely a score of towns of any considerable size.

[1] See the passages collected at *Vinaya Texts*, 3. 220; and also Jāt. 2. 149, 367, 5. 193, 6. 487.

It will have been seen, however, that the mass of the people, the villagers, occupied a social grade quite different from, and far above, our village folk. They held it degradation, to which only dire misfortune would drive them, to work for hire. They were proud of their standing, their family, and their village. And they were governed by headmen of their own class and village, very probably selected by themselves, in accordance with their own customs and ideals.

CHAPTER IV

SOCIAL GRADES

PERHAPS the most important of these in their own eyes were the customs as to the holding and distribution of lands and property. But those as to religion on the one hand, and as to *connubium* and *commensality* on the other, had probably a greater effect on their real well-being and national progress.

We have learnt in recent years that among primitive peoples all over the world there exist restrictions as to the *connubium* (the right of intermarriage), and as to *commensality* (the right of eating together). Customs of endogamy and exogamy, that is, of choosing a husband or wife outside a limited circle of relationship, and inside a wider circle, were universal. A man, for instance, may not marry in his own family, he may marry within his own clan, he may not marry outside the clan. Among different tribes the limits drawn were subject to different customs, were not the same in detail. But the limits were always there. There were customs of eating together at sacred tribal feasts from which foreigners were excluded;

customs of not eating together with persons outside certain limits of relationship, except under special circumstances; customs by which an outsider could, by eating with men of a tribe, acquire certain rights of relationship with that tribe. Here again the details differ. But the existence of such restrictions as to commensality was once universal.

In India also in the seventh century B.C. such customs were prevalent, and prevalent in widely different forms among the different tribes,—Aryan, Dravidian, Kolarian, and others,—which made up the mixed population. We have unfortunately only Aryan records. And they, of course, take all the customs for granted, being addressed to people who knew all about them. We have therefore to depend on hints; and the hints given have not, as yet, been all collected and sifted. But a considerable number, and those of great importance, have been already observed; so that we are able to draw out some principal points in a sketch that requires future filling in.

The basis of the social distinctions was relationship; or, as the Aryans, proud of their lighter colour, put it, colour. Their books constantly repeat a phrase as being common amongst the people,—and it was certainly common at least among the Aryan sections of the people,—which divided all the world, as they knew it, into four social grades, called Colours (*Vaṇṇā*). At the head were the Kshatriyas, the nobles, who claimed descent from the leaders of the Aryan tribes in their invasion of the continent. They were most particular as to the purity of their descent through seven generations, both on the father's and the mother's side; and are described as "fair in colour, fine in presence, stately to behold."[1] Then came the brahmins, claiming descent from the sacrificing priests, and though the majority of them followed then other pursuits, they were equally with the nobles distinguished by high birth and clear complexion. Below these were the peasantry, the people, the Vaiśyas or Vessas. And last of all came the Śūdras, which included the bulk of the people of non-Aryan descent, who worked for hire, were engaged in handicraft or service, and were darker in colour.

In a general way this classification corresponded to the actual facts of life. But there were insensible gradations within the borders of each of the four Colours, and the borders themselves were both variable and undefined.

And this enumeration of the populace was not complete. Below all four, that is below the Śūdras, we have mention of other "low tribes" and "low trades"—*hīna-jātiyo* and *hīna-sippāni*. Among the first we are told of workers in rushes, bird-catchers, and cart-makers—aboriginal tribesmen who were *hereditary* craftsmen in these three ways. Among the latter—mat-makers, barbers, potters, weavers, and leather-workers—it is implied that there was no hard and fast line, determined by birth. People could, and did, change their vocations by adopting one or other of these "low trades." Thus at Jāt. 5. 290, foll., a love-lorn Kshatriya works successively (without any dishonour or penalty) as a potter,

[1] *Dialogues of the Buddha*, i. 148; Vin. II. 4. 160.

basket-maker, reed-worker, garland-maker, and cook. Also at Jāt. 6. 372, a *seṭṭhi* works as a tailor and as a potter, and still retains the respect of his high-born relations.

Finally we hear in both Jain and Buddhist books of aboriginal tribes, Chandālas and Pukkusas, who were more despised even than these low tribes and trades.[1]

Besides the above, who were all freemen, there were also slaves: individuals had been captured in predatory raids and reduced to slavery,[2] or had been deprived of their freedom as a judicial punishment[3]; or had submitted to slavery of their own accord.[4] Children born to such slaves were also slaves; and the emancipation of slaves is often referred to. But we hear nothing of such later developments of slavery as rendered the Greek mines, the Roman *latifundia*, or the plantations of Christian slave-owners, scenes of misery and oppression. For the most part the slaves were household servants, and not badly treated; and their numbers seem to have been insignificant.[5]

Such were the divisions of the people. The three upper classes had originally been one; for the nobles and priests were merely those members of the third class, the Vessas, who had raised themselves into a higher social rank. And though more difficult probably than it had been, it was still possible for analogous changes to take place. Poor men

[1] Anguttara, 1. 162. Jacobi, *Jaina Sutras*, 2. 301.
[2] Jāt. 4. 220.
[3] Jāt. 1. 200.
[4] *Vinaya Texts*, 1. 191; Sum. 1. 168.
[5] *Dialogues of the Buddha*, 1. 101.

could become nobles, and both could become brahmins. We have numerous instances in the books, some of them unconsciously preserved even in the later priestly books which are otherwise under the spell of the caste theory. And though each case is then referred to as if it were exceptional, the fact no less remains that the line between the "Colours" was not yet strictly drawn. The members of the higher Colours were not even all of them white. Some, no doubt, of the Kshatriyas were descended from the chiefs and nobles of the Dravidian and Kolarian tribes who had preserved, by conquest or by treaty, their independence or their social rank. And others of the same tribes were, from time to time, acquiring political importance, and with it an entry into a higher social grade.

That there was altogether a much freer possibility of change among the social ranks than is usually supposed is shown by the following instances of occupation[1]:

1. A Kshatriya, a king's son, apprentices himself successively, in pursuance of a love affair, to a potter, a basket-maker, a florist, and a cook, without a word being added as to loss of caste when his action becomes known.[2]

2. Another prince resigns his share in the kingdom in favour of his sister, and turns trader.[3]

3. A third prince goes to live with a merchant and earns his living "by his hands."[4]

[1] Collected in the *J. R. A. S.*, 1901, p. 868.

[2] Jāt. II. 5. 290.

[3] Jāt. 4. 84.

[4] Jāt. 4. 169.

4. A noble takes service, for a salary, as an archer.[1]

5. A brahmin takes to trade to make money to give away.[2]

6. Two other brahmins live by trade without any such excuse.[3]

7. A brahmin takes the post of an assistant to an archer, who had himself been previously a weaver.[4]

8, 9. Brahmins live as hunters and trappers.[5]

10. A brahmin is a wheelwright.[6]

Brahmins are also frequently mentioned as engaged in agriculture, and as hiring themselves out as cowherds and even goatherds. These are all instances from the Jātakas. And *a fortiori* — unless it be maintained that Buddhism brought about a great change in this respect — the state of things must have been even more lax at the time when Buddhism arose.

The customs of *connubium* were by no means coextensive with the four Colours. They depended among the Aryans on a quite different idea, that of the group of agnates (the Gotta); and among the other people either on the tribe, or on the village. No instance is known of the two parties to a marriage belonging by birth to the same village. On the other hand, there were numerous instances of irregular unions. And in some cases the offspring of such unions took rank even as nobles (Kshatriyas) or as brahmins.[7]

[1] Jāt. 2. 87. [2] Jāt. 4. 15. [3] Jāt. 5. 22; 471.
[4] Jāt. 5. 127. [5] Jāt. 2. 200; 6. 170. [6] Jāt. 4. 207.
[7] Jāt. 4. 38, 146, 305; 6. 348, 421.

As to customs of eating or not eating together, the books contain only a few hints. We have clear instances of a brahmin eating with a Kshatriya;[1] another of a brahmin eating the food of a Chandāla, and repenting of doing so.[2] The whole episode of the marriage of the Sākiya maiden to Pasenadi, King of Kosala, turns on the belief that a Kshatriya will not eat, even with his own daughter, if she be slave-born. And we hear of sending people to Coventry (as we should say) for breach of such customs. Thus at J. 4. 388, brahmins are deprived, by their brother brahmins, of their status as brahmins, for drinking water mixed with the rice water a Chandāla had used. And in an older document, one of the Dialogues, we are told how this was done. Three brahmins "for some offence or other, outlaw a brahmin, shaving him and cutting him dead by pouring ashes over him, thus banishing him from the land and from the township."[3] And the passage goes on to state that if Kshatriyas had done this to a Kshatriya the brahmins would still admit him to *connubium*, and allow him to eat with them at their sacred feasts. It then adds that "whosoever are in bondage to the notions of birth or of lineage, or to the pride of social position or connection by marriage, they are far from the best wisdom and righteousness." We see, therefore, that the whole passage is tinged with Buddhist views. But it is none the less good evidence that at the time when it was written such customs, and such pride of birth,

[1] Jāt. 2. 319, 320. The verses recur 3. 81, 355. So also 6. 33.
[2] Jāt. 2. 82.
[3] *Dialogues of the Buddha*, 1. 120.

were recognised as a factor in the social life of the people.

Again at Jāt. 5. 280, we have, as the central incident of a popular story, the detail, given quite as a matter of course, that a brahmin takes, as his only wife, the discarded consort of a Kshatriya. The people laugh at him, it is true, but not because he is acting in any way unworthy of his social standing, only because he is old and ugly.

There are also numerous instances, even in the priestly manuals of custom, of unions between men and women of all degrees of social importance. These are not only between men of rank and girls of a lower social grade, but also between men of a lower, and women of a higher, position; and we ought not to be in the least surprised to find such cases mentioned in the books. Even without them we should know, from the existing facts, what must have happened. It is generally admitted that there are now no pure Aryans left in India. Had the actual custom been as strict as the brahmin theory this would not be so. Just as in England we find Iberians, Kelts, Angles, Saxons, Danes, and Normans now fused, in spite of theoretical restrictions on intermarriage, into one nation, so in Northern India the ancient distinctions, Aryan, Kolarian, and Dravidian, cannot, at the time of the rise of Buddhism, any longer be recognised. Long before the priestly theory of caste had been brought into any sort of working order, a fusion, sufficient at least to obliterate completely the old landmarks, was an accomplished fact; and the modern divisions, though race has also its share in them, use different names, and are based on different ideas.

We may remark incidentally that there can have been no such physical repulsion as obtains between the advanced and savage races of to-day—a repulsion arising partly from great difference in customs and in intellectual culture, but still more largely dependent on difference of colour.[1] On the other hand, though the fact of frequent intermarriage is undoubted; though the great chasm between the proudest Kshatriya on the one hand and the lowest Chandāla on the other was bridged over by a number of almost imperceptible stages, and the boundaries between these stages were constantly being overstepped, still there were also real obstacles to unequal unions. Though the lines of demarcation were not yet drawn hard and fast, we still have to suppose, not a state of society where there were no lines of demarcation at all, but a constant struggle between attracting and repelling forces.

It will sound most amazing to those familiar with brahmin pretensions (either in modern times in India, or in priestly books such as Manu and the epics) to hear brahmins spoken of as "low-born." Yet that precisely is an epithet applied to them in comparison with the kings and nobles.[2] And it ought to open our eyes as to their relative importance in these early times.

The fact is that the claim of the priests to social

[1] See the discussion in Bryce's *Romanes Lecture*, 1902, on the "Relations of Advanced and Backward Races of Mankind."

[2] *Hīna-jacco*. See, for instance, Jāt. 5. 257. The locus is Benares.

superiority had nowhere in North India been then, as yet, accepted by the people. Even such books of the priests themselves as are pre-Buddhistic imply this earlier, and not the later, state of things with which we are so much familiar. They claim for the north-western, as distinct from the easterly, provinces a most strict adherence to ancient custom. The ideal land is, to them, that of the Kurus and Panchālas, not that of the Kāsis and Kosalas. But nowhere do they put forward in their earlier books those arrogant claims, as against the Kshatriyas, which are a distinctive feature of the later literature. The kings are their patrons to whom they look up, from whom they hope to receive approval and rewards. And it was not till the time we are now discussing that they put forward claims, which we find still vigorously disputed by all Kshatriyas — and by no means only by those of noble birth (a small minority of the whole) who happen also to be Buddhists.

We find, for instance, that the Jain books take it throughout as a matter of course, that the priests, as regards social standing, are below the nobles. This was the natural relation between the two, as we find throughout the world. Certain priests, in India as elsewhere, had very high social rank — Pokkharasādi and Sonadaṇḍa for instance. They were somewhat like the great abbots and bishops in our Middle Ages. But as a class, and as a whole, the priests looked up to the nobles, and were considered to be socially beneath them.

Restrictions as to marriage and as to eating

together, such as then existed in North India, existed also everywhere throughout the world, among peoples of a similar stage of culture. They are, it is true, *the key to the origin* of the later Indian caste system. But that system involves much more than these restrictions. And it is no more accurate to speak of caste at the Buddha's time in India, than it would be to speak of it as an established institution, at the same time, in Italy or Greece. There is no word even for caste. The words often wrongly rendered by that modern expression (itself derived from a Portuguese word) have something to do with the question, but do not mean caste. The Colours (*Vaṇṇā*) were not castes. No one of them had any of the distinctive marks of a caste, as the term is now used, and as it always has been used since it was first introduced by Europeans, and there was neither *connubium* nor *commensality* between the members of each. *Jāti* is "birth"; and pride of birth may have had to do with the subsequent building up of caste prejudices; but it exists in Europe today, and is an idea very different from that of caste. *Kula* is "family" or "clan" according to the context. And though the mediæval caste system had much to do with families and clans, it is only misleading to confuse terms which are so essentially different, or to read back a mediæval idea into these ancient documents. The caste system, in any proper or exact use of the term, did not exist till long afterwards.[1]

[1] For the discussion of this question see also Senart, *Les Castes dans l'Inde;* Fick, *Sociale Gliederung im nordöstlichen Indien zu Buddha's Zeit;* and Rhys Davids, *Dialogues of the Buddha*, I. 95–107.

CHAPTER V

IN THE TOWN

WE have, unfortunately, no detailed description of the outward appearance of an ancient city. We are told of lofty walls, and strong ramparts with buttresses and watch-towers and great gates; the whole surrounded by a moat or even a double moat, one of water and one of mud. In a bas-relief on the Sanchi tope, dating from the second or perhaps the third century B.C., we have a representation of such city walls, and it is very probable that in earlier times the fortifications were often similar in kind. But we are nowhere told of the length of the fortifications or of the extent of the space they enclosed. It would seem that we have to think, not so much of a large walled city, as of a fort surrounded by a number of suburbs. For there is frequent mention of the king, or a high official, going out of the city when he wants to take an afternoon's pleasure jaunt. And from the equally frequent mention of the windows of the great houses opening directly on to the streets or squares, it would appear that it was not the custom to have them surrounded by any private grounds. There were, however, no doubt, enclosed spaces behind the fronts of the houses, which latter abutted on the streets.

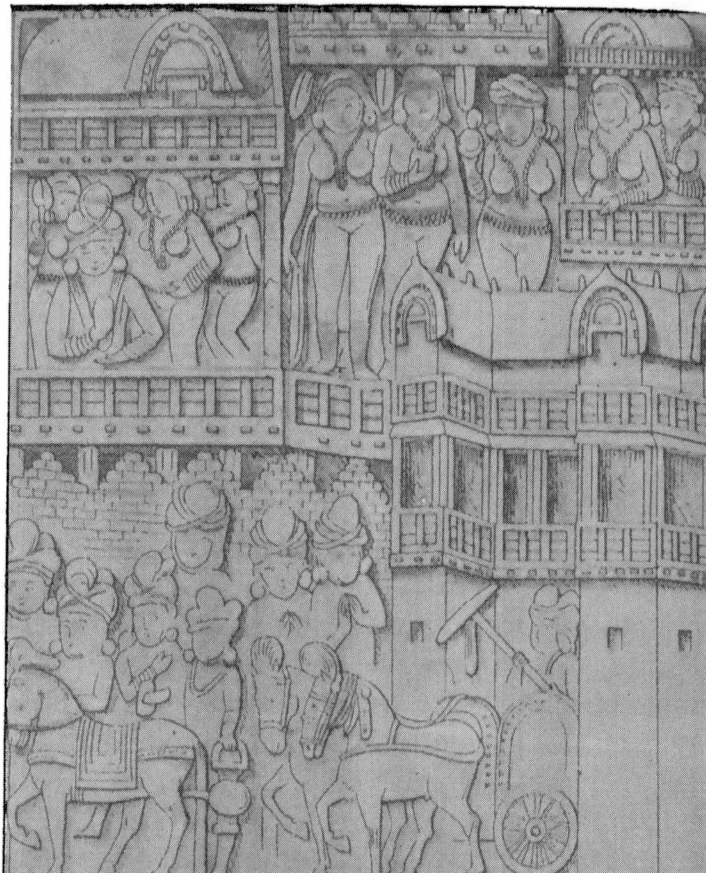

FIG. 3.—KING AND QUEENS WATCHING A PROCESSION AS IT LEAVES A FORT.

[From the Sanchi Tope.]

We have several descriptions of the building of a house, showing the materials used, and we have bas-

FIG. 4.—FAÇADE OF MANSION.

[From the Bharahat Tope. Pl. xxxi.]

reliefs showing the general design of the frontage. The elaborate description of the underground palace, a sort of Welbeck Abbey of ancient days, constructed by Mahosadha in his famous tunnel, is full of points of interest in this connection.[1] And the detailed account of the residences of members of the Order given in *Vinaya Texts* (3. 96, 104–115, 160–180) goes farther into minute details of the construction and ornamentation of the various portions of a human habitation. Then we have descriptions and bas-reliefs of the palace of the gods. And as gods are made in imitation of men, these are fair evidence also of the buildings in use by men at the time when the books were written, or the sculptures made. We have no space to enter fully into detail here. But the annexed illustration shows the ideas of a sculptor on the Bharahat tope as to the façade of a mansion, and the next shows his notion of what the meeting-hall of the gods, part of Vejayanta, the palace in heaven, was like.[2]

It is not easy to determine from these illustrations whether the pillars and railings depicted are intended to represent woodwork, or stone carved in imitation of wood. I am inclined to think the latter is meant. If so, that would show that in the third century B.C. (the date of the bas-reliefs), stone was already much used. We have an extant example of stone walls surrounding a hill fortress before the sixth century B.C. (at Giribbaja, see above, p. 37). But in the

[1] Jāt. 6. 430 ; translated in Yatawara's *Ummagga Jātaka*.

[2] These gods must have been made by the clansmen in the free republics, or they would not have had a mote-hall.

FIG. 5.—SUDHAMMO; THE MOTE-HALL OF THE GODS.

[From the Bharahat Tope. Pl. xvi.]

books referring to this earlier period, there is no mention of stone except for pillars or staircases. A palace of stone is only once mentioned, and that is in fairy land.[1] We must suppose that in earlier times the superstructure at least, of all dwellings was either of woodwork or brickwork. In either case it was often covered, both internally and externally, with fine chunam plaster-work, and brilliantly painted, in fresco, with figures or patterns. Elaborate directions are given in the Vinaya[2] for the construction of this smooth plaster basis on which the frescoes were painted. And the names of four of the commoner patterns have been preserved.[3] They are Wreath-work, Creeper-work, Five-ribbon-work, and Dragon's-tooth-work. When figures predominated the result is often called a picture-gallery (*cittāgāra*). And though we cannot suppose that the art had reached the perfection afterwards attained in the Ajanta frescoes, the descriptions show that it had already advanced to a stage far removed from the early beginnings of pictorial ornamentation.

The entrance to the great houses was through a large gateway. To the right and left of the entrance passage were the treasury and grain stores. The gateway led into an inner courtyard round which were chambers on the ground-floor. And above these chambers was a flat roof called the *upari-pāsāda-tala*, the upper flat surface of the house, where the owner sat, usually under a pavilion, which

[1] Jāt. 6. 269.
[2] Translated in *Vinaya Texts*, 3. 170–172.
[3] Vin. 2. 67; 4. 47.

FIG. 6.—ANCIENT OPEN-AIR BATH AT ANURĀDHAPURA (NO. 1).

answered the purpose at once of a drawing-room, an office, and a dining-hall.

In the king's palace there was accommodation also for all the business of the State, and for the numerous retinue and the extensive harem. We hear of no offices, in which the business of the nation could be carried on, outside the palace. And the supplementary buildings included three institutions which are strange to us, and of considerable historical interest.

We are told several times of a building of seven stories in height—a *satta-bhūmaka-pāsāda.*[1] No one of these has survived in India. But there is one of later date still standing at Pulasti-pura in Ceylon; and the thousand stone pillars on which another was erected in the second century B.C. at Anurādhapura form one of the most interesting monuments of the same island.[2] It seems almost impossible to avoid the conclusion that these curious buildings were not entirely without connection with the seven-storied Ziggarats which were so striking a feature among the buildings of Chaldæa. We know in other ways of connections between the civilisation of the Ganges Valley and that of Mesopotamia; and it would seem that in this case also the Indians were borrowers of an idea. But in India the use to which such seven-storied palaces was put was entirely private, and had nothing to do with any worship of the stars.

We hear in several places that a public gambling

[1] Jāt. 1. 227, 346; 4. 378; 5. 52, 426; 6. 577, etc.

[2] This illustration (see Fig. 9) from Mr. Cave's *Ruined Cities of Ceylon* (Plate XIII.). This beautiful volume ought to be in the hands of every Indian archæologist.

71 Fig. 7.—Ancient open-air bath at Anurādhapura (No. 2).

hall formed an ordinary part of a king's palace, either separately or as part of a great reception hall. It was especially laid down in Āpastamba, ii. 25, that it is the king's duty to provide such a place; and later law books disclose a custom by which

FIG. 8.—OLD INDIAN SCROLLWORK.

a share of the winnings went to the treasury. The gambling was with dice on a board with thirty-six squares; and the best description of the game, the details of which are very obscure, is at Jātaka, vi. 281.[1] There is a curious old bas-relief in which

[1] Comp. 1. 290; 3. 91.

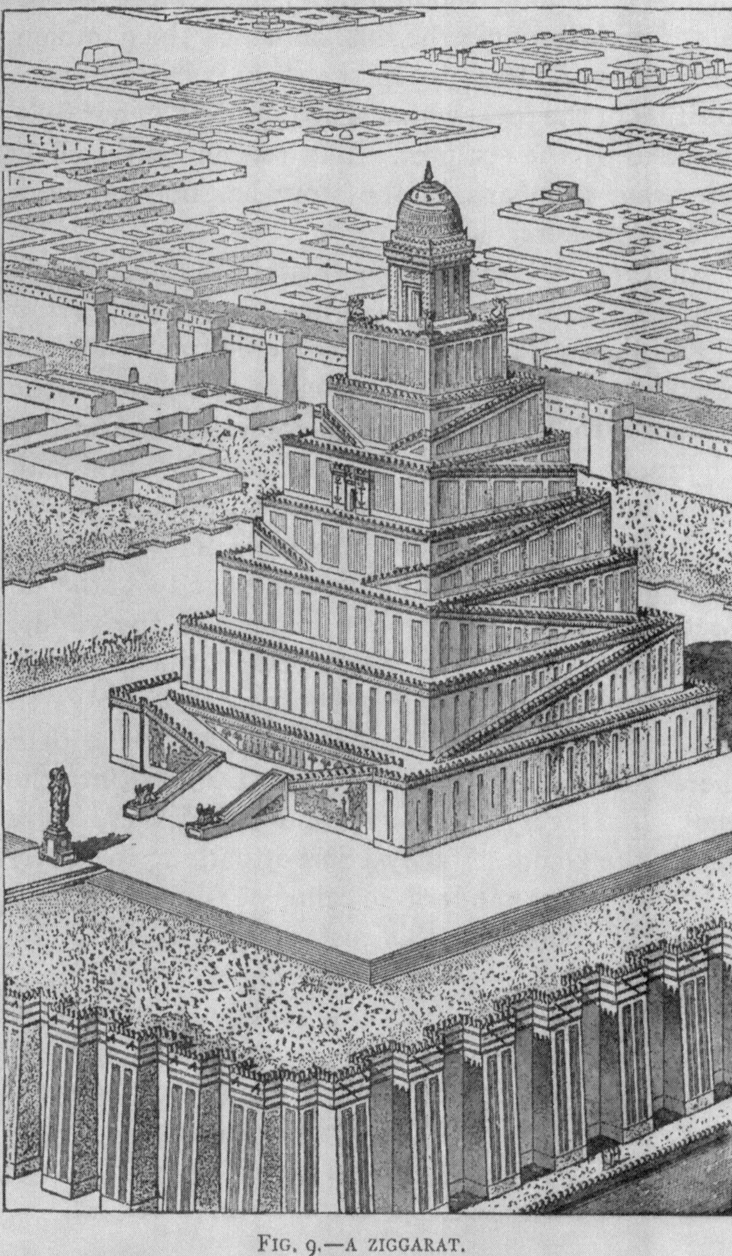

FIG. 9.—A ZIGGARAT.
[From Ragozin's *Story of Chaldea*.]

such a gambling saloon in the open air is represented with a split in the rock on which the gamblers are playing. The point of the story is evidently the splitting of the rock, which is not accidental, but fully intended by the sculptor. But we can only conjecture what it means, as the story has not yet been found elsewhere. (Fig. 11.)

Another sort of building historically interesting were the hot-air baths, described in full in *Vinaya Texts*, iii. 105–110, 297. They were built on an elevated basement faced with brick or stone, with stone stairs up to it, and a railing round the verandah. The roof and walls were of wood, covered first with skins, and then with plaster; the lower part only of the wall being faced with bricks. There was an antechamber, and a hot room, and a pool to bathe in. Seats were arranged round a fireplace in the middle of the hot room; and to induce perspiration hot water was poured over the bathers, whose faces were covered with scented *chunam* (fine chalk). After the bath there was shampooing, and then a plunge into the pool. It is very curious to find at this very early date in the Ganges Valley a sort of bathing so closely resembling our modern so-called "Turkish Baths." Did the Turks derive this custom from India?

In another of our oldest documents, the Dīgha Nikāya, there is a description of another sort of bath, an open-air bathing tank, with flights of steps leading down to it,[1] faced entirely of stone, and ornamented both with flowers and carvings. These bathing places must have been beautiful objects in the

[1] See the translation in my *Buddhist Suttas*, pp. 262, foll.

FIG. 10.—THE THOUSAND PILLARS. RUINS OF THE FOUNDATION OF THE SEVEN-STORIED, GREAT BRAZEN PALACE AT ANURĀDHAPURA.

[From Cave's *Ruined Cities of Ceylon.*]

private grounds of the rich. Several very ancient ones are still to be seen at Anurādhapura in a fair state of preservation in spite of the more than two thousand years that have elapsed since they were first constructed.

In the illustration of the first of these two bathing ponds, the platform, which appears as if built out into the pond, was, no doubt, the basement of a dressing pavilion supported on wooden pillars. It will be observed that it was cooled, in its turn, by a special little pond constructed to fill up one side of the platform. In the other illustration the pediments to support a canopy or awning over the steps leading down into the bath are still perceptible. (Fig. 7.)

One other detail of these ancient buildings, especially noticed by Buddhaghosa in his enumeration of the parts of a palace in olden times,[1] is the curious scroll work or string course in common use as exterior decoration. The details differ; so also do the materials used; they are usually wood or plaster, but occasionally stone, as in the annexed examples from the Bharhut Tope. (Figs. 8, 11, 12.)

But the great houses must have been few in number. There was probably a tangle of narrow and evil-smelling streets of one-storied wattle and daub huts with thatched roofs, the meagre dwelling-places of the poor. And we must imagine long lines of bazaars, the shops (without windows, of course, and indeed with very little wall on that side) open to the streets, and mostly devoted, in the same street, to the sale of wares of a similar kind.

[1] Âttha Sālinī, p. 107.

FIG. II.—THE SPLIT ROCK. GAMBLING SCENE FROM THE BHARAHAT TOPE.

Crowded the city must have been, and noisy. The oldest records boast of the fact,[1] and we are not surprised to learn that a corner house, abutting on two streets, was highly prized.[2] But the size of the few large cities is represented as so large, including the suburbs, that the crowding and noise were less probably in those days, at least outside the fortifications, than they are now.

So far as the records at present show there seem to have been few sanitary arrangements. There is constant mention of drains; but they are for water only—either small ones to carry off the water from a bathroom or a chamber,[3] or large ones to carry off the rain from within the fortifications. It was through these last that dogs[4] and jackals[5] got into the citadel; and sometimes even men used them as means of escape, at night, when the gates were closed.[6] It is not likely that they at all corresponded, therefore, to the Roman *cloaca*. On the other hand the at present obscure arrangements to obviate the various sanitary difficulties arising from the living together of a number of members of the Order[7] render it probable that in the palaces and larger mansions, at least similar arrangements may have been in use.

The disposal of the dead was, in some respects, very curious. Deceased persons of distinction, either by birth or wealth or official position, or as

[1] Rh. D. *Buddhist Suttas*, 248, 249.

[2] Jāt. 5. 350.

[3] *Vinaya Texts*, 3. 108, 110.

[4] Jāt. 1. 175.

[5] Jāt. 1. 425; 3. 415.

[6] Jāt. 1. 409, 489.

[7] *Vinaya Texts*, 3. 155, 298.

79 FIG. 12.—SCROLLWORK ORNAMENT AS USED OUTSIDE HOUSES AND ON TOPES IN BUDDHIST INDIA.

[From the Bharahat Tope. Pl. xliii.]

public teachers, were cremated; and the ashes were buried under a so-called tope (in Pāli *thūpa*, in Buddhist Sanskrit *stūpa*). But the dead bodies of ordinary people were disposed of in a unique way. They were put away in a public place (*sīvathikā* or *āmaka-susāna*, both of which, for want of a better word, are usually translated cemetery). There, as a rule, the bodies, or the remains of the pyre, were not buried, but left to be destroyed by birds or beasts, or dissipated by the process of natural decay.[1] This spot was also used as the public place of execution especially by impalement.[2] It was quite open to the public. But as we can readily understand, it was believed to be haunted; and was only frequented by the more austere sort of ascetics.

Sometimes Dāgabas or topes were erected in these cemeteries.[3] But more usually they were put up in the suburbs, either in private grounds,[4] or, in cases of special honour, at some place where four cross-roads met.[5] We are accustomed to think of them as especially Buddhist monuments. They were, in fact, pre-Buddhistic; and indeed only a slight modification of a world-wide custom. The use of barrows or cairns to mark a place of interment was not universal; but it was certainly very frequent in ancient times. And marked differences in their shape or size is rightly held to be evidence of race. The Aryans in India still used the round form. And the only curious point is that, in India, at the period under discussion, certain sections of the

[1] D. 2. 295–297; Jāt. 1. 264; 3. 330; 5. 458. [2] Jāt. 4. 29; 6. 10.
[3] Vin. 4. 308. [4] Jāt. 3. 155. [5] *Buddhist Suttas*, 93.

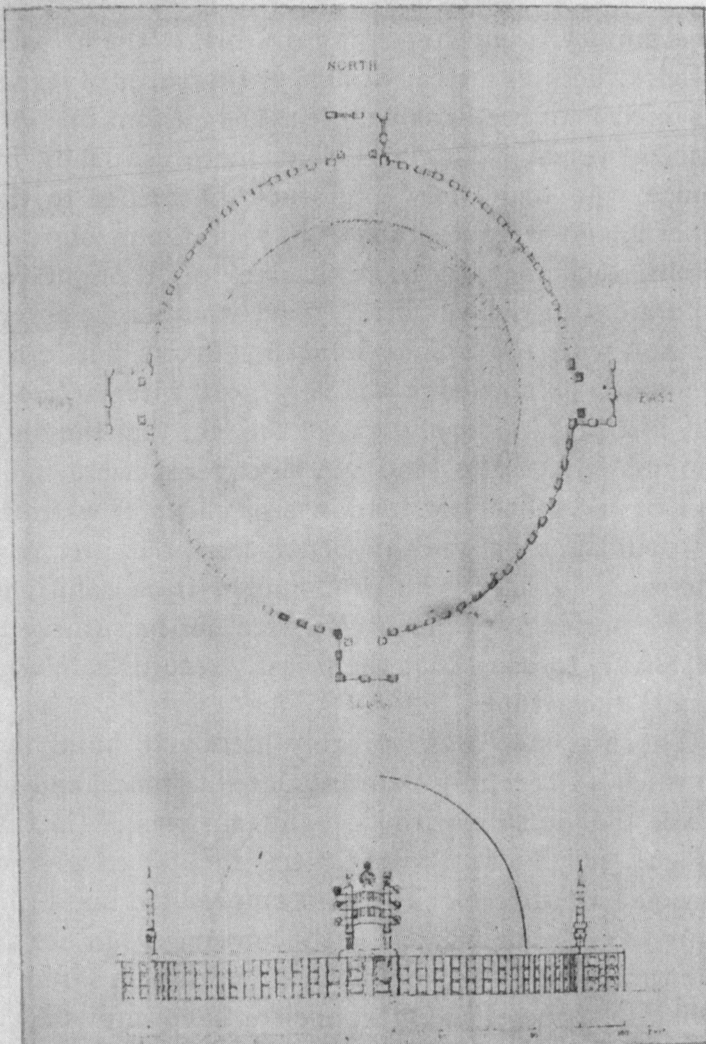

FIG. 13.—GROUND PLAN AND RESTORATION OF THE BHARAHAT STŪPA.

[From Cunningham's *Stūpa of Bharhut*. Pl. iii.]

6

community were beginning to make them solid brick structures instead of heaps of earth, or of stones covered with earth, as had been the custom in more ancient times.[1] This was done more especially by those who had thrown off their allegiance to the priests, and were desirous to honour the memory of their teachers, who were leaders of thought, or reformers, or philosophers. And whether we agree, or not, with the opinions these thinkers put forth, we must acknowledge the very great interest, from the historical point of view, of the fact that the only monuments of the kind yet discovered were built out of reverence, not for kings or chiefs or warriors or politicians or wealthy benefactors, but precisely for such thinkers, who propounded fresh solutions of the problems of life. We need not be surprised, therefore, to learn that the priestly records carefully ignore these topes.

The first step was probably merely to build the cairn more carefully than usual, with stones, and to cover the outside with fine chunam plaster (in the use of which the Indians were adepts) to give a marble-like surface. The next step was to build the cairn of concentric layers of the huge bricks in use at the time, and to surround the whole with a wooden railing. None of the most ancient have survived, or been explored sufficiently to enable a restoration to be drawn. But we can tell very much about what they were from the later examples. This, for instance, is Cunningham's plan and restoration of the famous Bharahat Stūpa.

[1] White Yajur Veda, chap. 35.

And among the bas-reliefs carved on the stone railing are several topes as the sculptor of the day imagined they ought to be.

We should notice however in the first of these carvings, designed to fill up the post of a stone railing, that the artist, in order to fill up the tall and

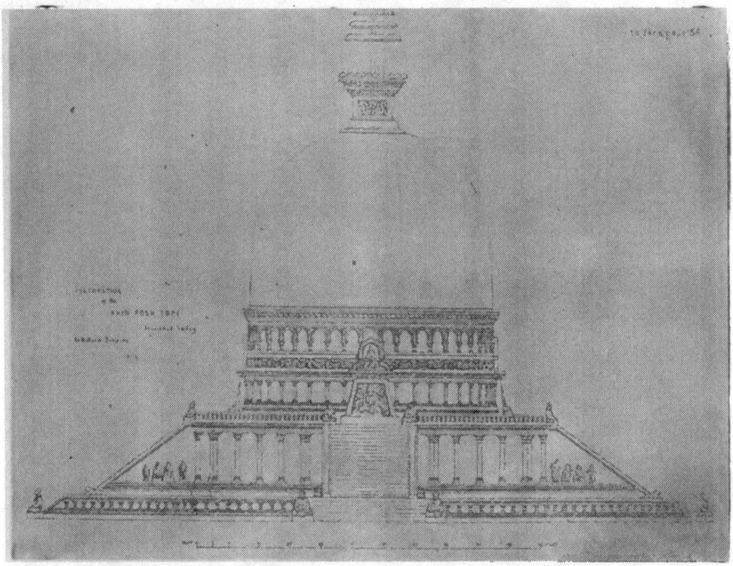

FIG. 14.—RESTORATION (BY W. SIMPSON) OF THE AHIN POSH TOPE.
[From the Proceedings of the R. I. B. A.]

narrow space he has to deal with, has allowed himself to give a disproportionate height to the ornamentation at the top of the dome.

Even in the Buddha's time the size of these monuments had already reached very considerable dimensions. The solid dome erected by the Sākiyas over their share of the ashes from the Buddha's funeral pyre must have been about the same height as the dome of St. Paul's, measured from the roof.[1] And it is that dome, as seen from Waterloo Bridge, where the intervening houses hide the view of the

FIG. 15.—A STŪPA AS CARVED ON THE BAS-RELIEFS.
[From Cunningham's *Stūpa of Bharhut*. Pl. xxxi.]

church, and only the beautiful outline of the dome itself is seen against the sky, which gives to those who have never seen them the best idea of what these domes must have been. Unfortunately no one

[1] See Mr. Peppé's measurements in the *J. R. A. S.* for 1898. The present state of the ruins of this important monument is shown in the above Fig.

FIG. 16.—THE JETAVANA DAGABA.

has yet attempted to make a restoration of one of these of the most ancient date. But Mr. W. Simpson has given us one of later date, and this is here appended for the sake of comparison.

The appearance of such a dāgaba in the landscape is also well shown in the annexed plate, from Mr. Cave's *Ruined Cities of Ceylon*, of the Jetavana Dāgaba. (Fig. 16.)

This dāgaba itself dates from the third century A.D., but the large irrigation "tank" shown in the foreground is probably the oldest dated one in India, as it was constructed before the time of Asoka.

CHAPTER VI

ECONOMIC CONDITIONS

THERE has been as yet no attempt to reconstruct a picture of the economic conditions at any period in the early history of India. Professor Zimmer, Dr. Fick, and Professor Hopkins have dealt incidentally with some of the points on the basis respectively of the Vedas, the Jātakas, and the Epics. But generally speaking the books on India have been so exclusively concerned with questions of religion and philosphy, of literature and language, that we seem apt to forget that the very necessities of life, here as elsewhere, must have led the people to occupy their time very much, not to say mostly, with other matters than those, with the earning of their daily bread, with the accumulation and distribution of wealth. The following remarks will be chiefly based on Mrs. Rhys-Davids's articles on this important subject in the *Economic Journal*, for 1901, and in the *Journal of the Royal Asiatic Society*, for 1901. And numbers given in this chapter as references, without letters referring to other sources, refer to the pages of the latter article.

When the King of Magadha, the famous (and infamous) Ajātasattu, made his only call upon the Buddha, he is said[1] to have put a puzzle to the teacher to test him—a puzzle characteristic of the King's state of mind. It is this:

"What in the world is the good of your renunciation, of joining an Order like yours? Other people (and here he gives a list), by following ordinary crafts, get something out of them. They can make themselves comfortable in this world, and keep their families in comfort. Can you, Sir, declare to me any such immediate fruit, visible in this world, of the life of a recluse?"

The list referred to is suggestive. In the view of the King the best examples of such crafts were the following:

1. Elephant-riders.
2. Cavalry.
3. Charioteers.
4. Archers.
5–13. Nine different grades of army folk.
14. Slaves.
15. Cooks.
16. Barbers.
17. Bath-attendants.
18. Confectioners.
19. Garland-makers.
20. Washermen.
21. Weavers.
22. Basket-makers.
23. Potters.
24. Clerks.
25. Accountants.

These are just the sort of people employed about a camp or a palace. King-like, the King considers chiefly those who minister to a king, and are dependent upon him. In the answer he is most politely reminded of the peasant, of the tax-payer, on whom both he and his depended. And it is evident enough

[1] D. I. 51.

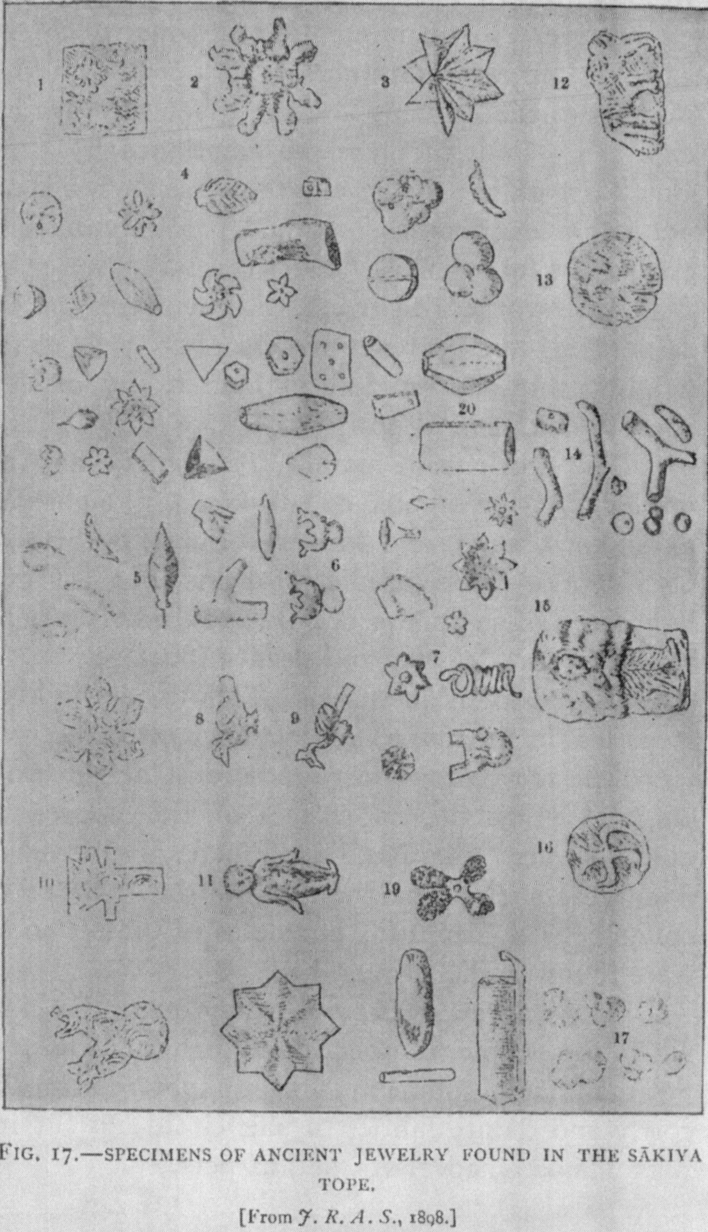

FIG. 17.—SPECIMENS OF ANCIENT JEWELRY FOUND IN THE SĀKIYA TOPE.

[From *J. R. A. S.*, 1898.]

from other passages that the King's list is far from exhaustive. There is mention, in other documents of the same age, of guilds of work-people; and the number of these guilds is often given afterwards as eighteen. Four of these are mentioned by name.[1] But a list of the whole eighteen has unfortunately not yet been found. It would probably have included the following:

1. The workers in wood. They were not only carpenters and cabinet-makers, but also wheelwrights; and the builders of houses, and of ships, and of vehicles of all sorts (863).

2. The workers in metal. They made any iron implements—weapons of all kinds, ploughshares, axes, hoes, saws, and knives. But they also did finer work—made needles, for instance, of great lightness and sharpness, or gold and (less often) silver work of great delicacy and beauty (864).

3. The workers in stone. They made flights of steps, leading up into a house or down into a reservoir; faced the reservoir; laid foundations for the woodwork of which the upper part of the houses was built; carved pillars and bas-reliefs; and even did finer work such as making a crystal bowl, or a stone coffer (864). Beautiful examples of these two last were found in the Sākiya Tope.

4. The weavers. They not only made the cloths which the people wrapped round themselves as dress, but manufactured fine muslin for export, and worked costly and dainty fabrics of silk cloth and fur into rugs, blankets, coverlets, and carpets.[2]

[1] At Jāt. 6. 427.

[2] D. 1. 7.

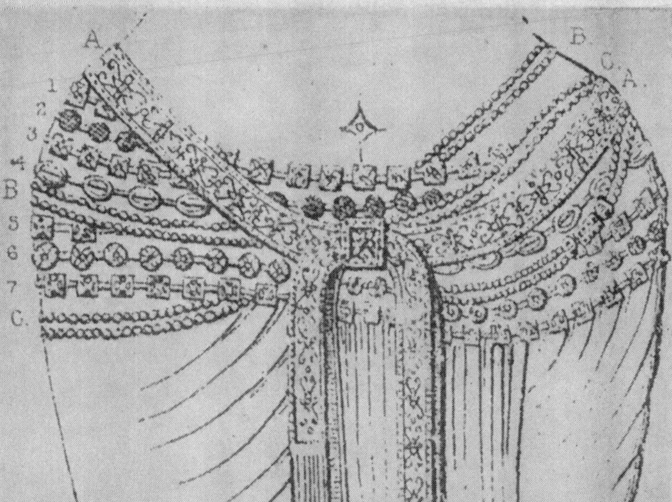

FIG. 18.—OLD INDIAN GIRDLE OF JEWELS.
[From the figure of Sirimā Devatā on the Bharahat Tope. Pl. li.]

5. Leather workers, who made the numerous sorts of foot-covering and sandals worn by the people mostly in cold weather; and also the embroidered

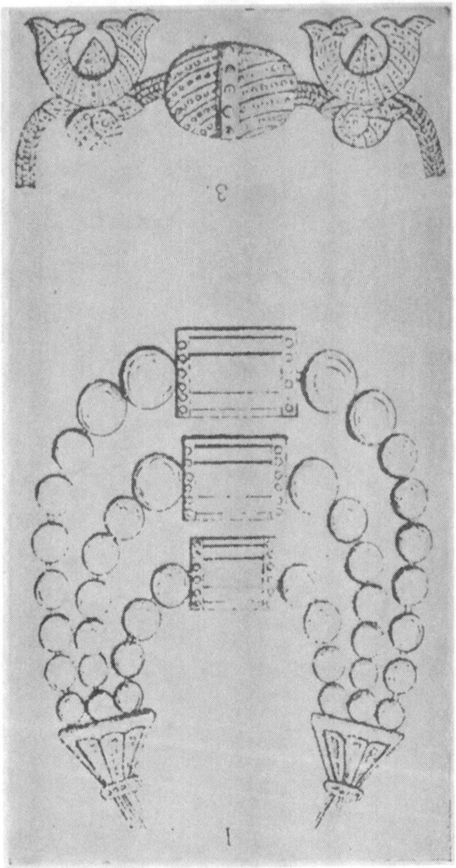

FIG. 19.—OLD INDIAN NECKLACES.

and costly articles of the same kind mentioned in the books (865).

6. Potters, who made all sorts of dishes and bowls for domestic use; and often hawked their goods about for sale.

7. Ivory workers, who made a number of small articles in ivory for ordinary use, and also costly carvings and ornaments such as those for which India is still famous (864).

8. Dyers, who coloured the clothes made by the weavers (864).

9. Jewellers, some of whose handiwork has survived, and is also so often represented in bas-

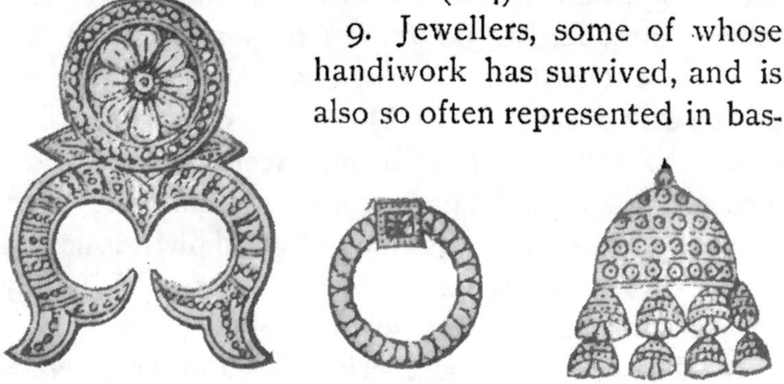

FIG. 20.

OLD INDIAN LOCKET. OLD INDIAN EARRING. OLD INDIAN LOCKET.
[Size of original.]

reliefs that we know fairly well the shape and size of the ornaments they made.

10. The fisher folk. They fished only in the rivers. There is no mention of sea-fishing known to me.

11. The butchers, whose shops and slaughter-houses are several times mentioned (873).

12. Hunters and trappers, mentioned in various passages as bringing the animal and vegetable products of the woods, and also venison and game, for sale on carts into the city (873). It is doubtful whether they were formed into guilds. But their industry was certainly a very important one. The

large stretches of forest, open to all, separating most of the settlements; the absence of any custom of breeding cattle for the meat-market; the large demand for ivory, fur, sinews, creepers, and all the other produce of the woods; and the congeniality of the occupation, all tended to encourage the hunters. And there is no reason to suppose that the very ancient instinct of the chase was confined to the so-called savages. The kings and nobles also, whether Aryan by blood or not, seem to have taken pleasure in it, quite apart from the economic question of food supply. But men of good birth followed it as a trade; and when brahmins did so (868) they are represented as doing so for profit.

13. The cooks and confectioners, a numerous class, probably formed a guild. But there is no passage saying that they did.

14. The barbers and shampooers had their guilds. They dealt in perfumes, and were especially skilled in arranging the elaborate turbans worn by the wealthier classes. (Figs. 21, 22.)

15. The garland-makers and flower-sellers (866).

16. Sailors, occupied for the most part in the traffic up and down the great rivers, but also going to sea. In some of our earliest documents[1] we hear of sea voyages out of sight of land; and in the later documents, such as the Jātakas, the mention of such voyages is frequent (872). So the earlier documents speak of voyages lasting six months made in ships (*nāvā*, perhaps "boats") which could be drawn up on

[1] Dīgha, I. 222 (translated in *Dialogues of the Buddha*, I. 283); Anguttara, 3. 368.

FIG. 21.—MEDALLION ON THE BHARAHUT TOPE.

Pl. xxiv. Fig. 3.

shore in the winter.[1] And later texts, of about the third century B.C., speak of voyages down the Ganges from Benares to the mouth of the river and thence across the Indian Ocean to the opposite coast of Burma; and even from Bharukaccha (the modern Baroch) round Cape Comorin to the same destination (871). It is clear, therefore, that during the whole of this period the occupation of sailor was neither unfrequent nor unimportant.

17. The rush-workers and basket-makers (868).

18. Painters (865). They were mostly house-painters. The woodwork of the houses was often covered with fine chunam plaster and decorated with painting. But they also painted frescoes.[2] These passages tell us of pleasure-houses, adorned with painted figures and patterns, belonging to the kings of Magadha and Kosala; and such frescoes were no doubt similar in character to, but of course in an earlier style than, the well-known ancient frescoes of the seventh and eighth centuries A.D. on the Ajanta Caves, and of the fifth century on the Sīgiri Rock in Ceylon.

It is doubtful with regard to two or three in this list whether they were organised in guilds (*seniyo, pūgā*). But it is certain that these were among the most important branches of handicraft apart from agriculture; and most of them had, no doubt, their guilds not unlike the mediæval guilds in Europe. It is through their guilds that the king summons the people on important occasions (865). The Aldermen

[1] Saṃyutta, 3. p. 155, 5. 51; Anguttara, 4. 127.

[2] Vin. ii. 151; iv. 47, 61, 298; Sum. 42, 84.

or Presidents (*jeṭṭhakā* or *pamukhā*) of such guilds are sometimes described as quite important persons, wealthy, favourites at the court. The guilds are said to have had powers of arbitration between the mem-

FIG. 22.—ANCIENT INDIAN HEAD-DRESS.

[From a medallion on the Bharahat Tope. Pl. xxiv. Fig. 2.]

bers of the guild and their wives. And disputes between one guild and another were in the jurisdiction of the *mahā-seṭṭhi*, the Lord High Treasurer, who acted as a sort of chief Alderman over the Aldermen of the guilds (865).

Besides the peasantry and the handicraftsmen there were merchants who conveyed their goods either up and down the great rivers, or along the coasts in boats; or right across country in carts travelling in caravans. These caravans, long lines of small two-wheeled carts, each drawn by two bullocks, were a distinctive feature of the times.[1] There were no made roads and no bridges. The carts struggled along, slowly, through the forests, along the tracks from village to village kept open by the peasants. The pace never exceeded two miles an hour. Smaller streams were crossed by gullies leading down to fords, the larger ones by cart ferries. There were taxes and octroi duties at each different country entered (875); and a heavy item in the cost was the hire of volunteer police who let themselves out in bands to protect caravans against robbers on the way (866). The cost of such carriage must have been great; so great that only the more costly goods could bear it.

The enormous traffic of to-day in the carriage of passengers, food-stuffs, and fuel was non-existent. Silks, muṣlins, the finer sorts of cloth and cutlery and armour, brocades, embroideries and rugs, perfumes and drugs, ivory and ivory work, jewelry and

[1] The accompanying plate (Fig. 23) shows, in four scenes on the same bas-relief, Anātha Piṇḍika's famous gift of the Jetavana Park to the Order. To the left is the park, the ground of which is being covered with *Kahāpaṇas*. In front is the bullock cart which has brought them. In the centre the donor holds in his hand the water of donation, the pouring out of which is to complete the legality of the gift. To the right are the huts to be afterwards put up in the park for the use of the Wanderers.

FIG. 23.—ANĀTHA PIṆḌIKA'S GIFT OF THE JETAVANA PARK.

[From the Bharahat Tope. Pl. lxvii.]

gold (seldom silver), — these were the main articles in which the merchant dealt.

The older system of traffic by barter had entirely passed away never to return. The later system of a currency of standard and token coins issued and regulated by government authority had not yet arisen. Transactions were carried on, values estimated, and bargains struck in terms of the *kahāpaṇa*, a square copper coin weighing about 146 grains, and guaranteed as to weight and fineness by punch-marks made by private individuals.[1] Whether these punch-marks are the tokens of merchants, or of guilds, or simply of the bullion dealer, is not certain (874). (Fig. 24.)

No silver coins were used (877). There were half and quarter kahāpaṇas, and probably no other sort. The references to gold coins are late and doubtful; and no such coins have been found. Some thin gold films with punch marks on them were found in the Sākiya Tope, but these are too flimsy to have been used in circulation as coins (878). It is interesting to notice that Alexander, when in India, struck a half kahāpaṇa copper piece, square (in imitation of the Indian money), and not round like the Greek coins of the time.

It is only in later times that we hear (as for instance in Manu, 8. 401) of any market price being fixed by government regulation. In the sixth century B.C. there is only an official called the Valuer, whose duty it was to settle the prices of goods

[1] See Figs. 1, 3, and 8 in the plate annexed to this chapter for examples of these oldest *Kahāpaṇas*.

ordered for the palace—which is a very different thing (875). And there are many instances, incidentally given, of the prices of commodities fixed, at different times and places, by the haggling of the market (875). These are all collected together in the article referred to (at pp. 882, foll.); and the general result seems to be that though the kahāpaṇa would be worth, at the present value of copper, only five sixths of a penny, its purchasing power then was about equivalent to the purchasing power of a shilling now.

Besides the coins, there was a very considerable use of instruments of credit. The great merchants in the few large towns gave letters of credit on one another. And there is constant reference to promissory notes (879). The rates of interest are unfortunately never stated. But interest itself is mentioned very early; and the law books give the rate of interest current at a somewhat later date for loans on personal security as about eighteen per cent. per annum (881).

There were no banking facilities. Money was hoarded either in the house, or buried in jars in the ground, or deposited with a friend, a written record of the transaction being kept (881).

The details of prices above referred to enable us to draw some conclusion as to the spending power of the poor, of the man of the middle classes, and of the wealthy merchants and nobles respectively. Of want, as known in our great cities, there is no evidence. It is put down as the direst misfortune known that a free man had to work for hire. And there was plenty of land to be had for the trouble of clearing it, not far from the settled districts.

On the other hand, the number of those who could be considered wealthy from the standards of those times (and of course still more so from our own) was very limited. We hear of about a score of monarchs, whose wealth consisted mainly of the land tax, supplemented by other dues and perquisites; of a considerable number of wealthy nobles, and some priests, to whom grants had been made of the tithe arising out of certain parishes or counties[1] or who had inherited similar rights from their forefathers; of about a dozen millionaire merchants in Takkasilā, Sāvatthi, Benares, Rājagaha, Vesāli, Kosambi, and the seaports (882), and of a considerable number of lesser merchants and middlemen, all in the few towns. But these were the exceptions. There were no landlords. And the great mass of the people were well-to-do peasantry, or handicraftsmen, mostly with land of their own, both classes ruled over by local headmen of their own selection.

Before closing this summary of the most important economic conditions in Northern India in the sixth century B.C. it may be well to bring together the few notices we have in the books about the trade routes. There is nothing about them in the pre-Buddhistic literature. In the oldest Pali books we have accounts of the journeys of the wandering teachers; and as, especially for longer journeys, they will generally have followed already established routes, this is incidental evidence of such as were then in

[1] D. 1. 88; M. 2. 163, 3. 133; S. 82.

use by traders. Later on, we have accounts of routes actually followed by merchants, either on boats, or with their caravans of bullock carts. We can thus draw up provisionally the following list:

1. *North to South-west.* Sāvatthi to Patiṭṭhāna (Paithan) and back. The principal stopping places are given [1] (beginning from the south) as Māhissati, Ujjeni, Gonaddha, Vedisa, Kosambi, and Sāketa.

2. *North to South-east.* Sāvatthi to Rājagaha. It is curious that the route between these two ancient cities is never, so far as I know, direct, but always along the foot of the mountains to a point north of Vesāli, and only then turning south to the Ganges. By taking this circuitous road the rivers were crossed at places close to the hills where the fords were more easy to pass. But political considerations may also have had their weight in the original choice of this route, still followed when they were no longer of much weight.[2] The stopping places were (beginning at Sāvatthi), Setavya, Kapilavastu, Kusinārā, Pāvā, Hatthi-gāma, Bhaṇḍagama, Vesāli, Pātaliputta, and Nālandā. The road probably went on to Gaya, and there met another route from the coast, possibly at Tāmralipti, to Benares.[3]

3. *East to West.* The main route was along the great rivers, along which boats plied for hire. We even hear of express boats. Upwards the rivers were used along the Ganges as far west as Sahajāti,[4] and along the Jumna as far west as Kosambi.[5] Downwards, in later times at least, the boats went

[1] In S. N. 1011-1013.
[2] Sutta Nipāta *loc. cit.*, and Dīgha, 2.
[3] *Vinaya Texts*, 1. 81.
[4] *Ibid.* 3. 401.
[5] *Ibid.* 3. 382.

right down to the mouths of the Ganges, and thence either across or along the coast to Burma.[1] In the early books we hear only of the traffic downward as far as Magadha, that is, to take the farthest point, Champā. Upwards it went thence to Kosambi, where it met the traffic from the south (Route 1), and was continued by cart to the south-west and north-west.

Besides the above we are told of traders going from Videha to Gandhāra,[2] from Magadha to Sovīra,[3] from Bharukaccha round the coast to Burma,[4] from Benares down the river to its mouth and thence on to Burma,[5] from Champā to the same destination.[6] In crossing the desert west of Rājputāna the caravans are said[7] to travel only in the night, and to be guided by a "land-pilot," who, just as one does on the ocean, kept the right route by observing the stars. The whole description of this journey is too vividly accurate to life to be an invention. So we may accept it as evidence not only that there was a trade route over the desert, but also that pilots, guiding ships or caravans by the stars only, were well known.

In the solitary instance of a trading journey to Babylon (Baveru) we are told that it was by sea, but the port of departure is not mentioned.[8] There is one story, the world-wide story of the Sirens, who

[1] That is at Thaton, then called Suvanna-bhūmi, the Gold Coast. See Dr. Mabel Bode in the *Sāsana Vamsa*, p. 12.

[2] Jāt. 3. 365.
[3] V. V. A. 370.
[4] Jāt. 3. 188.
[5] *Ibid.* 4. 15–17.
[6] *Ibid.* 6. 32–35.
[7] *Ibid.* 1. 108.

[8] *Ibid.* 3. 126. Has the foreign country called Seruma (Jāt. 3. 189) any connection with Sumer or the land of Akkad?

are located in Tambapaṇṇi-dīpa, a sort of fairy land, which is probably meant for Ceylon.[1] Lankā does not occur. Traffic with China is first mentioned in the Milinda (pp. 127, 327, 359), which is some centuries later.

APPENDIX TO CHAPTER VI

THE MOST ANCIENT COINS OF INDIA

EXPLANATION OF FIGS. 24 AND 25.

This explanation, being too long to be inserted here, has been transferred to pp. 321, 322.

[1] Jāt. 2. 127.

FIG. 24 —ANCIENT INDIAN COINS.
[See Appendix, pp. 321, 322.]

CHAPTER VII

WRITING—THE BEGINNINGS

LITERATURE of all kinds laboured under a curious disability. There were, for a long time, no writing materials—that is, none that could be used for the production and reproduction of books. And the Indians not only did not feel the want of them, but even continued, for centuries after materials had become available, to prefer, so far as books are concerned, to do without them. The state of things thus disclosed, being unique in the history of the world, deserves a detailed exposition.

The oldest reference to writing is in a tract called the *Sīlas*, embodied in each of the thirteen Dialogues which form the first chapter of the first division of the Suttantas, or conversational discourses of the Buddha. This tract must therefore have been already in existence as a separate work before those Dialogues were put together by the early disciples within the first century after the Buddha's death. The tract on the *Sīlas* may be dated, therefore, approximately about 450 B.C. The tract contains lists of things a member of the Buddhist Order would not do. And among these is a list of games, one of which is called *Akkharikā* (Lettering), explained as "Guessing at letters traced in the air, or on a playfellow's back." As the context[1] gives a number of children's games, this was almost certainly regarded as such. And for children to have such a game, and to call it by the name "Lettering," shows that the knowledge of an alphabet was fairly prevalent at the time in question.

The collection of canon law laid down for members of the Order under the generic name of *Vinaya* (Discipline) is in its present shape somewhat, perhaps two or three generations, younger. In it there are several suggestive references.

For instance, writing (*lekha*) is praised at Vin. iv. 7, as a distinguished sort of art; and whereas the sisters of the Order are, as a rule, to abstain from worldly arts, there are exceptions; and one of these is learning to write.[2] A criminal "who had been written up in the king's porch" (as we should say "who was wanted by the police") was not to be received into the Order.[3] In a discussion as to what career a lad should adopt, his parents say that if he adopt the profession of a "writer" he will dwell at ease and in comfort; but then, on the other hand, his fingers will ache.[4] Were a member of the Order to write to a man setting out the

[1] The whole tract is translated in my *Dialogues of the Buddha*, vol. i. pp. 3–26. The passage in question is on p. 11.

[2] Vin. iv. 305. [3] *Ibid.* i. 75. [4] *Ibid.* i. 77; iv. 128.

advantage of suicide, then, for each letter in the writing, he commits an offence.[1]

It is evident, therefore, that writing was in vogue at the time these passages were composed: that it was made use of for the publication of official notices, and for the communication by way of letter between private individuals: that the ability to write was a possible and honourable source of livelihood: that the knowledge of writing was not confined to any particular class, but was acquired by ordinary folk, and by women: and that it was sufficiently prevalent to have been made the basis of a game for children. A long period, probably centuries, must have elapsed between the date when writing first became known to the few, and the date when such a stage could have been reached.

But it is a long step from the use of writing for such notifications, public or private, to the use of it for the purpose of writing down any books, much less an extensive literature. And the very same texts we have just quoted show, and show in a manner equally indisputable, that, for such purposes, writing, however well known, had not yet come into use.

For if books had been known and used in India at the period in question, then the manuscripts themselves, and the whole industry connected with

[1] Vin. iii. 76. The expression used for writing is here *lekham chindati*, "scratches a writing." From this Bühler (*Indische Päleographie*, p. 88) concludes that the material implied is wood. But the reference is to scratching with a style on a leaf.

them, must have played an important part in the daily life of the members of the Buddhist Order. Now the extant rules of the Order place clearly enough before our eyes the whole of the "personal property" of the community, or of its individuals. Every movable thing, down to the smallest and least important domestic utensil, is referred to, and its use pointed out. And articles in ordinary use among laymen, but not allowed to members of the Order, are mentioned also, in order to be disallowed. But nowhere do we find the least trace of any reference to books or manuscripts.

This is really decisive. It is one of those rare cases where negative evidence, the absence of the mention of something where the mention of it would be reasonably expected, is good evidence. But this is not all. Positive evidence comes in at the precise point where it is wanted. There is pretty constant reference to the texts as existing, but existing only in the memory of those who had learnt them by heart. Here we have the explanation of how the difficulty was met.

Thus at Anguttara, 3. 107, the dangers that may eventually fall upon the faith are being discussed. One is that the members of the Order will listen and give heed when poetical, pretty, ornate Suttantas are being repeated, and think them worthy of the trouble of being learnt by heart; but will neglect the deeper, more subtle, more philosophical treatises.

So at Anguttara, 2. 147, among four causes of the decay of religion one is that "those Bhikshus who have learnt much (literally, heard much), to whom the tradition has been handed on, who carry (in their memory) the doctrine, and the discipline, and the indices thereto (that is, the tables of contents drawn up to assist the memory) they (those Bhikshus) may not be careful to make others repeat some Suttanta; and so, when they shall themselves have passed away, that Suttanta will become cut off at the root, without a place of refuge."

Again at Anguttara, 5. 136, we have the "nutriment" of a list of mental states, the conditions precedent without which they cannot be and grow. One of these states is learning, scholarship. One would expect to find that study, the reading of books, would be its "nutriment." Not at all. It is said to be "repeating over to oneself." A chance expression of this sort has particular value. For it implies that the basis of learning was what a man carried in his head, in his memory; and that constant repetition was required to prevent his losing it. It is a sort of expression that would have been impossible if books had been in general use.

In the canon law also we find two suggestive rules. In the *Vinaya Texts*, I. 267, the rule is that the Pātimokkha, consisting of the 227 Rules of the Order, is to be recited monthly in each "residence" or monastic settlement. And if, among the brethren there, none should know the rules by heart, then they are (not to send for a copy, but) to send one of their younger members to some neighbouring fraternity, there to learn the Pātimokkha, either with or without the explanations of the several rules, by heart.

Shortly afterwards we have a rule forbidding the brethren to travel in the rainy season. But among the exceptions[1] we find the case put that a layman knows how to recite some celebrated Suttanta. "If he send a messenger to the brethren, saying: 'Might their reverences come and learn this Suttanta, otherwise this Suttanta will fall into oblivion?'"—then they may go, so important is the emergency, even during the rains.

It is evident from such passages—and many others might be quoted to a like effect—that the idea of recording, by writing, even a Suttanta, the average length of which is only about twenty pages of the size of this work, did not occur to the men who composed or used the canonical texts. They could not even have thought of the possibility of using writing as a means of guarding against such painful accidents. Yet, as we have seen, the Indian peoples had been acquainted with letters, and with writing, for a long time, probably for centuries before; and had made very general use of writing for short communications. It seems extraordinary that they should have abstained from its use on occasions which were, to them, so important. Now the reason why they did so abstain is twofold.

In the first place writing was introduced into India at a late period in the intellectual development of its people—so late that, before they knew of it, they had already brought to perfection, to a perfection

[1] *Vinaya Texts*, I. 305.

unparalleled in the history of the world, another method, and in some respects a very excellent method, of handing down literary productions. They would not lightly give up, for a new-fangled expedient, this tried and ancient one.

In the second place, even had they desired to do so, they could not. For they did not become acquainted, at the same time when they came to know of writing, with the necessary materials for writing lengthy records.

We have only just been able to see clearly this very curious state of things. But we now have three different lines of evidence all converging to a certain date as that of the introduction of writing into India: and it is the knowledge of that date which has led to the true explanation.

The first line is that of the oldest references to writing in Indian literature as set out above.

The second line is the discovery, due originally to Professor Weber, and lately greatly extended and confirmed by Hofrath Dr. Bühler,[1] that a certain proportion of the oldest Indian letters are practically identical with letters on certain Assyrian weights, and on the so-called Mesa inscription of the seventh and sixth centuries B.C. About one-third of the twenty-two letters of the so-called Northern Semitic alphabet of that period are identical with the oldest forms of the corresponding Indian letters. Another third are somewhat similar. And the remaining third can, with great difficulty, be more or less—gene-

[1] In Part III. of his *Indian Studies* (2d ed., 1898), and in his *Indische Päleographie*, 1896.

8

rally less—harmonised. Other scholars have made similar, but not such satisfactory, comparisons between the Indian letters and those of the Southern forms of the Semitic alphabet. And the conclusion hitherto drawn has been either, with Weber and Bühler, that the Indian alphabet is derived from the Northern Semites; or, with Dr. Deecke, Isaac Taylor, and others, that it is derived from that of the Southern Semites, in South Arabia.

Now direct intercourse, at the requisite date, was possible, but not probable, along the coast, between India and South Arabia, where the resemblance is least. No one contends that the Indians had any direct communication with the men who, on the borders of Palestine, inscribed the Mesa stone, where the resemblance is greater. I venture to think, therefore, that the only hypothesis harmonising these discoveries is that the Indian letters were derived, neither from the alphabet of the Northern, nor from that of the Southern Semites, but from that source from which these, in their turn, had been derived — from the pre-Semitic form of writing used in the Euphrates Valley.

As to the date, the derivation must have taken place at a time when the resemblance between the forms of the letters is greatest. It must have been, therefore, in the seventh century B.C. or earlier; for a comparison of *later* Babylonian or Semitic forms shows no sufficient agreement. And it is to be supposed that the origin of the Indian alphabet is previous to the time when the parent script was written from right to left. For the Indian, like our own, runs from left to right. Only the legend on one coin (described in Cunningham's *Coins of Ancient India*)[1] and a few short inscriptions in Ceylon, not yet published,[2] run from right to left. Certain groups of letters also, in the third century B.C., are intended to be read, as

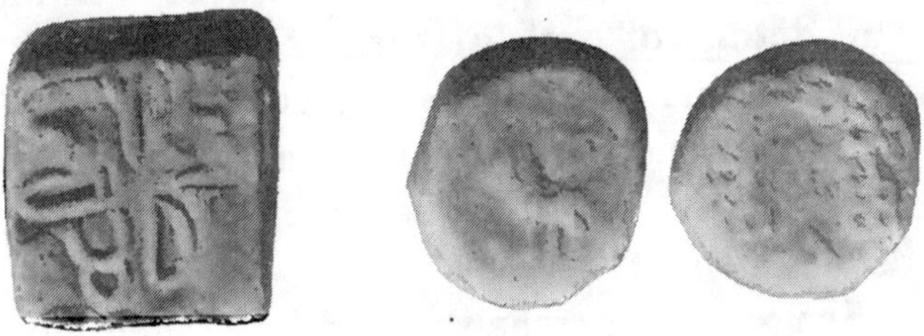

FIG. 25.—ERAN COINS.

[See pp. 321, 322.]

we should say, backwards.[3] The direction of the writing was open to fluctuation when these (by no means the most ancient) records were made.

The third line of evidence is that best brought together by Mr. Kennedy in his article in the *Journal of the Royal Asiatic Society* for 1898. It tends to show:

1. That continued and extensive trading took place in the seventh century B.C. between Babylon and ports on the west coast of India.

2. That it is highly improbable that there was any such trade much before that time.

3. That it is not at all likely that the Indian

[1] The coin No. 1 is reproduced here by the kindness of Mr. Head and Mr. Rapson, from the coin itself, now in the British Museum; No. 2 is in Mr. White King's collection.

[2] See Mr. Wickramasinha's letter in the *J. R. A. S.* 1895.

[3] See Mr. Wickramasinha's article in the *J. R. A. S.* 1901.

merchants who went to Babylon went also farther inland, from Babylon to the west; or that they continued their voyages as far as Yemen; or that they reached Babylon overland, by way of the passes, across Afghanistan.

There is still much to be done in the working out of the details of each of these three lines of evidence. No one of them is yet conclusive by itself. But the consensus of all three lends confirmation to each. And it may now be accepted as a working hypothesis that:

1. Sea-going merchants, availing themselves of the monsoons, were in the habit, at the beginning of the seventh (and perhaps at the end of the eighth) century B.C., of trading from ports on the south-west coast of India (Sovīra at first, afterwards Suppāraka and Bharukaccha) to Babylon, then a great mercantile emporium.

2. These merchants were mostly Dravidians, not Aryans. Such Indian names of the goods imported as were adopted in the west (Solomon's ivory, apes, and peacocks, for instance, and the word "rice") were adaptations, not of Sanskrit or Pāli, but of Tamil words.

3. These merchants there became acquainted with an alphabetic writing derived from that first invented and used by the white pre-Semitic race now called Akkadians.

4. That alphabet had previously been carried, by wandering Semitic tribes, from Babylon to the west, both north-west and south-west. Some of the particular letters learnt by the Indian merchants

are closely allied to letters found on inscriptions recorded by those Semitic tribes, and also on Babylonian weights, both of a date somewhat earlier than the time when the Indians made their trading journeys.

5. After the merchants brought this script to India it gradually became enlarged and adapted to suit the special requirements of the Indian learned and colloquial dialects. Nearly a thousand years afterwards the thus adapted alphabet became known as the Brāhmī Lipī, the Sublime Writing. What name it bore in the interval—for instance, in Asoka's time—is not known. From it all the alphabets now used in India, Burma, Siam, and Ceylon have been gradually evolved.

6. When this script was first brought to India in the eighth or seventh century B.C., the Indians had already possessed an extensive Vedic literature handed down in the priestly schools by memory, and by memory alone. The alphabet soon became known to the priests. But they continued as before to hand down their books by the old method only. It is probable, however, that they began to make use of written notes to aid the memory on which they still, in the main, depended.

7. The material on which the signs had been traced in Babylon was clay. They were traced in India with an iron style, on leaves, or on pieces of bark, chiefly birch bark. No ink was used; and these mere scratchings on such fragile substances were not only difficult to make out, but the leaves or bark were apt easily to be broken up or destroyed.

8. It was not till long afterwards that a method of preparing large pieces of bark or the leaves of the Corypha talipot palm so as to prevent their breaking was discovered. It was not till long afterwards that an ink was discovered, which could be rubbed over such a leaf with letters scratched upon it, and would then remain in the scratches, thus making the writing easily legible. Till these discoveries had been made there were really no materials practically available for use as books. And it was probably chiefly because of the fact that the need of such materials was not felt that the discoveries were not much sooner made.

9. To say indeed that the need was not felt is, as regards the Vedic schools, not nearly strong enough. The priests were, as a body, exceedingly keen to keep the knowledge of the *mantras* (the charms or verses), on which the magic of the sacrifice depended, in their own hands. There are some pretty rules about this in the later priestly law-books — rules that received, it should be noted, the cordial approval of Shankara.[1]

"The ears of a Sudra who listens, intentionally, when the Veda is being recited are to be filled with molten lead. His tongue is to be cut out if he recite it. His body is to be split in twain if he preserve it in his memory."[2] The priestly view was that God himself had bestowed the exclusive right of teaching upon the hereditary priests[3]; who claimed to be, each of them, great divinities,[4] even to the gods.[5]

[1] On the Vedānta Sūtras, I. 3. 38. [2] Gautama, xii. 4–6.
[3] Manu, I. 88. [4] *Ibid.* ix. 317, 319. [5] *Ibid.* xi. 85.

We cannot, therefore, be far wrong if we suppose they were not merely indifferent to the use of writing as a means of handing on the books so lucrative to themselves, but were even strongly opposed to a method so dangerous to their exclusive privileges. And we ought not to be surprised to find that the oldest manuscripts on bark or palm leaf known in India are Buddhist; that the earliest written records on stone and metal are Buddhist; that it is the Buddhists who first made use of writing to record their canonical books; and that the earliest mention of writing at all in the voluminous priestly literature is in the Vāsishṭha Dharma Sūtra[1]—one of the later law books, and long posterior to the numerous references quoted above from the Buddhist canon.

It is, of course, not impossible, *a priori*, that the priests in India had developed an alphabet of their own out of picture writing; and that it was on to such an alphabet that the borrowed letters were grafted. General Cunningham went even farther. He thought the alphabet was altogether developed, independently, on Indian soil. But we have at present, not only no evidence to that effect, but much the other way. All the present available evidence tends to show that the Indian alphabet is not Aryan at all; that it was introduced into India by Dravidian merchants; and that it was not, in spite of their invaluable services in other respects to Indian literature, to the priests, whose self-interests were opposed to such discoveries, but to traders, and to less prejudiced literary circles, that India

[1] xvi. 10. 14.

owes the invention of those improvements in the mechanical aids to writing that enabled the long previously existent knowledge of letters to be applied at last to the production and preservation of books.

CHAPTER VIII

WRITING — ITS DEVELOPMENT

IT may be asked why the Indian merchants who brought the knowledge of the alphabet from Babylon to Western India did not also bring the method, then carried in Babylon to so great a degree of success, of writing — and of writing not only mercantile memoranda but also books — on clay tablets, on bricks.

The problem is not without difficulty. But it does not arise only in India. Elsewhere also the traders or tribes who learnt the alphabet in the Euphrates Valley never adopted the habit of writing on bricks. Bricks and tablets and seals, all of them of clay, have been found, indeed, in widely separated parts of India, with letters, and even sentences, inscribed upon them. But the letters on the bricks, though most interesting as palæographic evidence, are merely mason's marks; the inscribed clay tablets contain only short sentences of scripture; and the legends on the seals are only of the usual kind. The fact remains, therefore, that clay was not in any general use among the people as a material for writing books upon, or even short communications. As a specimen of writing on clay the annexed figure of a tablet discovered by Dr. Hoey,

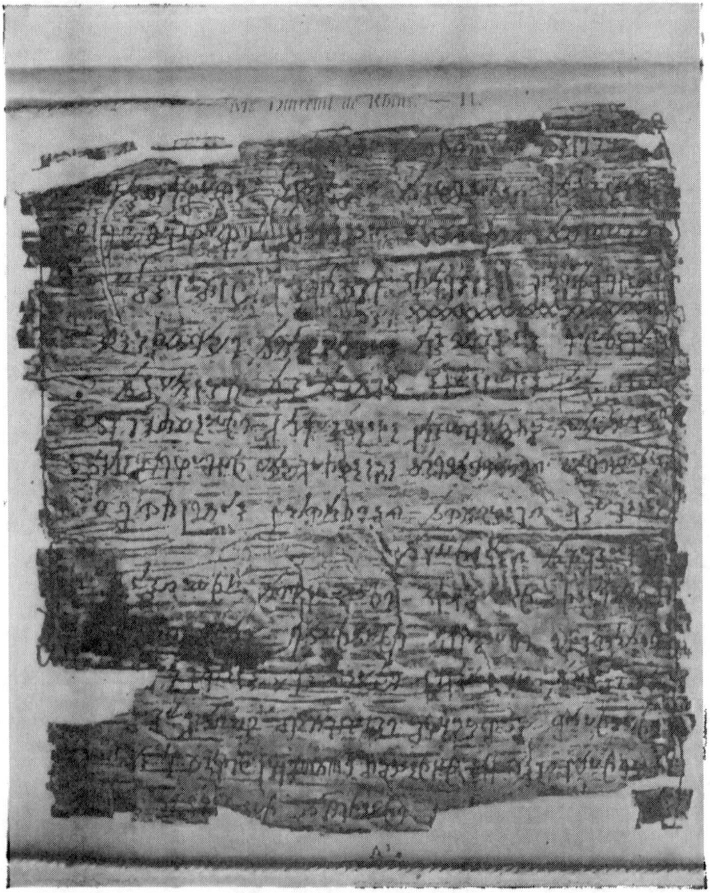

FIG. 26.—LEAF OF MS. FROM THE GOSINGA VIHĀRA OF AN OLD BUDDHIST ANTHOLOGY.

by whose kindness I am allowed to reproduce it, is interesting. It contains a Buddhist tract. Of course copper and gold plates were early and often

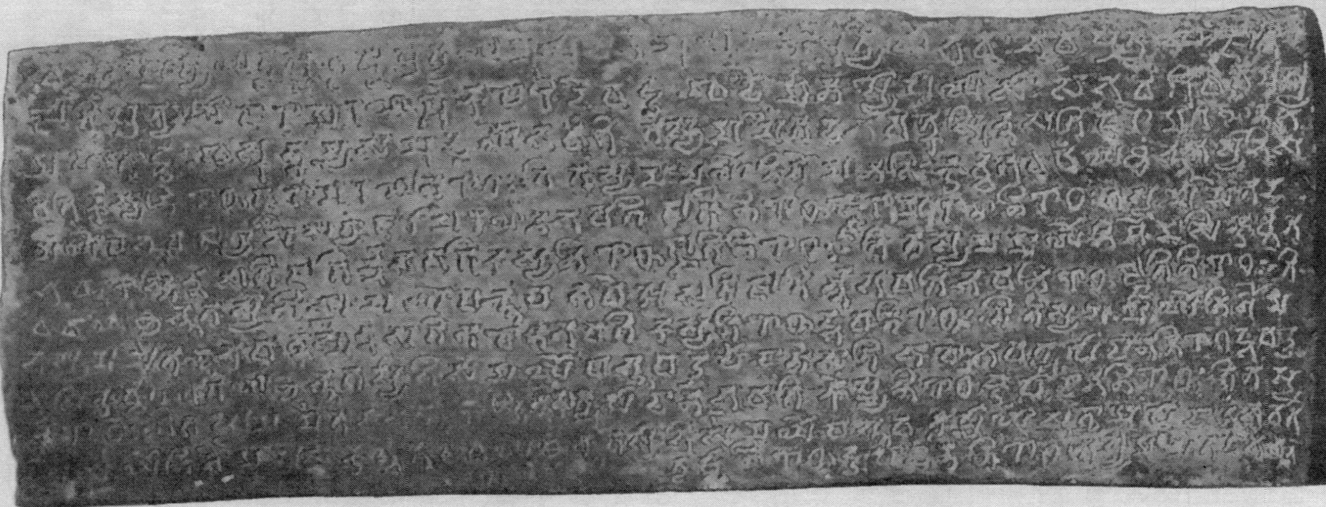

FIG. 27.—DR. HOEY'S BRICK TABLET, WITH BUDDHIST SUTTA INSCRIBED ON IT.

used, of which the Takshila copper plates and one of the Maung-gon gold plates are here shown.

On the other hand we have abundant evidence, both literary and archæological, of the use for such purposes of birch bark and palm leaves. The oldest specimen of a book in such writing hitherto discovered is the MS. found in the ruins of the Gosinga Vihāra, thirteen miles from Khotan. This MS. is written with ink on birch bark in letters of the Kharoṣṭrī alphabet, an alphabet introduced overland into the extreme north-west of India about 500 B.C., and used locally in Gandhāra (side by side with the other alphabet to which reference has been made above, and to which all existing Indian alphabets can be traced back).[1] This MS., portions of which have just found their way both to Paris and St. Petersburg, must have been written in Gandhāra shortly before or after the Christian era. And it contains an anthology of Buddhist religious verses taken from the canonical books, but given in a local dialect, younger than the Pāli of the texts.[2]

The next MS. in point of age is much younger. It is the one discovered by Captain Bower in Mingai, near Kuchar, containing medical receipts and formulas for snake-charming, and written in characters of the fourth or perhaps the fifth century A.D., with

[1] The name of this alphabet has always been spelt *Kharoṣṭhī*. But Professor Sylvain Lévi in his just published article in the *Bulletin de l'école français d'extrême-orient* for 1902 has clearly shown that the right spelling is as above, and that the Kharostra is simply the name of a country, to wit, Kashgar.

[2] See Senart in the *Journal Asiatique* for 1898; and compare Rh. D.'s note in the *J.R.A.S.* for 1899.

FIG. 28.—THE COPPER PLATE FROM TAKKA-SILĀ.

[*Epigraphia Indica*, Vol. IV.]

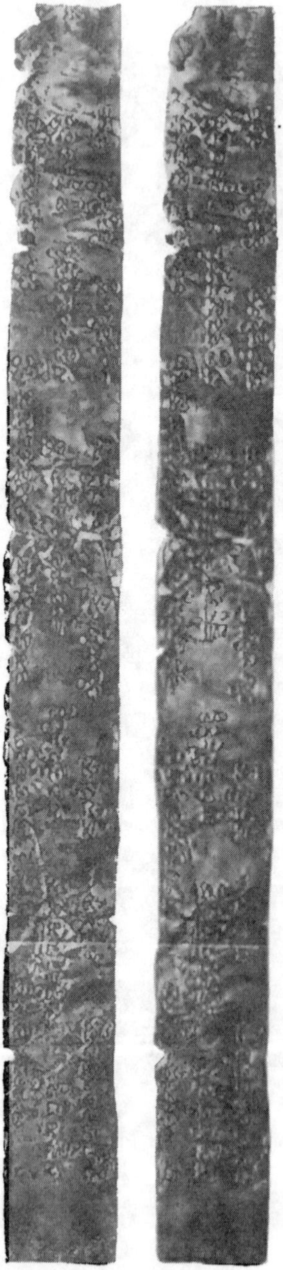

FIG. 29.—THE MAUNG-GON GOLD PLATE. [From *Epigraphia Indica*, Vol. V., p. 101.]

ink, on birch bark cut to imitate palm leaves. These leaves are also pierced with holes, through which a string can be passed to keep the leaves together — a plan always adopted for palm leaves, but very unsuitable for birch bark, which is so brittle that the string is apt to tear and break the leaves, as it had done in this case. The language used in this MS. is sufficiently near to classical Sanskrit for it to be called Sanskrit. But the five different short treatises of which this MS. consists contain, in varying degree, a good many colloquialisms.[1] Other MSS. of great

[1] See now, on this MS., Dr. Hoernle's magnificent edition of the texts, with lithographed reproductions, transliterations, and translations. Professor Bühler's preliminary remarks on it are in the fifth volume of the *Vienna Oriental Journal*.

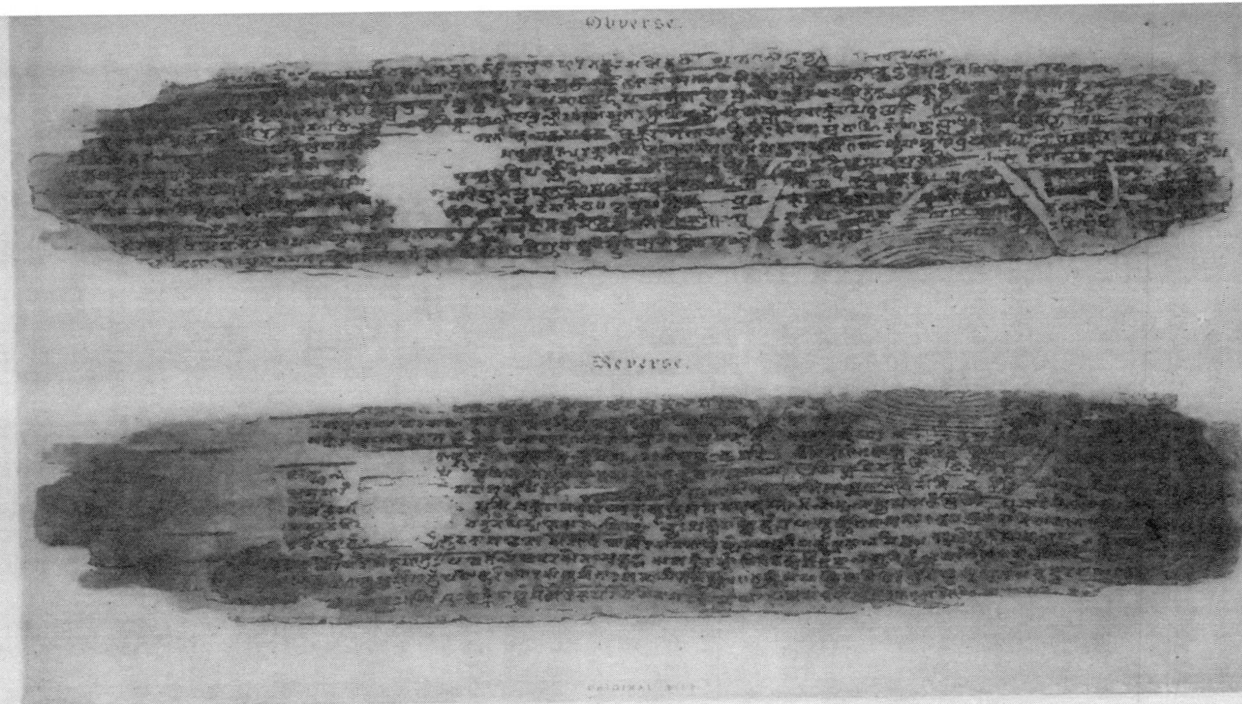

FIG. 30.—LEAF FROM THE BOWER MS. BIRCH BARK CUT TO IMITATE PALM LEAVES, WITH HOLES FOR STRINGS TO TIE THEM UP WITH.

age have been recently discovered in Turkestan; but these are the oldest ones so far deciphered and edited. The others are still awaiting decipherment, and are in the hands of Dr. Hoernle for that purpose.

Now as the Bower MS. is in Sanskrit (though not good Sanskrit), and the Gosinga MS. is in a dialect allied to, but younger than Pāli, the natural conclusion would seem to be that, as Sanskrit is older than Pāli, the texts contained in the Bower MS. must be older. That the MS. itself, the particular copy that has survived, is some centuries later, does not matter. Pāli is to Sanskrit about as Italian is to Latin. Whatever the age of the MSS. in which the copies of them may be written, the text of a work by Vergil must be older than the text of a work by Dante. The conclusion seems, therefore, obvious that a work in Sanskrit, whatever the age of the MS. in which it is written, must be older than a work in Pāli, and, *a fortiori*, older than a work in a dialect that is, philologically speaking, younger than Pāli.

Oddly enough the exact contrary is the case. Not only is the Gosinga MS. older than the Bower MS., but the verses contained in it are also older than the texts contained in the Bower MS., and that *precisely because they are written in a dialect closely allied to Pāli.* And we should know this for certain even if we had only printed copies of these two works, that is, even if we had not the palæographic evidence of the age of the handwriting to guide us. For, in the period we are considering, the more closely a book or an inscription approximates to

Fig. 31.—The inscribed vase from the Sākiya tope.

pure Sanskrit, unalloyed by colloquialisms, by Pāli phrases and grammatical forms, the *later* it is—notwithstanding the fact that Sanskrit is, etymologically speaking, older than Pāli.

The explanation of this apparent anomaly is really perfectly plain and simple. It is clear enough from a comparison of the literature, but it is more easily shown, perhaps, by a comparison of the inscriptions. Take the inscription, for instance, on the vase discovered by Mr. Peppé in the Sākiya Tope—which is in my opinion the oldest inscription yet discovered in India—and what do we find?[1]

1. As to the language. It is entirely in the living language, in the vernacular.

2. As to the orthography. The consonants are roughly and rudely written.

3. The only vowels expressed, by signs hung on to the consonants, are *i* and *u* and (in one doubtful case) either *e* or *o*.

4. No consonants are written double, in spite of the fact that double consonants, pronounced double (as in Italian of to-day), were a marked feature of the vernacular.

5. No groups of consonants (such as the *ndr* in our word *hundred* or the *pl* and *st* in our word *plastic*, are written as groups. Thus the word for "of the Sākiyas" is written *s ki y n*ᵐ, which is the nearest orthography the writer could get, or troubled

[1] See the *Journal of the Royal Asiatic Society*, 1898 and 1899.
The annexed illustrations are from photographs by Mr. Peppé to whose skill and enterprise we owe this most interesting and important addition to our knowledge.

himself to get, for the word as spoken in the living local dialect. This may have been either *Sākiyānaṃ* or *Sakkiyānaṃ* (pronounced Sak-kiyānang).

It will be noticed that the orthography, therefore, is very imperfect. It is, strictly speaking, not so much an alphabet as a syllabary. The light

FIG. 32.—THE PEPPÉ VASES.
Found by Mr. Peppé in the Sākiya Tope.

vowel *a*, pronounced as in our word *vocal*, is supposed inherent in every consonant on to which no other vowel is hung. No attempt is yet made to distinguish between long and short vowels. No diphthongs are written. There is no expedient as yet to show that a consonant is to be pronounced as a final, that is, without the inherent *a;* and this, together with the absence of groups, is what renders it impossible to express the double consonants so frequent in the actual language.

The next stage we have (that is, at present; no doubt as soon as archæological explorations are carried on systematically in India intermediate stages will be available) are the Asoka inscriptions. Of these thirty-four have so far been found, and M. Senart, in his *Inscriptions de Piyadasi*, has subjected all those discovered before 1886 to an exhaustive and detailed analysis. With these ought to be compared the greater number of the inscriptions on the Bharhut Tope, some of which are a little older, some a little younger, and only one or two a good deal younger than Asoka.

Two tendencies are very marked in these inscriptions of the third century B.C. In the first place the orthographical expedients are very much improved. All the long vowels are now marked as such. Once we have a diphthong. Numerous groups of consonants are written as such. The letters as a whole are engraved much more neatly and regularly. The alphabet tends, therefore, to be much more accurate, more phonetic, fuller, more complete.

On the other hand, the scribes or engravers, or both, have fallen into the habit of giving expression in their orthography to what they conceived to be the more learned and more proper forms of words, and of grammatical inflexions, rather than to the forms actually in use in the real, living language. The alphabet tends, therefore, to be much less accurate, to give a less faithful picture of the living speech.

This last tendency is exactly analogous to what happened when our own spelling was being set-

Fig. 33.—Ruins of the Sākiya Tope, put up by his relatives over their portion of the ashes from the funeral pyre of the Buddha.

tled. Englishmen probably pronounced *would* and *could* much as they do now. But some one knew there had been an *l* in the earlier form of *would* (as in the German *wollte*). And so he spelt it with an *l*, which no longer existed in the real, living speech. Somebody else (who thought he would be quite learned, and proper, and on the safe side), spelt *could* also with an *l*, though the *l* existed, in this case, neither in the older form of the word nor in the living speech. And now we are saddled with the *l* in both words whether we like it or not. It was this latter tendency which won the day in India. Very gradually the efforts to represent the real facts of the language gave way to another effort altogether, the effort to give expression to the learned phraseology. The past history of the words came to be considered more than their actual sound. Both the language in the inscriptions, and the methods of spelling adopted in them, became more and more artificial. The double process went on through the centuries, until at last, at the very time when the alphabet had been so continually improved that it had become the most perfect instrument of phonetic expression the world has yet seen, the other process had also reached its climax, the living speech had completely disappeared from the monuments, and all the inscriptions are recorded in a dead language, in the so-called classical Sanskrit. The oldest inscription in pure Sanskrit so far discovered, that of Rudradāman at Girnar in the Kathiawad, is dated (no doubt in the Saka Era) in the year 72. It belongs, therefore, to the middle of the second century after Christ. It had taken four centuries from Asoka's time to reach this stage. And though the end was not yet, and inscriptions in

FIG. 34.—FRAGMENT OF THE 13TH ROCK EDICT OF ASOKA, DISCOVERED BY PROFESSOR RHYS-DAVIDS AT GIRNAR.

the vernacular, pedantically contorted, are still met with, from the fifth century onwards the dead language reigns supreme.

The case of the coins is, if possible, even more instructive. The oldest coin which bears an inscription in Sanskrit is a unique coin of Satyadāman, belonging to the western Kshatrapa dynasty, whose approximate date is 200 A.D.[1] Of the seven words contained in the inscription on this coin all have Sanskrit terminations, and only one offends against the rules of *sandhi* as observed in Sanskrit. All coins previous to this one bear legends either in Pāli or in the vernacular. So, also, oddly enough, do all subsequent coins for a period of about two centuries. The experiment was evidently found to have been a failure, and was not repeated. Sporadically we find single words in Sanskrit occurring in legends, otherwise in the vernacular. These are evidence of the desire of the mint authorities, or of the mint officials, to appear learned. But the people did not fancy the innovation of Sanskrit legends, and the authorities apparently did not care to go on issuing coins not popular with the people.

So in our own country up to as late as the end of the nineteenth century any important monumental record in honour of a wealthy or successful personage was almost always written in Latin. Coins still, for the most part, have their legends in Latin. And throughout Europe, up to a date not so very remote, works on a great variety of subjects were written, and education was often carried on, in that language.[2] We have never reached the point, reached in the fifth century A.D. in India, that the

[1] Rapson in the *J. R. A. S.* 1899, p. 379.

[2] Even in 1855, the first Pāli text edited in Europe was edited with Latin introduction, Latin notes, and a Latin translation.

dead language was exclusively used. But we were not so very far from it. And the conditions as to this matter in the two continents—for India is more of a continent than a country—were more similar than is often supposed. The dead language in each case was the language used in the sacrifice. The greater credit attaching to it was largely of a religious nature. But it was also a sort of *lingua franca* widely understood through many countries in which many various languages were respectively the language of the people. There was a time in each case when the clergy were in great part the main custodians of the learning of the day, so that the language of the church was the most convenient language in which to appeal to a larger circle of educated people than could be reached through any one vernacular. And in each case those who first used the vernacular were the men who wished to appeal to the people, who were advocating what they deemed to be reforms.

There are, of course, differences also in these two cases. The most important of these is that, in India, the use of the vernacular came first in order of time. And one result of this was the curious dialect half-way between the vernacular and the dead language, which may be called equally well either mixed Sanskrit or mixed vernacular, according as it approximates more or less to the one or to the other. Another result was that, the vernacular being taken so early, the grammatical terminations still survived in it in a shape more or less akin to those in use in the dead language. When

Dr. Johnson overlaid his English with a mass of Latin words, the process stopped at a kind of hybrid vernacular. When the Indian writers before and after the Christian Era did the same sort of thing, and began to adopt also the Sanskrit grammatical terminations, the end was inevitable. When they made use of a mixture of some real forms and words drawn from the vernacular, some such words slightly altered to make them look more learned, and some forms wholly artificial with no existence at all in living speech, the only possible consequence was that the first sort were called vulgar, the second blunders, and only the third declared to be right. The hybrid they thus made use of became increasingly too like Sanskrit to be able to contend against it; and from the end of the fourth century the latter alone was used. Then, linguistically speaking, death reigned supreme. The living language was completely overshadowed by the artificial substitute. The changeling had taken the place of the rightful heir. The parasite had overgrown and smothered the living tree from which it drew its sustenance, from which it had derived its birth.

The loss, from the point of view of intellectual advancement, must have been very great. Who can doubt that Europe was fortunate in escaping (and it was a very narrow escape) a similar bondage? Classical Sanskrit, in consequence very largely of the rich fortune it had inherited from the vernacular as previously cultivated,—for Pali is not much farther removed from the vernacular than, say, Hume's *Essay* from the spoken English of the day,

—is rich in varied expressions. But, with its long compounds and its poverty in syntax, it is cumbrous and unwieldy as compared even with the Latin of the Middle Ages, and much more so if compared with any living tongue. It must be a disadvantage to write in any language in which one does not habitually speak and think. And the disadvantage is not lessened when the existing works in that language are charged with an unprogressive (not to say reactionary) spirit in religion, philosophy, and social views of life.

It is therefore clear why Pali books written in India, or books in a dialect allied to Pali, or in a mixture of such a dialect and forms taken from pure Ṡanskrit, are each of them older than the books written in classical Sanskrit; and why a coin, a book, or an inscription, in so far as its language approximates to the regular Sanskrit, is later, and not earlier. The vernacular was used first. Then, gradually, what were considered more learned forms (taken from the dead language used in the priestly schools) were, in a greater and greater degree, made use of, till, finally, the regular Sanskrit became used exclusively.

CHAPTER IX

LANGUAGE AND LITERATURE

I. GENERAL VIEW

IN early times there must have been several systems of literature preserved independently among the followers of different schools. No one of these schools preserved (that is, learnt by heart) the literature of the others. But each knew of the others, talked over the opinions maintained in them, considered in their own Suttas what was preserved in the Suttas of their opponents. We have a fair number of well-established instances of men who had received a long training in one school passing over to another. These men at least had thus acquired a familiarity, more or less complete, with two literatures.

In the forests adjoining the settlements, the disciples of the various schools, living a hermit life, occupied themselves, according to the various tendencies of the schools to which they belonged, either in meditation or in sacrificial rites, or in practices of self-torture, or in repeating over to themselves, and in teaching to their pupils, the Suttas containing the tenets of their school. Much time was spent in gathering fruits and roots for their sustenance, or in going into the village for alms. And there was difference of opinion, and of practice, as to the comparative importance attached to the learning of texts. But the hermitages where the learning, or the repeating, of texts was unknown were the exceptions.

Then, besides the Hermits, there was another body of men, greatly respected throughout the country, quite peculiar to India, and not known even there much before the rise of Buddhism, called the Wanderers (*Paribbājakā*). They were teachers, or sophists, who spent eight or nine months of every year wandering about precisely with the object of engaging in conversational discussions on matters of ethics and philosophy, nature lore and mysticism. Like the sophists among the Greeks, they differed very much in intelligence, in earnestness, and in honesty. Some are described as "Eel-wrigglers," "Hair-splitters," and not without reason if we may fairly judge from the specimens of their lucubrations preserved by their opponents.[1] But there must have been many of a very different character, or the high reputation they enjoyed, as a body, would scarcely have been maintained. We hear of halls put up for their accommodation, for the discussion by them of their systems of belief. Such was "The Hall" in Queen Mallikā's park at Sāvatthi,[2] and the "Gabled Pavilion" put up by the Licchavi clan in

[1] *Dialogues of the Buddha*, I. 37, 38. [2] *Ibid.*, p. 244.

the Great Wood adjoining their capital of Vesāli, and often mentioned in the books as the resort of the Wanderers. Or a special space was set apart for them in the groves adjoining the settlement,—such were the sweet-smelling Champaka Grove on the borders of the lake dug out by Queen Gaggarā at Champā[1]; the Mora-nivāpa, the place where the peacocks were fed, at Rājagaha,[2] and others.

The Wanderers are often represented as meeting one another at such places, or at the rest-houses (*chowltries*) which it was a prevalent custom for villagers to put up on the roadside for the common use of travellers. And they were in the habit, on their journeys, of calling on other Wanderers, or on the learned brahmins, or on the Hermits, resident in the neighbourhood of the places where they stopped. So Dīgha-nakha calls on the Buddha,[3] the Buddha visits Sakuludāyi,[4] Vekhanassa calls on the Buddha,[5] Keniya does the same,[6] and Potali-putta calls on Samiddhi.[7] The residents also, both to testify respect and to listen to their talk, used to call on the Wanderers when the latter stayed in or near a village—evidence both of the popularity of the Wanderers, and of the frequent interchange of opinion.

The Wanderers, some of whom were women, were not ascetics, except so far as they were celibates. The practices of self-mortification are always referred to as carried out by the Hermits in the woods. The Buddha, before he attained Nirvana under the

[1] *Dialogues of the Buddha*, 144. [4] M. 2. i. 29. [6] S. N. p. 99.
[2] M. 2. 1. [3] M. 1. 497. [5] M. 2. 40. [7] M. 3. 207.

Tree of Wisdom, had been such a self-torturer (*tāpasa*) in the woods on the banks of the Nerañjarā. Thenceforward he became a Wanderer. It was easy to pass from one career to the other. But they were quite distinct, were spoken of by different names, and in the priestly law-books we find quite different regulations laid down for the Hermits on the one hand, and the Wanderers on the other.[1]

We have the names of a considerable number of the individuals in both of these classes. And not only the personal names. In those cases when a number of individuals acknowledged the leadership of one teacher, or adhered to the same set of opinions (whether attributed to one teacher or not), they had also corporate names. Thus the members of that Order which we call the Buddhist Order were called *Sākyaputtīya Samaṇas*. Each order was called a Sangha. The members of the Sangha which we call the Jain Order were called the *Nigaṇṭhas*, "The Unfettered." There was an Order the members of which were called the *Ājīvakā*, the "Men of the Livelihood." Both of these orders were older than the Buddhist. The Jains have remained as an organised community all through the history of India from before the rise of Buddhism down to to-day. The Ājīvakās still existed as an organised community down to the time of Asoka's grandson Dasaratha, who gave them, as we learn from the inscriptions on the caves, certain cave-hermitages. They have long ago died out. And with the dis-

[1] The references are collected in *Dialogues of the Buddha*, I. pp. 208–212, 221.

appearance of the Order, the Suttas containing their ideas have vanished also. For during a long period they existed only in the memories of the members of the Order; and even after writing was applied to the preservation of such literary works, it was only the members of the Order or lay adherents of the school who would copy them. There are many references[1] in Jain and Buddhist books to this Order, and to the opinions they professed. And it will be possible, when these have been fully compared and summarised, to arrive at a more or less complete and accurate view of their tenets.

The names of other orders, of which we know little more than the names, have been preserved in the Anguttara.[2] And the existence of at least two or three others can be inferred from incidental references. There is still in existence a Vaikhānasa Sūtra, of about the third century A.D., which purports to contain the rules of an Order founded by one Vikhanas. It has just been mentioned that a certain Vekhanassa, a Wanderer, called on the Buddha. It is not improbable that he belonged to that Order. In a note on Pāṇini, iv. 3. 110, there are mentioned two brahmin orders, the Karmandinas and the Pārāsāriṇas. Now in the Majjhima (3. 298) the opinions of a certain Pārasāriya, a brahmin teacher, are discussed by the Buddha. It is very probable that he was either the founder or an adherent of the second of these schools. In any case the Order still existed at the time when the note

[1] Collected in *Dialogues of the Buddha*, I. pp. 71, 221.

[2] *Ibid.* p. 220.

to Pāṇini was made; and it is probably referred to in an inscription mentioned by Cunningham.[1]

Of the other schools or corporate bodies of Wanderers, or of Hermits, only the names are known. But as even the names throw light on the movement they may here be mentioned.[2] They are:

1. *Muṇḍa-sāvakā.*—"The disciples of the Shaveling."

2. *Jaṭilakā.*—"Those who wear their hair in braids." To do so was the rule for those of the Hermits who were brahmins, and perhaps other hermits also did so. In that case they cannot have formed one corporate body.

3. *Magaṇḍikā.*—This name is probably derived from the name of the founder of a corporate body. But all their records have perished, and we know nothing of them otherwise.

4. *Tedaṇḍikā.*—"The bearers of the triple staff." This is probably the name given, in the Buddhist community, to those of the Wanderers (not Hermits) who were brahmins. They were not allowed, by their rules, to wear their hair in braids, but must either have their heads shaved entirely, or so shaved as to leave a forelock only.

5. *Aviruddhakā.*—"The friends." We know as yet nothing otherwise about them.

6. *Gotamakā.*—"The followers of Gotama." These are almost certainly the followers of Devadatta, the Buddha's cousin, who founded an Order in opposition to the Buddhist Order, on the ground that the

[1] *Archæological Reports*, xx. 105.

[2] For references see *Dialogues of the Buddha*, pp. 220–222.

latter was too easy-going in its regulations as to food, and did not favour asceticism.

7. *Devadhammikā.*—"Those who follow the religion of the gods" or perhaps "of the god." On neither interpretation do we know the exact meaning of the term.

We find in this curious list several names, used technically as the designation of particular orders, or bodies of *religieux*, but in meaning applicable quite as much to most of the others. They all claimed to be pure as regards means of livelihood (like the Ājīvakās); to be unfettered (like the Nigaṇṭhas); to be friends (like the Aviruddhakās); they were all, except the Jaṭilakās, Wanderers, they were all mendicants (Bhikshus). The names can only gradually have come to have the special meaning of the member of one division or order, only. We find a similar state of things in the names of Christian sects in England to-day. And a considerable time must have elapsed before the names could thus have become specialised.

All this is very suggestive from more than one point of view. And as some of these points are of the first importance for a right understanding of the questions of language and literature, I may be allowed to enlarge a little on one or two of them. It is clear, in the first place, that there was no obstacle, arising from diversity of language, to intercourse—and that not merely as regards ordinary conversation about the ordinary necessities of daily life, but as regards philosophical and religious discussions of a subtle and earnest kind. The common language thus widely understood — used from the land of the Kurus in the west to Magadha in the east, northwards at Sāvatthi and Kusinārā in the Nepal hills, and southwards in one direction as far as Ujjen — could not have been Sanskrit. Classical Sanskrit was not yet in existence; and the language used in the Brāhmaṇas was neither sufficiently known outside the widely scattered schools of the brahmins, nor of a nature to lend itself easily to such discussions. The very last thing one would say of it would be to call it a conversational idiom. Neither is it probable that each one could have spoken in the dialect of the peasantry of his own place of origin. It would have been impossible to use such a dialect for the discussion of such subjects as are described as the matter of these dialogues.

The only reasonable and probable explanation is that the Wanderers talked in a language common among the cultured laity (officials, nobles, merchants, and others), which bore to the local dialects much the same relation as the English of London, in Shakespeare's time, bore to the various dialects spoken in Somersetshire, Yorkshire, and Essex. The growth of such a language had only just then become possible. It was greatly promoted by (if not, indeed, the immediate result of) the growth of the great kingdom of Kosala. This included, just before the rise of Buddhism, all, and more than all, of the present United Provinces. And it gave occasion and security for peaceful intercourse, both of a commercial and of an official kind, from one end to the other of its extensive territory. It was precisely these political conditions which favoured also the rapid growth of the institution or custom of the Wanderers, of whom we have no evidence prior to the establishment of the Kosalan power, and who doubtless contributed much to the cultivation of the more intellectual side of the common language which was enabled to grow up under the protective shield of the Kosalan peace.

The question has been much complicated and obscured by the impressions derived from the Sanskrit dramas which early in the history of our acquaintance with Indian literature became known to Europeans. In them the men of any social standing speak Sanskrit, except occasionally when addressing women. And even the women, especially those of higher rank, are supposed to understand, and occasionally, mostly when verses are put into their mouths, to speak it. Otherwise in the dramas the characters talk, not the vernacular, but the literary Prakrits.[1]

It is probable, even at the time when the dramas were written, that as a matter of fact every one, in ordinary daily life, spoke neither Sanskrit nor Prakrit, but simply the vernaculars. It is only the authors, when addressing a cultured public at a date when Sanskrit had become the paramount literary language, who thought it proper, in their dramas, to divide up the speeches between Sanskrit and the equally unreal literary Prakrits. But however that may be, even if Sanskrit were then used

[1] See the instances collected by Pischel, *Grammatik der Prakritsprachen*, pp. 31, 32.

by ordinary people in their daily intercourse,—which seems to me quite incredible,—that is still of no value at all as evidence of the condition of things twelve centuries before, in a much more simple and natural state of society.

Another point is that though brahmins take part in the religious and philosophical conversations of those early times, and in the accounts of them are always referred to with respect, and treated with the same courtesy that they always themselves (with one or two instructive exceptions) extended also to others, yet they hold no predominant position. The majority of the Wanderers, and the most influential individuals among them, are not brahmins. And the general impression conveyed by the texts is that the Wanderers and other non-priestly teachers were quite as much, if not more esteemed than the brahmins by the whole people—kings, nobles, officials, merchants, artisans, and peasantry.

"But that is only a matter of course," will be the obvious objection. "The books you quote, if not the work of bitter opponents, were at least composed under rajput influence, and are prejudiced against the brahmins. The law-books and the epics represent the brahmins as the centre round which everything in India turns; and that not only because of the sacredness of their persons, but because of their marked intellectual superiority to the rest of the people. Or take the European books on Indian literature and religion. They treat these subjects as practically identical with literature and religion *as shown in brahmin books.* Surely, then, the brahmins must have been predominant in the intellectual life of the period you are considering."

"These are not two independent testimonies," one would reply. "The European writers would be perfectly willing to consider other texts, if they only had them. They have been perfectly right in using the material before them. And in editing texts they naturally chose first those nearest at hand. But even so, with practically only priestly books to judge by, they are by no means unanimous in accepting the views of those texts as to the exclusive supremacy of the brahmins in early times."

Consider, for instance, the opinion of Professor Bhandarkar—himself, be it noted, a high-caste brahmin, and not only the most distinguished of native scholars, but so versed in the methods of historical criticism that his opinion is entitled to special weight. In a strikingly suggestive and important paper[1] he calls attention to the evidence of the inscriptions. In the second century *after* Christ they begin to record grants of land to brahmins. In the third there are also a few instances. From the fourth century onwards there are quite numerous inscriptions showing a marked rise in brahmin influence. The Gupta kings are then stated to have carried out the most complicated and expensive sacrifices, such as the Horse-sacrifice. Each of two inscriptions records the

[1] *Journal of the Bombay Branch of the Royal Asiatic Society* for 1901.

erection of a sacrificial post, another an endowment for lighting lamps in a temple to the sun. There are grants of villages for the performance of sacrificial rites; and numerous grants of land to brahmins, and to the temples in their charge. But for the four centuries before that (that is to say, from 300 B.C. to 100 A.D.) no brahmin, no brahmin temple, no brahmin god, no sacrifice or ritualistic act of any kind is ever, even once, referred to. There is a very large number of gifts recorded as given by kings, princes, and chiefs, by merchants, goldsmiths, artisans, and ordinary householders; but not one of them is given in support of anything—of any opinion or divinity or practice—with which the brahmins had anything to do. And whereas the later inscriptions, favouring the brahmins and their special sacrifices, are in Sanskrit, these earlier ones, in which they are not mentioned, are in a sort of Pāli—not in the local vernacular of the place where the inscriptions are found, but in a dialect similar, in many essential respects, to the dialect for common intercourse, based on the vernacular, which, I suggest, the Wanderers must have used, in their discussions, at the time when Buddhism arose.

This marked distinction in the inscriptions of the two periods—both as to the object of the gifts they record, and as to the language in which they are written—leads Professor Bhandarkar to the following conclusion:

"The period that we have been speaking of [that is,

from the beginning of the second century B.C. to the end of the fourth century after] has left no trace of a building or sculpture devoted to the use of the Brahmin religion. Of course Brahminism existed; and it was probably, during the period, being developed into the form which it assumed in later times. But the religion certainly does not occupy a prominent position, and Buddhism was followed by the large mass of the people from princes down to the humble workman." And he goes on to say that the language of the earlier inscriptions "indicates a greater deference for the people who used it, than for Brahmanic learning."

If this opinion be accepted as accurate for that period (200 B.C.–400 A.D.)—and it certainly seems incontrovertible—then, *a fortiori*, it must be accepted in yet larger measure for the period four centuries earlier. As Professor Hopkins says[1]:

"Brahminism has always been an island in a sea. Even in the Brahmanic age there is evidence to show that it was the isolated belief of a comparatively small group of minds. It did not even control all the Aryan population."

With regard to the inscriptions, M. Senart has shown conclusively, by an exhaustive study of the whole subject, that they at no time, either in spelling or in vocabulary, present us with a faithful picture of any vernacular. The degree in which they become more and more nearly allied to Sanskrit is a curious and interesting barometer by which we can gauge the approach of the impending revolution in politics, religion, and literature. And the gradual change in

[1] *Religions of India* (1896), p. 548.

their form, though that form never gives us the real vernacular, is an invaluable assistance in establishing the linguistic history of India. To treat that question at all fully, even in an elementary manner, would demand at least a volume. But the main features may be summarised as follows. We have, in the following order (as to time):

1. The dialects spoken by the Aryan invaders of India, and by the Dravidian and Kolarian inhabitants they found there.

2. Ancient High Indian, the Vedic.

3. The dialects spoken by the Aryans, now often united by marriage and by political union with the Dravidians, in their settlements either along the spurs of the Himālaya range from Kashmir to Nepal, or down the Indus Valley and then across to Avanti, or along the valleys of the Jumna and the Ganges.

4. Second High Indian, Brahmanic, the literary language of the Brāhmaṇas and Upanishads.

5. The vernaculars from Gandhāra to Magadha at the time of the rise of Buddhism, not so divergent probably as not to be more or less mutually intelligible.

6. A conversational dialect, based probably on the local dialect of Sāvatthi, the capital of Kosala, and in general use among Kosala officials, among merchants, and among the more cultured classes, not only throughout the Kosala dominions, but east and west from Delhi to Patna, and north and south from Sāvatthi to Avanti.

7. Middle High Indian, Pāli, the literary language

based on No. 6, probably in the form in which it was spoken in Avanti.

8. The Asoka dialect, founded on No. 6, especially as spoken at Patna, but much influenced by the aim at approximation to Nos. 7 and 11.

9. The Ārdha-Māgadhi, the dialect of the Jain Angas.

10. The Lena[1] dialect of the cave inscriptions from the second century B.C. onwards, based on No. 8, but approximating more and more to the next, No. 11, until it merges altogether into it.

11. Standard High Indian, Sanskrit—elaborated, as to form and vocabulary, out of No. 4; but greatly enriched by words first taken from Nos. 5 to 7, and then brought back, as to form, into harmony with No. 4. For long the literary language only of the priestly schools, it was first used in inscriptions and coins from the second century A.D. onwards; and from the fourth and fifth centuries onwards became the literary *lingua franca* for all India.

12. The vernaculars of the India of the fifth century A.D. and onwards.

13. Prakrit, the literary form of these vernaculars, and especially of Mahārāshtri. These are derived, not from No. 11 (Sanskrit), but from No. 12, the later forms of the sister dialects to No. 6.

The technical terms Sanskrit and Prakrit are used strictly, in India, as shown in Nos. 11 and 13. Sanskrit is never used for No. 2 or No. 4. Prakrit is never used for No. 7 or No. 8. Sanskrit was, and is,

[1] This is the name suggested by Professor Pischel, *Grammatik der Prakritsprachen*, 1901, p. 5.

written in India in various alphabets, a scribe in the north using that form of the Brāhmī alphabet current in the district in which he wrote, and a scribe in the south using the corresponding form of the Dravidian alphabet. The particular one of these many alphabets usually selected for use in Europe is an alphabet from Western India of the ninth century A.D.; and it is, therefore, often called the Sanskrit alphabet.

As appears from the foregoing list, the centre of linguistic predominance has naturally shifted, in India, with political power. At first it was in the Panjāb; then in Kosala; then in Magadha; and finally, when Sanskrit had become the *lingua franca*, it was in Western India that the most important vernacular was found. It is only in Ceylon that we have documents sufficient to follow the continuous development of a vernacular that has been able to hold its own against the depressing influence of the dead language used in the schools. And the relation there between the vernacular, the language of the inscriptions (based on the vernacular, but subject to the constant and increasing influence of a desire to show knowledge of the "higher" languages), the language used in poetry, Elu (the Prakrit of Ceylon), and Pali, which was there a dead language, used in the schools, is most instructively parallel, throughout, to the history of language in India.

Throughout the long history of Aryan speech Dravidian dialects were also spoken; and in the north, I venture to think, to a much larger extent and much later in time than is usually supposed. Our No. 2, Vedic, is largely subject to Dravidian influence, both in phonetics and in vocabulary. The Aryan vernaculars throughout, and all the literary forms of speech,—Pāli, Sanskrit, and Prakrit,—are charged with it in a degree no less than that in which the descent and the blood-relationships of the many peoples of India are charged with non-Aryan elements—and that is saying a great deal.

The fact that south of the Godāvari we find the reverse state of things—Dravidian dialects charged with Aryan elements—shows that the Aryan settlements there were late, and not very important in regard to numbers. And it took a long time, in spite of a fair sprinkling of brahmin colonists, for the brahmin influence, now so supreme, to reach its supremacy in those parts. The mass of the more wealthy classes, and the more cultured people, in the south, were Buddhists and Jain before they were Hindu in faith. As late as the fifth and sixth centuries we have Pāli books written in Kāñcipura and Tañjūr; and as Buddhism declined Jainism became predominant. It was only after the rise of brahmin influence in Northern India in the fourth and fifth centuries, and after it had become well established there, that it became the chief factor also in the south. But when once it had reached that stage, it developed so strongly as to react with great results on the north, where the final victory was actually won during the period from Kumārila to Sankara (700 to 830 A.D.), both of them born in the south, and one of them, apparently, of half Dravidian blood.

The victory was won. But how far was it a victory? The brahmins had become the sole arbiters in law and social institutions. Their theory of castes had been admitted, and to their own castes was accorded an unquestioned supremacy. Their claim to the exclusive right to teach was practically acknowledged. Of those rajputs who had disputed their authority, the Buddhists and Jains were both reduced to feeble minorities, and the rest had become mostly subservient. All philosophy, except their own pantheistic theosophy, had been driven out of the field. But Vedic rights and Vedic divinities, the Vedic language and Vedic theology, had also gone under in the struggle. The gods of the people received now the homage of the people. Bloody sacrifices were still occasionally offered, but to new divinities; and brahmins no longer presided over the ritual. Their literature had had to be recast to suit the new worship, to gain the favour and support of those who did not reverence and worship the Vedic gods. And all sense of history had been lost in the necessity of garbling the story of the past so as to make it tally with their own pretensions. It was when they had ceased to depend on their rights as priests of those sacrifices not much used by the people (who preferred the less costly cult of their local gods), when they had become the champions, the literary defenders, the poets, of the popular gods, that they succeeded in their aim. They had probably gained what most of them wanted most. And in deserting the faith of their forefathers to adopt other views it is by no means certain that they were not first really converted, that they gave up anything they themselves still wanted to keep. The most able of them had ceased philosophically to care for any such divinities as the Vedic ones, and it was a matter of indifference to them what gods the people followed. A small and decreasing minority continued to keep alive the flickering lamp of Vedic learning; and to them the Indian peoples will one day look back with especial gratitude and esteem.

This rapid sketch of the general history of language and literature in India is enough to show that there also, precisely as in Europe, a dominant factor in the story is the contest between the temporal and spiritual powers. Guelph and Ghibelin, priest and noble, rajput and brahmin, these are the contending forces. From India we had had hitherto only that version of the long war, of its causes and of its consequences, which has been preserved by the priestly faction. They make out that they were throughout the leading party. Perhaps so. But it is well to consider also the other side; and not to forget the gravity of the error we should commit if we should happen, in reliance on the priestly books, to antedate, by about a thousand years, the victory of the priests; to suppose, in other words, that the condition of things was the same at the beginning of the struggle as it was at the end.

It is difficult to avoid being misunderstood. So I would repeat that the priests were always there, were always militant, were always a power. Many of them were learned. A few of them, seldom the learned ones, were wealthy. All of them, even those neither learned nor wealthy, had a distinct prestige. There was never wanting among them a minority distinguished, and rightly distinguished, for earnestness or for intellectual power, or for both. This minority contributed largely to the influence of forward movements both in philosophy and in ethics. Certain members of it were famous as leaders, not only in the brahmin schools, but also among the Wanderers. Even among the Jains and Buddhists a minority of the most influential men were brahmins. But it is a question of degree. Their own later books persistently exaggerate, misstate, above all (that most successful method of *suggestio falsi*) omit the other side. They have thus given a completely distorted view of Indian society, and of the place, in it, of the priests. They were not the only learned, or the only intellectual men, any more than they were the only wealthy ones. The religion and the customs recorded in their books were not, at any period, the sole religion, or the only customs, of the many peoples of India. The intellectual movement before the rise of Buddhism was in large measure a lay movement, not a priestly one. During the subsequent centuries, down to the Christian era, and beyond it, the priests were left high and dry by the vigorous current of the national aims and hopes. Even later than that how different is the colouring of the picture drawn by the Chinese pilgrims from that of the priestly artists. And we shall continue to have but a blurred and confused idea of Indian history unless, and until, the priestly views are checked and supplemented throughout by a just and proportionate use of the other views now open to research.

CHAPTER X

LITERATURE

II. THE PĀLI BOOKS

IN the last chapter we have seen that in the sixth century B.C. there was in India a very considerable amount of literature of a special sort. Hampered as it was by the absence of written books, by the necessity of learning by heart, and of constantly repeating, the treatises in which it was contained, the extent of the literature is evidence of a considerable degree both of intelligence and of earnestness in effort among the people of India in those days. A great deal of it, perhaps the larger portion of it, has absolutely perished. But a considerable part of the results of the literary activity of each of three different schools has survived. It is by a comparison of three sets of documents, each of them looking at things from a different point of view, that we have to reconstruct the history of the time.

Of these three the surviving books — if books they may be called which had never yet been written — composed and used by those of the brahmins who earned their livelihood by the sacrifices, have been now, for the most part, edited and translated; and a large part of the historical results to be won from them have been summarised and explained. But much remains to be done. The documents of the other two schools may be expected to throw fresh light on passages in the brahmin books now misunderstood. The unhappy system of taking these ancient records in the sense attributed to them by modern commentators with much local knowledge but no historical criticism, with great learning but also with considerable party bias, was very naturally adopted at first by European scholars who had everything to learn. The most practical, indeed the only then possible, course was to avail oneself of the assistance of those commentaries, or of the living pandits whose knowledge was entirely based upon them. In the interpretation of the Vedic hymns this method, followed in Wilson's translation, has now been finally abandoned. But it still survives in many places in the interpretation of the documents nearest to the date of the rise of Buddhism. And we still find, for instance, in the most popular versions of the Upanishads, opinions that are really the outcome of centuries of philosophic or theosophic discussions, transplanted from the pages of Śankara in the ninth century A.D. into these ancient texts of the eighth or seventh century B.C.

This method of interpretation takes effect in two ways. A passage in the vague and naïve style of those old thinkers (or, rather, poets) is made more exact and precise, is given what is, no doubt, a clearer meaning, by putting into it the later ideas. And in the translation of single words, especially those of philosophic or ethical import, a connotation, which they had really acquired many centuries afterwards, is held applicable at the earlier date. In both these cases a better commentary could be drawn from the general views, and from the exact meaning of philosophic terms, preserved in documents much nearer in time to the Upanishads, though opposed to them on many essential points. As Professor Jacobi says[1]:

"The records of the Buddhists and Jainas about the philosophic ideas current at the time of the Buddha and the Mahāvīra, meagre though they be [he is speaking of the incidental references to the ideas they did not accept], are of the greatest importance to the historian of that epoch."

Of these records the Pāli ones (thanks, in great part, to the continuous efforts, during the past twenty years, of the Pāli Text Society), are very nearly all now available. We can say not only what they do, but (which is often of even more importance) what they do not, contain. The Jain records are unfortunately as yet known only in fragments. It is the greatest desideratum for the history of this period that they should be made accessible in full. The philosophical and religious speculations contained in them may not have the originality, or intrinsic value, either of the Vedānta or of Buddhism. But they are none the less historically important because they give evidence of a stage less

[1] *Jaina Sutras*, 2. xxvii.

cultured, more animistic, that is to say, earlier. And incidentally they will undoubtedly be found, as the portions accessible already show, to contain a large number of important references to the ancient geography, the political divisions, the social and economic conditions of India at a period hitherto very imperfectly understood.

It is difficult to appreciate the objections made to the authenticity and authority of these documents. The arguments advanced in 1884 by Professor Jacobi[1] seem quite incontrovertible, and indeed they have not been seriously disputed. The books purport to be substantially the ones put together in the fourth century B.C. when Bhadrabāhu was head of the community. The Jains themselves, of all divisions or schools, acknowledge that there had been older books (the Pūrvas, the Former Ones), now lost. Had they been inventing the story this is not the way in which they would have put it. They would have claimed that the existing books were the original literature of their Order. The linguistic and epigraphic evidence so far available confirms in many respects both the general reliability of the traditions current among the Jains, and the accuracy of this particular detail. Of course the name given in this tradition to the older books cannot have been the original name. They were only "former" as compared with the eleven Angas that are still preserved. And the existing books, if of the fourth century, can only be used with critical care as evidence of institutions, or events, of the sixth century B.C. Still,

[1] *Jaina Sūtras*, I. xxxvii.–xlv.

even so, we have here important materials for Indian history, at present only very imperfectly utilised.

It is really much the same with the existing records of the other school, of the men we now call Buddhists. They have as yet been only very imperfectly utilised, though they are better and more completely known than the last. This is partly, no doubt, because we call them Buddhists, and imagine them, therefore, to belong to a separate class, quite distinct from other Indians of that epoch. The Buddhists were, as a matter of fact, characteristically and distinctively Indian. They probably, at least during the fourth and third centuries B.C., formed the majority of the people. And the movement of thought out of which all these schools arose, so far from being a negligible quantity, as the priestly books suggest, was one of the most dominant factors the historian of the fourth, fifth, and sixth centuries B.C. has to consider.

As to the age of the Buddhist canonical books, the best evidence is the contents of the books themselves—the sort of words they use, the style in which they are composed, the ideas they express. Objection, it is true, has recently been raised against the use of such internal evidence. And the objection is valid if it be urged, not against the general principle of the use of such evidence, but against the wrong use of it. We find, for instance, that Phallus-worship is often mentioned, quite as a matter of course, in the Mahābhārata, as if it had always been common everywhere throughout Northern India. In the

Nikāyas, though they mention all sorts of what the Buddhists regarded as foolish or superstitious forms of worship, this particular kind, Siva-worship under the form of the Linga, is not even once referred to. The Mahābhārata mentions the Atharva Veda, and takes it as a matter of course, as if it were an idea generally current, that it was a Veda, the fourth Veda. The Nikāyas constantly mention the three others, but never the Atharva. Both cases are interesting. But before drawing the conclusion that, therefore, the Nikāyas, as we have them, are older than the existing text of the Mahābhārata, we should want a very much larger number of such cases, all tending the same way, and also the certainty that there were no cases of an opposite tendency that could not otherwise be explained.

On the other hand, suppose a MS. were discovered containing, in the same handwriting, copies of Bacon's *Essays* and of Hume's *Essay*, with nothing to show when, or by whom, they were written; and that we knew nothing at all otherwise about the matter. Still we should know, with absolute certainty, which was relatively the older of the two; and should be able to determine, within a quite short period, the actual date of each of the two works. The evidence would be irresistible because it would consist of a very large number of minute points of language, of style, and, above all, of ideas expressed, all tending in the same direction.

This is the sort of internal evidence that we have before us in the Pali books. Any one who habitually reads Pali would know at once that the Nikāyas are older than the Dhamma Sangaṇi; that both are older than the Kathā Vatthu; that all three are older than the Milinda. And the Pali scholars most competent to judge are quite unanimous on the point, and on the general position of the Pali literature in the history of literature in India.

But this sort of evidence can appeal, of course, only to those familiar with the language and with the ideas. To those who are not, the following points may be suggestive:

On the monuments of the third century B.C. we find the names of donors—donors of different parts of the building—inscribed on those parts (pillars, rails, and bas-reliefs). When the names are common ones, certain epithets are added, to distinguish the donors from other persons bearing the same name. Such epithets are either local (as we might say, John of Winchester) or they specify an occupation (as we might say, John the carpenter, or John the clerk) or are otherwise distinctive. Among these epithets have been found the following:

1. *Dhamma-kathika.*—"Preacher of the System" (the Dhamma)—the "System" being a technical term in the Buddhist schools to signify the philosophical and ethical doctrine as distinguished from the Vinaya, the Rules of the Order.

2. *Peṭakin.*—"One who had (that is, knew by heart) the Piṭaka." The Piṭaka is the traditional statements of Buddhist doctrine as contained in the Sutta Piṭaka. The word means basket, and as a technical term applied to a part of their literature: it is used exclusively by the Buddhists.

3. *Suttantika.*—"A man who knows a Suttanta by heart."

4. *Suttantakinī.*—"A woman who knows a Suttanta by heart." Suttanta is, again, a technical term used exclusively of certain portions of the Buddhist canonical books, more especially of the Dialogues. It means literally the "end of the Suttas." In its technical sense it is the aim, object, outcome of them; and is applied to the Dialogues as giving, in a more complete and elaborate form, the general result of those shorter Suttas on which they are based.

The brahmins have an analogous term, Vedānta, applied, in post-Buddhistic writings, at first in the Śvetāśvatara and Muṇḍaka Upanishads and often afterwards, to the Upanishads, as being the highest outcome of the Vedas. Previously to this the word is only found in its literal sense, "the end of the Veda," and the secondary sense is, therefore, probably adapted from the corresponding (and earlier) Buddhist term.

5. *Panca-nekāyika.*—"One who knows the Five Nikāyas by heart." The five Nikāyas, or "Collections," as a technical term used of literary works, is applied to the canonical Buddhist texts, and to them only. Of the five, the first two contain the Suttantas, the next two are made up of Suttas arranged in two different ways, and the fifth is a supplementary collection, mostly of later works.[1] As the word Nikāya also means a school, or sect, it is somewhat ambiguous, and was gradually replaced by the word Āgama, continually used in the later Sanskrit litera-

[1] See *American Lectures*, pp. 60–62.

ture. The same remark holds good of the technical term Suttanta. That also was gradually replaced by the shorter and easier phrase Sutta.

The expressions here explained are used on Buddhist monuments and refer to Buddhist books. They are conclusive proof that some time before the date of the inscriptions (that is, roughly speaking, before the time of Asoka), there was a Buddhist literature in North India, where the inscriptions are found. And further, that that literature then had divisions known by the technical names of Piṭaka, Nikāya, and Suttanta, and that the number of Nikāyas then in existence was five.

But this is not all. Asoka, in his Bhabra Edict, addressed to the Buddhist Order (the Sangha), recommends to the Brethren and Sisters of the Order, and to the lay disciples of either sex, frequently to hear (that is to learn by heart), and to meditate upon, certain selected passages. And of these, he, most fortunately, gives the names. They are as follows:

Ariya-vasāni (now found in the Dīgha Nikāya, in the portion called the Sangīti Suttanta).

Anāgata-bhayāni (now found in the Anguttara Nikāya, vol. iii. pp. 105–108).

Muni Gāthā (now found in the Sutta Nipāta, verses 206–220).

Moneyya Sutta (now found in the Iti-vuttaka, p. 67, and also in the Anguttara Nikāya, vol. i. p. 272).

Upatissa Pasina.—"The question put by Upatissa" (more commonly known as Sāriputta). There are so many such questions in the books that opinions differ as to which of them is the one most probably referred to.

There is a word at the commencement of this list which may either be an adjective applied to the whole list, or the name of another passage. However this may be, this Edict of Asoka's gives the actual titles of some of the shorter passages included, in his time, in those books, the larger divisions of which are mentioned in the inscriptions just referred to.

Now the existing literature, divided into the same larger divisions, contains also the shorter passages. To suppose that it was composed in Ceylon is to suppose that, by an extraordinary series of chances, the Ceylon writers happened to hit upon just the identical technical terms, two of them then almost fallen out of use, that had been used in these old inscriptions (of which they knew nothing) for the names they gave to the larger divisions of the literature they made. And we must further suppose that, by another extraordinary series of chances, they happened to include in those divisions a number of shorter passages, each of them corresponding exactly to those mentioned by name, long before their time, in Asoka's Edict, of which also they knew nothing. To adopt such a theory as the most probable explanation of the facts would be nothing less than absurd.

How is it, then, will be the immediate question, that this theory in almost, if not in all, the current books on Buddhism or on Indian history is taken for granted; that the Pali canonical literature is always called "the Southern Recension" or "the Singhalese Canon"?

The expression is ambiguous, and apt to be misleading. But though it is doubtless sometimes used in such a way as to suggest that these books were composed in Ceylon, this is not its real meaning, and it is never so used by careful writers. It simply means that of the few works known to the European scholars who first studied Buddhism, the MSS. of some came from Ceylon; and that such works were therefore called southern, to distinguish them from the others, known from MSS. which had come from Nepal, and therefore called northern.

It is very possible that Burnouf, to whom the popularity of this mode of speech is mainly due, leaned at first to the opinion that the canonical works had been actually written in Ceylon. He always spoke of them in his first work as "the Pali books of Ceylon," not as "the Pali books of India." But that phrase is also ambiguous. Very conscious how meagre, and for the most part how late, were the works he used, he was much too careful a scholar to express, at first, any clear opinion at all. At the end of his long labours, however, he certainly was quite clearly of the contrary opinion. For at the very close of his magnificent work, at p. 862 of the "Lotus," he suggests that the Pali works "may have been popular among inferior castes, and the great mass of the people, *in Magadha and Audh*, while the Buddhist Sanskrit works were in use among the brahmins." He at that time regarded them all, herefore, as North Indian works. And considering that he knew nothing of the inscriptions, and had only the internal evidence to guide him, this suggestion, though not exactly right, reflects the greatest credit on his literary judgment. Had he started with this view, we should probably have been saved the use of the ambiguous phrases, so suggestive of these works being written in Ceylon, which have had so great an influence in retarding the acceptance of the view that that great pioneer in Buddhist studies came at last, himself, to hold.

Not only ought such phrases to be dropt out of any works, on these subjects, claiming to be scholarly; but even the phrases "northern" and "southern" should be avoided. This seems a pity, for they look so convenient. But the convenience is delusive if they convey a wrong impression. And I venture to assert that most people draw the conclusion that we have two distinct Buddhisms to deal with, one made in Nepal, the other made in Ceylon. Every one now agrees that this is all wrong. What we have is not two, but very many different sorts of Buddhism; for almost every book gives us a different doctrine.

The more authoritative and ancient books, whether written in Pali or in Buddhist Sanskrit, are none of them either northern or southern. They all, without any exception,—if we disregard the absurdly unimportant detail of the place from which our modern copies of them are derived,—claim to belong, and do actually belong, to the Middle Country, as the Indians call it, that is, to the Ganges Valley.

Each differs from the next (in point of date) by small gradations in doctrine. There are such differences even within the Nikāyas themselves. Many Sanskrit books, though they differ, by containing certain details of later opinion, from the oldest Pali ones, still, on the whole, have to be classed with the Pali rather than with the other Sanskrit works. The Sanskrit Mahā Vastu, for instance (" The Sublime Story") is much nearer to the Pali Cariyā Piṭaka(" The Tradition as to Conduct ") than it is to such Sanskrit books as the " Lotus of the Good Law." All three alike had their origin in the Middle Country—where exactly, in that country, we cannot, with respect to any one of the three, determine. The only two ancient works we can specify as distinctly northern in origin, the Milinda and the Gosinga Anthology, are neither of them written in Sanskrit, and are identical in doctrine with what is called southern Buddhism. Is it not rather absurd to have to ticket as southern just the very two books we know to be the most northern in origin?

There is not now, and never has been, any unity either of opinion or of language in what is called northern, or in what is called southern Buddhism. There is a distinct disadvantage in continually suggesting a unity which has no existence in fact. In a word, the current division of Buddhist literature into northern and southern is entirely unscientific, and misleading. It contains a *suggestio falsi* in at least two important respects. It cuts across the only division that has a scientific basis, the division, not according to the locality whence we get our modern copies, but according to time, according to date of origin. Why then continue the use of an ambiguous phraseology which may be (and which we know, from experience, will be) misunderstood? The only way to avoid endless confusion is to drop the use of it altogether. And I take this opportunity of acknowledging my error in having used it so long myself. In my *Buddhism*, from the fifteenth edition onwards the mistake has been corrected. So slight is the change that no one is likely to have noticed it. The word "northern" has been replaced by "Tibetan," "Japanese," "Mahāyanist," etc., according to the context. There has been no loss in clearness, or in conciseness, and much gain in precision.

We must take our Pali canonical books then to be North Indian, not Singhalese in origin; and the question as to whether they have suffered from their sometime sojourn under the palm groves of the mountain *vihāras* in the south must be decided by a critical study of them in their present condition. Toward such a study there are some points that can already be made.

The books make no mention of Asoka. Had they undergone any serious re-editing after the reign of the great Buddhist Emperor (of whom the Buddhist writers, whether rightly or wrongly, were so proud), is it probable that he would have been so completely ignored?

The books never mention any person, or any place, in Ceylon; or even in South India. They tell us a goodly number of anecdotes, usually as introductions to, or in illustration of, some ethical point. It would have been so easy to bring in a passing reference to some Ceylon worthy—in the same way as the brahmin Buddhaghosa does so often, in his Attha Sālinī, which *was* revised in Ceylon.[1] If the Piṭaka books had been tampered with, would not opportunity have been taken to yield to this very natural impulse?

We know a great deal now of developed or corrupted doctrine current in Ceylon, of new technical terms invented, of new meanings put into the older phrases. Not one single instance has yet been found of any such later idea, any such later form of language, any such later technical term, in any one of the canonical books.

The philosophic ideas of the ancient Buddhism, and the psychological ideas on which they were based, were often curtly, naïvely, confusedly expressed. In Ceylon they had been much worked up, polished, elucidated, systematised. From several works now accessible we know fairly well the tone and manner of these later—and, as they must have seemed to Ceylon scholars, clearer, fuller—statements of the old ideas. In no single instance yet discovered has this later tone and manner found its way into the canonical books.

It would seem, then, that any change that may have been made in these North Indian books after they had been brought into Ceylon must have been insignificant. It would be a great advantage if we should be able to find even one or two instances of

[1] See Mrs. Rhys Davids's *Buddhist Psychology*, p. xxi.

such changes. We should then be able to say what sort and degree of alteration the Ceylon scholars felt justified in making. But it is clear that they regarded the canon as closed.

While the books were in North India, on the other hand, and the canon was not considered closed, there is evidence of a very different tone. One whole book, the Kathā Vatthu, was added as late as the time of Asoka; and perhaps the Parivāra, a mere string of examination questions, is not much older. One story in the Peta Vatthu [1] is about a king Pingalaka, said in the commentary to have reigned over Surat two hundred years after the Buddha's time; and another [2] refers to an event fifty-six years after the Buddha's death. The latter is certainly in its right place in this odd collection of legends. The former may (as the commentator thinks) have been added at Asoka's Council. Even if it were, that would be proof that they then thought no harm of adding to the legendary matter in their texts. And the whole of this little book of verses, together with the Vimāna Vatthu (really only the other half of one and the same work), is certainly very late in tone as compared with the Nikāyas.

The same must be said of two other short collections of ballads. One is the Buddha Vaṃsa, containing a separate poem on each of twenty-five Buddhas, supposed to have followed one another in succession. The other is the Cariyā Piṭaka, containing thirty-four short Jātaka stories turned into verse. Both of these must also be late. For in the Nikāyas

[1] IV. 3.

[2] V. 2.

only seven Buddhas are known; and Jātakas, in the technical sense, are not yet thought of. This particular set of Jātakas is also arranged on the basis of the *Pāramitās*, a doctrine that plays no part in the older books. The Ten Perfections (*Pāramitā*) are qualities a Buddha is supposed to be obliged to have acquired in the countless series of his previous rebirths as a Bodhisatva. But this is a later notion, not found in the Nikāyas. It gradually grew up as the Bodhisatva idea began to appeal more to the Indian mind. And it is interesting to find already, in these latest of the canonical books, the germs of what afterwards developed into the later Mahāyāna doctrine, to which the decline of Buddhism, in the opinion of Professor Bhandarkar, was eventually so greatly due.[1]

This question of the history of the Jātaka stories will be considered in greater detail in our next chapter. What has been here said (and other similar evidence will, no doubt, be hereafter discovered) is amply sufficient to show that some parts of the Canon are later than others; and that the books as we have them contain internal evidence from which conclusions may fairly be drawn as to their comparative age. Such conclusions, of course, are not always so plain as is the case in the four instances—the Peta and Vimāna Vatthus, the Buddha Vamsa, and the Cariyā Piṭaka—just considered. For example, let us take the case of the Sutta Nipāta.

This also is a short collection of poems. It contains fifty-four lyrics, each of them very short, ar-

[1] *J. R. A. S.*, Bombay Branch, 1900, p. 395.

ranged in four Cantos; and then sixteen others, as a fifth Canto, strung together by a framework of story. The last Canto (called the Pārāyana) had evidently once existed as a separate poem. It is so treated by the commentator, who calls it a Suttanta; and it is in fact about as long as one of those Suttantas in the Dīgha Nikāya which consist of verses strung together by a framework of story in prose. It is six times quoted or referred to by name, as a separate poem, in the Nikāyas.[1]

The preceding Canto, the fourth, is called "The Eights," most of the lyrics in it containing eight stanzas apiece. This Canto is also referred to by name as a separate work, in other parts of the Canon.[2] And it must in very earlier times have been already closely associated in thought with the fifth Canto, for the two together are the subject of a curious old commentary, the only work of the kind included in the Nikāyas. That this commentary, the Niddesa, takes no notice of the other three Cantos would seem to show that, when it was composed, the whole of the five Cantos had not yet been brought together into a single book.

Of the thirty-eight poems in the earlier three Cantos no less than six are found also in other parts of the Canon.[3] They had existed as separate hymns, popular in the community, before they were incor-

[1] Saṃyutta, 2. 49; Anguttara, 1. 144; 2. 45; 3. 399; 4. 63.

[2] Saṃyutta, 3. 12; *Vinaya*, 1. 196; Udāna, 5. 6.

[3] Poem No. 4=S. 1. 172; No. 8=Kh. P. No. 9; No. 13=Kh. P. No. 5; No. 15=Jāt. 3. 196; No. 16=Kh. P. No. 6; No. 33=M. No. 92.

porated into the several collections in which they are now found. When we find also that numerous isolated verses in these thirty-eight poems occur elsewhere in very ancient documents, the most probable explanation is that these were current as proverbs or as favourite sayings (either in the community, or perhaps among the people at large) before they were independently incorporated in the different poems in which they are now found.

We find, then, that single verses, single poems, and single Cantos, had all been in existence before the work assumed its present shape. This is very suggestive as to the manner of growth not only of this book, but of all the Indian literature of this period. It grew up in the schools; and was the result rather of communistic than of individual effort. No one dreamed of claiming the authorship of a volume. In the whole of the Buddhist canonical works one only, and that the very latest, has a personal name attached to it, the name of a leading member of the Order said to have lived in the time of Asoka. During the previous three centuries authorship is attributed not to treatises, or even poems, but only to verses; and to verses in two only out of the many collections of verses that have been preserved. Out of twenty-nine books in the Canon no less than twenty-six have no author at all, apart from the community.

This is decisive as to popular feeling on the point. And even in the priestly schools the then prevalent custom was not greatly different. Their works also were not produced by individuals, but grew up in the various schools of the priestly community. And no priestly work ascribed to an individual author can be dated much before the time of Asoka.

And yet another point, which will turn out, unless I am much mistaken, to be of striking importance for the history of Indian literature, arises in connection with the Sutta Nipāta. The fifth Canto regarded as a single poem, and about one-third of all the other poems in the collection, are of the nature of ballads. They describe some short incident, the speeches being always in verse, but the story itself usually in prose (though in a few instances this also is in verse). They resemble in this respect a very large number of Suttas found in other portions of the Canon. And even a few of the Suttantas — such as the "Riddles of Sakka," for instance (certainly one of our oldest documents, for it is quoted by name in the Saṃyutta[1]) — are characteristic specimens of this kind of composition. It is, in fact, next to the prose Sutta, the most popular style for literary effort during this period.

This manner of expressing one's ideas is now quite unknown. But it has been known throughout the world as the forerunner of the epic. Professor Windisch has subjected those of these ballads that are based on the temptation legends to an exhaustive study in his masterly monograph, *Mara und Buddha*. He says, apropos of the two ballads on this subject in the Sutta Nipāta :

"These two Suttas might have been regarded as a fragment of an epic had we otherwise found any traces of an ancient Buddha Epic. But that is not to be thought

[1] Saṃyutta, iii. 13.

of. Far rather are these Suttas to be looked upon as the early beginnings out of which, in certain circumstances, a Buddha Epic could eventually arise.

"We can mark with special ease how an Epic arises, and of what process an Epic, as a particular form of literature, is the consummation. Some years ago I drew attention to the historical points we have here to take into consideration in a lecture to the Congress of philologians at Gera on the Irish legends and the question of Ossian.[1] There I laid the chief stress on the old-Irish legends, but compared also the legends in ancient India. The latter subject was independently dealt with by Oldenberg in his well-known articles on the Ākhyāna hymns where the subject referred to (the relations of the Epic to previous literary forms) is dealt with in detail and thoroughly explained.[2] Professor Geldner then considered the same subject, partly from new points of view, inasmuch as he followed them out also in the case of the Avesta, in his article in the 'Vedische Studien.'[3] Now we find also in the Buddhist literature, as Oldenberg was the first to point out, this epic narrative in mixed prose and verse. . . . The persons who act, the place where they act, and the action itself form the constituent elements of the narrative. But the latter only springs into life when the persons acting are also represented as speaking. Now the speeches are frequently what it is least possible to keep historically accurate, where, therefore, the fancy of the narrator and the art of the poet come most into play. *Conversation* (*speech and rejoinder*) *is the first part of the narrative to be put into verse*, and that especially at the crucial points of the story. Here the beginnings of

[1] *Revue Celtique*, 5. 70.

[2] Z. D. M. G., vols. 37 and 39.

[3] 1. 284, foll.

epic and drama lie close together. That the more ancient epics in all countries contain many speeches and counter speeches can be seen too from the Iliad. It is only in the later epic form that this dramatic element is kept in the background. So in the old-Greek drama also we have an epic element in the speeches of the messengers. *But a poem becomes completely epical only when to the speeches in verse is added also the framework of the story in metrical form.* And the last stage is that the speeches grow shorter, or fall out, and only events are given in verse."[1]

Both the general accuracy and the great importance of this far-reaching generalisation will be admitted by all. Now we have in the Nikāyas all sorts of the earliest forms of the evolution referred to. We find (in the Thera- and Therī-Gāthā, for instance) only the speeches in verse in the canonical books, and the framework of prose, without which they are often unintelligible, handed on, by tradition, in the Commentary. We find (as in the Suttantas in the second volume of the Dīgha, or in the Udāna) speeches in verse, and framework in prose, both preserved in the canonical book. And we find ballads (such as the two Suttas discussed by Professor Windisch) in which speeches and framework are both preserved in verse. But it is not till long afterwards, in the time of Kanishka, that we have a fully developed Buddha Epic.

Are we then to suppose that the Indians had a mental constitution different from that of the other Aryan tribes (after all, their relatives in a certain

[1] Windisch, *Mara und Buddha*, pp. 222, foll.

degree) throughout the world? Or are we to suppose that the Buddhist community formed a section so completely cut off from the rest of the people that they were uninfluenced by the existence, in their immediate surroundings, of the great Indian Epics. The Rāmāyaṇa, as Professor Jacobi has shown, was composed in Kosala, on the basis of ballads popularly recited by rhapsodists throughout that district. But the very centre of the literary activity of the Buddhists was precisely Kosala. After the Rāmāyaṇa had become known there as a perfect epic, with the distinctive marks of the epic style, would such of the people in Kosala as had embraced the new doctrine have continued to use only the ancient method of composition? This would be quite without parallel. But we have to choose between this supposition (not a probable one) and the alternative proposition — that is to say, that whatever the date to be assigned to this ballad literature, in mixed prose and verse, preserved in the Nikāyas, the date of the Mahā-bhārata and of the Rāmāyaṇa, as Epics, must be later.

We may be pretty sure that if the Epics had existed at the period when this Buddhist literature was composed, they would have been referred to in it. But they are not. On the other hand, the ballads in prose and verse, such as those sung by the rhapsodists (the stage out of which the epics were evolved), are referred to under their technical name of *akkhānas* (Sanskrit *ākhyānas*) in one of the oldest documents.[1] Mention is there made of various

[1] *Dialogues of the Buddha*, I. 8.

sorts of public spectacles, and one of these is the reciting of such Ākhyānas. And when the commentator in the early part of the fifth century A.D. explains this as the reciting of the Bhārata, the Rāmāyaṇa, and so on, that is, as exegesis, perfectly right. This was the sort of thing referred to. But his remark is evidence of the existence of the perfect Epics, only at his own time, not at the time of the old text he is explaining.

This may seem, I am afraid, to have been a digression. But it is really very much to the purpose, when discussing Indian literature in this period, to bring out the importance of the wide prevalence of the versifying faculty, and to discuss the stage to which it had reached, the style of composition in which it was mostly used. We hear of four kinds of poets:—the poet of imagination (who makes original verses): the poet of tradition (the repeater of current verses); the poet of real life (or perhaps of worldly as distinct from religious topics); and the improvisatore.[1] We have several instances in the books of such impromptu verses. Though they were probably not quite so impromptu as they are described to be, we need not doubt the fact that the art was then a recognised form of ability. And when a man is charged with being "drunk with poesy"[2] (*kāveyyamatto*) the rapt and far-away look of the poet in the moment of inspiration cannot have been altogether unfamiliar.

It is interesting to notice that, just as we have evidence at this period of the first steps having been

[1] Anguttara, 2. 230; compare Sum. 95. [2] Saṃyutta, 1. 110.

taken towards a future Epic, so we have evidence of the first steps towards a future drama — the production before a tribal concourse on fixed feast days of shows with scenery, music, and dancing. There is ample evidence in the Buddhist and Jain records, and in Asoka inscriptions, of the existence of these *samajjas*, as they were called, as a regular institution.[1] That they are not mentioned in the priestly books need inspire no doubt upon the point. This is only another instance of the priestly habit of persistently ignoring what they did not like. We see from the Sigālovada Suttanta[2] that recitations, or the telling of stories, in mixed prose and verse (*akkhāna*), also took place at these meetings. But this seems, from the evidence at present attainable, to have been distinct; and the interpretation of the word I have rendered "scenery" is open to doubt. We cannot talk, therefore, as yet, of drama. When we see, however, that these meetings took place at sacred places, on the hilltops, and that high officials were invited and had special seats provided for them, we find ourselves in presence, not of private undertakings, but of such religious and communal ceremonies as those to which the beginnings of drama have elsewhere also been traced back. It is true that the kind of religion which we have here to consider is not the religion of the brahmins. The general prohibition which forbade a brahmin to see or hear

[1] See the passages quoted in *Dialogues of the Buddha*, I. 9. 10, and Jacobi's *Jaina Sutras*, 2. 303.

[2] In Grimblot's *Sept Suttas Palis*, p. 300, where the reading must be corrected accordingly.

dancing or music[1] must have included such performances. But it was at that time none the less on that account, a very vital and popular part of the national faith.[2]

I have dealt in this chapter, not with the contents, which I have described elsewhere,[3] but only with the outward form and style of the literature. It shows a curious contrast between the value of the ideas to be expressed and the childlike incapacity to express them well. We have here, as to style, only the untrained adolescence of the Indian mind. But what vigour it has! The absence of writing materials seems naturally to have affected less the short poems than the style of the prose, and there is much rough and rugged beauty both in the ballads and in the lyrics. Now the style, and much of the thought, is not Buddhist but Indian; and is in some respects the only evidence we possess of the literary ability, at that time, of the Indian peoples. If only we had still some of the ballads out of which the Epics were subsequently formed, they would, I am convinced, show equal limitations, but also equal power. In after times we have evidence of more successful study of the arts and methods of rhetoric and poetry. But never do we find the same virility, the same curious compound of humour and irony and love of

[1] See, for instance, the Pāraskara Gṛhya Sūtra, 2. 7. 3.

[2] The oldest dramas mentioned by name (second century B.C.) are mystery plays based on episodes in the life of Krishṇa. From this time onward there is more frequent mention of actors. But the earliest dramas are all lost. The oldest extant ones are of the sixth or seventh century A.D.

[3] *American Lectures*, chapter ii.

nature on the one hand, with a deadly earnestness, and really on the whole a surprisingly able grasp of the deepest problems of life, on the other. As we shall see presently in the case of the philosophy, so also is it true of the literature that it is in this period that India came nearest to having a Golden Age. And the learned, ornate poetry of later times is to the literature of this period what the systemisations and learned commentaries of Buddhaghosa and Śaṇkara are to the daring speculations and vivid life of the early Upanishads and of the Four Nikāyas.

APPENDIX TO CHAPTER X

CHRONOLOGICAL TABLE OF BUDDHIST LITERATURE FROM THE BUDDHA'S TIME TO THE TIME OF ASOKA

1. The simple statements of Buddhist doctrine now found, in identical words, in paragraphs or verses recurring in all the books.
2. Episodes found, in identical words, in two or more of the existing books.
3. The Sīlas, the Pārāyana, the Octades, the Pātimokkha.
4. The Dīgha, Majjhima, Anguttara, and Saṃyutta Nikāyas.
5. The Sutta Nipāta, the Thera- and Therī-Gāthās, the Udānas, and the Khuddaka Pāṭha.
6. The Sutta Vibhanga and the Khandakas.
7. The Jātakas and the Dhammapadas.
8. The Niddesa, the Itivuttakas, and the Paṭisambhidā.
9. The Peta- and Vimāna-Vatthus, the Apadānas, the Cariyā Piṭaka, and the Buddha Vaṃsa.
10. The Abhidhamma books; the last of which is the Kathā Vatthu, and the earliest probably the Puggala Paññatti.

The above table represents the probable order in which the extant Buddhist documents of this period were composed. They were not yet written, and a great deal has no doubt been lost.

CHAPTER XI

THE JĀTAKA BOOK[1]

THE Jātaka book, which we have now had before us for some years, in full, in the admirable edition of the Pali text by Professor Fausböll, is now also approaching its completion in the English translation published at Cambridge under the supervision of Professor Cowell. It is so full of information on the daily habits and customs and beliefs of the people of India, and on every variety of the numerous questions that arise as to their economic and social conditions, that it is of the utmost importance to be able to determine the period to which the evidence found in this book is applicable. The problem is somewhat complicated. But if only the right distinctions be drawn, the solution of it seems to me substantially sure, and really perfectly simple.

That we should have to draw distinctions between different parts of the same book is nothing sur-

[1] The following is an enlarged restatement of views first put forward in the introduction (written in August, 1878) to my *Buddhist Birth Stories*

prising. As Professor Deussen has said of the early Upanishads, and as Professor Winternitz has said of the Mahā-Bhārata, so also may be said of the Nikāyas and of the Vinaya (and even of some portions of the Abhidhamma), that "we must judge each separate piece by itself." And this is really only the very natural and necessary result of what has been pointed out above,[1] that the books grew up gradually, that they were not books in our modern sense, and that they had no single authors.

The distinctions we have to draw will best be shown by an example. The following is an abstract of a typical Jātaka.

THE BANYAN-DEER BIRTH STORY.[2]

'"*Follow rather the Banyan Deer.*" This the Master told when at Jetavana about the mother of Kumāra Kassapa,' and so on.

Then follows the story of this lady, how, after being wrongly found guilty of immoral conduct, she had been declared innocent through the intervention of the Buddha. Then it is said that the brethren talking this matter over at eventide, the Buddha came there, and learning the subject of their discourse said: "Not now only has the Tathāgata proved a support and protection to these two [the lady and her son]; formerly also he was the same." Then, on request, he revealed that matter, concealed by change of birth.

"Once upon a time, when Brahmadatta was reign-

[1] Above, p. 179. [2] No. 12.

ing in Benares, the Bodhisatta was reborn as a deer, a king of the deer, by name the Banyan Deer," and so on.

This is the Jātaka proper. It tells how there were two herd of deer shut in in the king's park. The king or his cook went daily to hunt for deer for venison. For each one killed many were wounded or harassed by the chase. So the golden coloured Banyan Deer, king of one of the herds, went to the king of the other herd, the Branch Deer, and persuaded him to a compact that lots should be cast, and that, every day, the one deer on whom the lot fell should go voluntarily to the cook's place of execution, and lay his head upon the block. And this was done. And so by the daily death of one the rest were saved from torture and distress.

Now one day the lot fell upon a pregnant doe in Branch Deer's herd. She applied to the king of that herd to order that the lot, "which was not meant to fall on two at once," should pass her by. But he harshly bade her begone to the block. Then she went to King Banyan Deer and told her piteous tale. He said he would see to it, and he went himself and laid his head on the block.

Now the king had decreed immunity to the two kings of the respective herds. When the cook saw King Banyan Deer lying there with his head on the block, he went hastily and told the king (the king of the men). The latter mounted his chariot, and with a great retinue went to the spot, and said:

"My friend, the king of the deer, did I not grant your life? Why are you here?" Then the king of the deer told him all. And the man-king was greatly touched, and said: "Rise up! I grant you your lives, both to you and to her!" Then the rejoinder came: "But though two be thus safe, what shall the rest of the herds do, O king of men?" So they also obtained security. And when the Banyan Deer had similarly procured protection for all the various sorts of living things, the king of the deer exhorted the king of men to justice and mercy, preaching the truth to him "with the grace of a Buddha."

And the doe gave birth to a son, beautiful as buds of flowers, and he went playing with the Branch Deer's herd. Then his mother exhorted him in a verse:

> "Follow rather the Banyan, dear;
> Cultivate not the Branch!
> Death, with the Banyan, were better far,
> Than, with the Branch, long life."[1]

And the Banyan Deer made a compact with the men that wherever leaves were tied round a field the deer should not trespass, and he made all the deer keep to the bargain. From that time, they say, the sign of the tying of leaves was seen in the fields.[2]

This is the end of the Jātaka proper, the "Story of the Past."

Then the Teacher identified the characters in the story as being himself and his contemporaries in a

[1] I have tried to imitate the form of riddle in which the verse appears in Pali.

[2] Very probably the origin of the fable is to be found in a popular explanation of this curious old custom.

former birth. "He who was then the Branch is now Devadatta, his herd the members of the Order who

FIG. 35.—THE BANYAN DEER JĀTAKA STORY.

[Three episodes on one bas-relief.]

followed Devadatta in his schism, the doe is now Kumāra Kassapa's mother, the deer she gave birth to is now her son Kumāra Kassapa, the king of the men is now Ānanda, but Banyan, the king of the deer, was I myself."

The bas-relief here reproduced from the Bharhut[1] Tope illustrates, on one picture, several scenes from this Jātaka.

In this story we have first the outer framework, constituted by the introductory episode and the concluding identification. Encased in this we have the Jātaka proper, the "Story of the past," as it is called in Pali. And in this again we have what is, in the existing canonical Jātaka book, the kernel of the whole, the verse. *Each of these has a separate history.*

The oldest form in which we find any Jātaka is, as might be naturally expected, the simple fable or parable itself, without the outer framework at all, and without the verse. Thus in one of the Nikāyas[2] we have an exhortation to maintain a constant presence of mind, for that is "the proper sphere" of a *religieux*. Should he do otherwise, should he allow worldly things to agitate his mind, then will he fall—as the field quail, when he left his customary and ancestral haunts, fell into the power of the hawk. And the fable is told as an introduction to the exhortation. It has, as yet, no framework. And it contains no verse.[3] It has not yet, therefore, become a Jātaka.

[1] Cunningham, *Stūpa of Bharhut*, Pl. xxv., Fig. 1.

[2] Saṃyutta, vol. 5, p. 146, of the M. Feer's edition for the Pali Text Society.

[3] M. Feer, indeed, prints two lines as if they were verse. But this is a mistake. The lines so printed are not verse.

But one of the Jātakas is precisely this very fable, in identical words for the most part. It is decked out with a framework of introductory story and concluding identification, just as in the example just given. And two verses are added, one in the fable itself, and one in the framework. And there can be no question as to which is the older document; for the Jātaka quotes as its source, and by name and chapter, the very passage in the Saṃyutta in which the fable originally occurs.[1]

This is not an isolated case. Of the Jātakas in the present collection I have discovered also the following in older portions of the canonical books, and no doubt others can still be traced.

2.	Jātaka No.	1. Apannaka	is based on	Dīgha	2. 342
3.	" "	9. Makhā-deva	" " "	Majjhima	2. 75
4.	" "	10. Sukha-vihari	" " "	Vinaya	2. 183
5.	" "	37. Tittira	" " "	Vinaya	2. 161
6.	" "	91. Litta	" " "	Dīgha	2. 348
7.	" "	95. Mahā-sudassana	" " "	Dīgha	2. 169
8.	" "	203. Khandha-vatta	" " "	Vinaya	3. 1095
9.	" "	253. Maṇi-kaṇṭha	" " "	Vinaya	3. 145
10.	" "	405. Baka-brahma	" "	Majjhima	1. 328
				Saṃyutta	1. 142

The heroes of two of these stories, Makhā Deva and Mahā-sudassana, are already in these older documents identified at the end of the stories with the Buddha in a previous birth. In the Mahā-sudassana, in the Litta, and in the second of the two older versions of the Baka story, the verses are given. In all the rest both identification and verses are still, as yet, wanting.

[1] Jātaka, vol. ii. p. 58.

The reverse case is about as frequent; that is to say, stories are told in the older documents, and the hero is expressly identified with the Buddha in a previous birth, and nevertheless these stories are not included in our Jātaka collection.[1] Such stories even before the Jātaka book grew up were called Jātakas. There is a very ancient division found already in the Nikāyas, of Buddhist literature into nine classes.[2] One of these is "Jātakaṃ," that is to say, Jātakas. And this must refer to such episodes in previously existing books. It cannot refer to the Jātaka book now included in the Canon, for that was not yet in existence. And it is important to notice that in no one of these instances of the earliest compositions that were called Jātakas is the Buddha identified in his previous birth with an animal. He is identified only with famous sages and teachers of olden time. This was the first idea to be attached to the word Jātaka. What we find in the canonical book is a later development of it.

Such are the oldest forms, in the Buddhist literature, of the Jātakas. And we learn from them two facts, both of importance. In the first place *these oldest forms have, for the most part, no framework and no verse.* They are fables, parables, legends, entirely (with two exceptions) in prose.

Secondly, *our existing Jātaka book is only a partial*

[1] So for instance Ghatikāra (M. 2. 53); Mahā-govinda (D. 2. 220); Pacetana's wheelwright (A. 1. 111); and Mahā-vijaya's priest (D. 1. 143). The story of Mahā Govinda occurs, as a Jātaka, in the Cariyā Piṭaka.

[2] Majjhima, &. 133; Anguttara, 2. 7, 103, 108,—P. P., 43. 178; Vinaya, 3. 8. The phrase *Navangaṃ Buddha-vacanaṃ* is later.

record. It does not contain all the Jātakas that were current, in the earliest period of their literature, among the Buddhist community.

So much is certain. But I venture to go farther and to suggest that the character of these ten earlier Jātakas, in their pre-Jātaka shape, enables us to trace their history back beyond the Buddhist literature altogether. None of them are specially Buddhist. They are modified, perhaps, more or less to suit Buddhist ethics. But even the Mahā-sudassana, which is the most so, is in the main simply an ancient Indian legend of sun worship. And the rest are pre-Buddhistic Indian folklore. There is nothing peculiarly Buddhist about them. Even the ethics they inculcate are Indian. What is Buddhist about them, in this their oldest shape, is only the selection made. There was, of course, much other folklore, bound up with superstition. This is left out. And the ethic is, of course, of a very simple kind. It is milk for babes. This comes out clearly in the legend of the Great King of Glory—the Mahā-sudassana. In its later Jātaka form [1] it lays stress on the impermanence of all earthly things, on the old lesson of the vanity of the world. In its older form, as a Suttanta, it lays stress also on the Ecstasies (the *Jhānas*), which are perhaps pre-Buddhistic, and on the Sublime Conditions (the *Brahma-Vihāras*), which are certainly distinctively Buddhistic (though a similar idea occurs in the later Yoga Sūtra, I. 33). These are much deeper, and more difficult, matters.

[1] It is translated both from the older and the later form in my *Buddhist Suttas*, pp. 238, foll.

So much for the earliest forms in which we find the Jātakas. The next evidence in point of date is that of the bas-reliefs on the Bharhut and Sānchi Stūpas— those invaluable records of ancient Indian archæology of which so much use has been made in this volume. Among the carvings on the railings round these stūpas are a number of scenes, each bearing as a title in characters of the third century B.C., the name of a Jātaka; and also other scenes, without a title, but similar in character. Twenty-seven of the scenes have been recognised as illustrating passages in the existing Jātaka Book.[1] Twenty-three are still unidentified, and some of these latter are meant, no doubt, to illustrate Jātaka stories current in the community, but not included in the canonical collection.

Now let the reader compare the bas-relief above (p. 193) with the Jātaka story given above (pp. 190, foll). In the background three deer are being shot at, two are running away, one is looking back in fear, one has fallen. In the foreground, to the left, a deer lies with its head on the block. In the centre foreground, the king of the deer, distinguished by his antlers, crouches beside the block, and close by him is a man, presumably the cook. In the centre the king of the deer exhorts the king of the men.

It may be noticed in passing that this strange device of putting several scenes of the same story on one plate is not confined to Indian art. The Greeks did the same, and it was common in Europe at the time of the revival of the arts after the dark ages.

[1] See the list at the end of this chapter.

But while the Indian artist has not hesitated to suggest in his plate so many points in the story, he omits all reference to the verse, or even to that episode in which the verse occurs. The bas-relief, however, resembles the verse in one important respect. It would be absolutely unintelligible to anyone not familar with the story as told in prose. It is the same with all these bas-reliefs. None of them, except as explained below, illustrate the verse, or the framework of the story. None are intelligible without a knowledge of the prose.

The exception referred to is the figure on the Bharhut Stūpa (Plate xxvi.), unfortunately broken, but bearing in clear letters the inscription, "*Yaṃ bamaṇo avayesi Jātaka.*" These are the opening words of the verse in this story which, in the printed edition, is called the Andhabhūta Jātaka.[1] This is exactly as if the deer story above were called the "Follow rather the Banyan" Jātaka. The fact is, as I pointed out already in 1880, that very great uncertainty prevails as to the titles of these stories, the same story being very often called in the existing collection by different names. Even one of these very old bas-reliefs itself has actually inscribed over it two distinct names in full. The carving illustrates a fable about a cat and a cock; and it is labelled, in Pali, both "Cat Jātaka" and "Cock Jātaka."[2] As I then said:

"The reason for this is very plain. When a fable about a lion and a jackal was told (as in No. 157) to show

[1] Fausböll, vol. i. p. 289.

[2] Cunningham, *Stūpa of Bharhut*, Pl. xlvii.

the advantage of a good character, and it was necessary to choose a short title for it, it was called the 'Lion Jātaka' or the 'Jackal Jātaka' or even the 'Good Character Jātaka.' And when a fable was told about a tortoise, to show the evil results which follow on talkativeness (as in No. 215), the fable might as well be called the 'Chatterbox Jātaka' as the 'Tortoise Jātaka'; and it is referred to accordingly under both those names. It must always have been difficult, if not impossible, to fix upon a short title which should at once characterise the lesson to be taught, and the personages through whose acts it was taught. And different names would thus arise, and become interchangeable."[1]

We should not be surprised, therefore, to find in this one instance the catchwords of the verse used also as a title. And it is a most fortunate thing that in this solitary instance the words of the verse are extant in an inscription of the third century B.C.

The next evidence we have to consider is that of the Jātaka Book itself. The canonical work, containing the verses only (and therefore quite unintelligible without a commentary), is very rare even in MSS., and has not yet been edited. It would be very interesting to see what it has to say about the titles, and whether it gives any various readings in the verses.

What we have, in the well-known edition by Professor Fausböll, is the commentary. We do not know its date. But as we know of no commentaries of this sort written before the fifth century A.D.—they were all handed down till then by word of

[1] *Buddhist Birth Stories*, p. lxi.

mouth — it is probable that this one also is of about the same date. The author gives a slight account of himself in the opening verses, but without mentioning his name. He names three scholars who instigated him to undertake the work, and says it is based on the tradition as then handed on in the Great Monastery at Anurādhapura in Ceylon. Twice in the seven long volumes he alludes to Ceylon scholars of the second century A.D.[1] And though he only does so in notes, we may fairly conclude from all this that he probably wrote in Ceylon. Professor Childers thought he was identical with the Buddhaghosa famous as the author of other great commentaries. But for reasons given elsewhere, this is, I think, impossible.[2]

How far, then, did our unknown author vary from the tradition handed down to him? How far had that tradition, with respect at least to the historical inferences suggested by it, preserved the tone and character of that much more ancient date to which the verses themselves can be assigned? It is a difficult question, and can only be finally solved when, by a careful and detailed study of the whole of these volumes, we shall have been able to discover every case of probable age, and to weigh the general result to be derived from them all. Dr. Lüders, in two admirable articles on the Isisinga Legend, has shown how, in two or three instances, the prose

[1] I have discussed these two difficult and interesting notes in an article entitled, "The Last to go Forth," *J. R. A. S.*, 1902.

[2] *Buddhist Birth Stories*, pp. lxiii., foll. Also the note in *Dialogues of the Buddha*, i. 17.

version in the commentary gives us a version of the story, later, in some respects, than that implied by the verses.[1] This is not exactly the point we are considering, but it is closely allied to it. Dr. Fick has subjected all the references contained in the Jātaka Book to the social conditions in North-eastern India to a detailed and careful analysis. He has come to the conclusion that, as regards the verses and the prose part of the stories themselves, as distinct from the framework, they have been scarcely altered from the state they were in when they were handed down from mouth to mouth among the early Buddhists, and that they can be referred undoubtedly, in all that relates to those social conditions, to the time of the Buddha himself.[2] Hofrath Bühler, perhaps the very highest authority we had in Indian history, and a scholar whom no one will accuse of partiality to Buddhism, says:

> "The chief point for consideration is if, in effecting the loan, the Buddhist monks altered much; and especially if the descriptions of life which the Jātakas contain have been made to agree with that of the times when Buddhism had become a power in India. The answer can only be that there are remarkably few traces of Buddhism in those stories, and that they do not describe the condition of India in the third or fourth century B.C., *but an older one.*"

[1] In the *Proceedings* of the Royal Academy at Göttingen, 1897 and 1901.

[2] Dr. Richard Fick, *Sociale Gliederung im nordöstlichen Indian zu Buddha's zeit*, pp. vi., vii.

And he gives his reasons:

"The descriptions of the political, religious, and social conditions of the people clearly refer to the ancient time before the rise of the great Eastern dynasties of the Nandas and the Mauryas, when Pāṭaliputra had become the capital of India. The Jātakas mention neither the one nor the other, and they know nothing of great empires which comprised the whole or large parts of India. The number of the kingdoms, whose rulers play a part in the Stories, is very considerable. The majority of the names, as Madra, the two Pañcālas, Kosala, Videha, Kāsi, and Vidarbha, agree with those mentioned in the Vedic literature; while a few others, like Kālinga and Assaka, occur, in brahminical literature, first in the Epics and in Pāṇini's Sutras. The characteristic names of the Andhras, the Pāṇḍyas, and the Keralas are not mentioned.

"Though a political centre was wanting, frequent statements regarding the instruction of the young brahmins and nobles show that there was an intellectual centre, and that it lay in Takkasilā, the capital of distant Gandhāra. . . . And it is very credible that Gandhāra, the native country of Pāṇini, was a stronghold of brahminical learning certainly in the fourth and fifth centuries B.C., and perhaps even earlier. The statements regarding the religious condition of India point to an equally early period. Just as the Three Vedas are the basis of the higher instruction, so the prevalent religion is that of the path of works with its ceremonies and sacrifices, among which several, like the Vājapeya and the Rājasūya, are specially and repeatedly mentioned. Side by side with these appear popular festivals, celebrated, when the Nakshatra had been proclaimed, with general merrymakings and copious libations of *surā*, as well as the worship of demons and trees, all of which go back to the earliest times. Nor are the hermits in the woods and the wandering ascetics unknown. . . . The state of civilisation described in the Jātakas is in various respects primitive, and particularly noteworthy is the prevalence of wood architecture, which, on the evidence of the earliest sculptures, had almost disappeared in the third century B.C. The Jātakas even describe the palaces of kings as usually constructed of wood. Many other details might be added, but the facts given are sufficient for our purpose."[1]

Professor Fausböll himself, the editor of the Jātaka book, expresses, in the preface to the last volume, a very similar opinion. The consensus of opinion among these distinguished scholars — the only ones who have written on this particular point —is sufficient, at least, to shift the burden of proof. Instead of neglecting altogether, for the history of India, what the Jātaka says, we may make historical inferences from statements made in the stories themselves (not in the framework) as presumptive evidence for the period in which, by a fortunate chance, the stories were preserved for us by their inclusion in the Basket of Buddhist tradition. That tradition is found to have preserved, fairly enough, in political and social matters, the earlier view. The verses, of course, are the most trustworthy, as being, in language, some centuries older. But the prose, which must have accompanied them throughout, and is

[1] Georg Bühler, *Indian Studies*, No. 5 (Vienna, 1895).

taken for granted in the illustrations on the ancient bas-reliefs, ought also, in such questions, to have due weight attached to it.

We may already note some points in the comparative age of the Jātakas, as compared one with another, especially at two stages in the formation of the tradition. The whole of the longer stories, some of them as long as a modern novelette, contained in vol. vi. of the edition, are later, both in language and in their view of social conditions in India, than those in the earlier volumes. Yet several of those latest in the collection are shown by the bas-reliefs to have been already in existence in the third century B.C. And this holds good, not only of the verses, but also of the prose, for the bas-reliefs refer to the prose portions of the tales.[1]

So also, at an earlier stage, it is possible to conclude that some of the tales, when they were first adopted into the Buddhist tradition (that is, certainly, not later than the beginning of the third century, B.C.), were already old. We have seen above that, out of those tales of which we can trace the pre-Jātaka book form, a large proportion, 60 to 70 per cent., had no verses. Now, in the present collection, there are a considerable number of tales which, as tales, have no verses. The verses (necessarily added to make the stories into Jātakas) are found only in the framework.[2] And there are

[1] See in the Appendix, under Vidhura, Sama, Ummagga, and Vessantara Jātakas.

[2] See now M. Senart's article on these Abhisambuddha-Gāthā, in the *Journal Asiatique* for 1902.

other tales, where the verses do not occur in the story itself, but are put, like a chorus, into the mouth of a fairy (a *devatā*) who has really nothing else to do with the story. It follows, I think, that these stories existed, without the verses, before they were adopted into the Buddhist scheme of Jātakas by having verses added to them; and that they are, therefore, probably, not only pre-Buddhistic, but very old.

On the other hand, as we have seen in the last chapter, the very custom, on which the Jātaka system is based, of handing down tales or legends in prose, with only the conversation in verse, is itself pre-Buddhistic. And the Jātaka Book is only another example, on a very extensive scale, of that pre-Epic form of literature of which there are so many other, shorter, specimens preserved for us in the earlier canonical texts.

To sum up:

1. The canonical Book of the Jātakas contains only the verses. It was composed in North India, in the so-called 'Middle Country,' before the time of Asoka. It is still unpublished.

2. It is absolutely certain that, with these verses, there must have been handed down, from the first, an oral commentary giving the stories in prose; for the verses without the stories are unintelligible.

3. Bas-reliefs of the third century B.C. have been found illustrating a number of these prose stories. One of these bas-reliefs gives also half of a verse.

4. There are Jātaka stories in those canonical books that are older than the Jātaka Book.

5. These oldest extant Jātakas are similes, parables,

or legends. They usually give us neither framework nor verses. In them the Buddha, in his previous birth, is never identified with an animal, or even with an ordinary man. He is identified only with some famous sage of bygone times.

6. Our present edition is not an edition of the text, but of the commentary. It was written probably in the fifth century A.D. in Ceylon by an author whose name is not known.

7. This commentary, which contains all the verses, contains also the prose stories in which they occur. To each such story it further gives a framework of introductory episode (stating when and where and on what occasion the story is supposed to have been spoken by the Buddha); and of final identification (of the characters in each story with the Buddha and his contemporaries in a previous birth).

8. This commentary is a translation into Pali of the commentary as handed down in Ceylon. That earlier commentary, now lost, was in the Singhalese language throughout, except as regards the verses, which were in Pali.

9. The Pali commentary, as we now have it, has in the stories preserved, for the most part, the tradition handed down from the third century B.C. But in one or two instances variations have already been discovered.

10. As regards the allusions to political and social conditions, they refer, for the most part, to the state of things that existed in North India in and before the Buddha's time.

11. When the original Jātaka was being gradually

formed most of the stories were taken bodily over from the existing folklore of North India.

12. Some progress has already been made in determining the relative age, at that time, of the stories. Those in the sixth and last volumes are both the longest and latest. Some of these were already selected for illustration on the bas-reliefs of the third century B.C.

13. All the Jātakas have verses attached to them. In a few instances these verses are in the framework, not in the stories themselves. Such stories, without the verses, have probably preserved the original form of the Indian folklore.

14. In a few instances, the verses, though in the stories, are in them only as a sort of chorus, and do not form part of the narrative. In these instances, also, a similar conclusion may be drawn.

15. The whole collection forms the most reliable, the most complete, and the most ancient collection of folklore now extant in any literature in the world.

APPENDIX TO CHAPTER XI

JĀTAKAS ILLUSTRATED BY BAS-RELIEFS ON THE BHARAHAT STŪPA

	Plate in Cunningham's *Stūpa of Bharhut*		Title inscribed on the bas-relief	No. of Jātaka in Fausböll	Name of Jātaka in Pali
1.	XVIII.		Vitura Punakiya Jātaka	545	Vidhūra Paṇḍita Jātaka
2.	XXV.	Fig. 1	Miga Jātaka	12	Nigrodha Miga "
3.	"	" 2	Nāga Jātaka	267	Kakkaṭa "
4.	"	" 3	Yavamajhakiya Jātaka	546	Episode in Mahā Ummagga "
5.	"	" 4	Mugapakaya Jātaka	538	Mūgapakkha "
6.	XXVI.	" 5	Latuvā Jātaka	357	Latukikā "
7.	"	" 6	Chadantiya Jātaka	514	Chaddanta "
8.	"	" 7	Isisingiya Jātaka	523	Alambusa "
9.	"	" 8	Yaṃ bamaṇo avayesi Jātaka	62	Andha-bhūta "
10.	XXVII.	" 9		206	Kurunga-Miga "
11.	"	" 10		349	Sandhi-bheda "
12.	"	" 11	Hansa Jātaka	32	Nacca "
13.	"	" 12	Kinara Jātaka	485	Caṇḍa Kinnara "
14.	"	" 13		181	Asadisa "
15.	"	" 14		461	Dasaratha "
16.	XXXIII.	" 15		407	Mahā Kapi "
17.	XLI.	" 1.3		324	Camma-Sataka "
18.	XLIII.	" 2.8	Isimigo Jātaka	372	Miga-Potaka "
19.	XLIV.	" 2	Janako rājā Sivali devī	539	Mahā-Janaka "
20.	XLV.	" 5		46 & 268	Ārāma-Dūsaka "
21.	"	" 7		42	Kapota "
22.	XLVI.	" 2	Uda Jātaka	400	Dabbha-Puppha "
23.	"	" 8	Secha Jātaka	174	Dūbhiya-Makkaṭa "
24.	XLVII.	" 3	Sujato gahuto Jātaka	352	Sujāta "
25.	"	" 5	Biḍala Jātaka Kukuta Jātaka	383	Kukkuṭa "
26.	XLVIII.	" 2	Maghādeviya Jātaka	9	Makhā Deva "
27.	"	" 7	Bhisa Haraniya Jātaka	488	Bhisa "
28.	L.			547	Vessantara "

The above table is taken, with a few alterations, from Professor Serge d'Oldenburg's table published in the *Journal of the American Oriental Society*, vol. xviii. 1897. It is later and better than the one in my *Buddhist Birth Stories*, p. cii. As the number of Jātakas in the printed collection is 547 it will be seen that rather more than five per cent. of them are represented in this list as having been illustrated in the third century B.C.

As to the spelling of the name of the stūpa the more correct form is Bharahat.

CHAPTER XII

RELIGION—ANIMISM

IT is the accepted belief that it is in the literature of the brahmins that we find the evidence as to the religious beliefs of the peoples of India in the sixth and seventh centuries B.C. This seems to me more than doubtful. The priests have preserved for us, not so much the opinions the people actually held, as the opinions the priests wished them to hold. When we consider the enormous labour of keeping up and handing down the priestly books—and this had to be done, as we have seen,[1] entirely through learning the books by heart—we are filled with admiration for the zealous and devoted students who have thus preserved for us a literature so valuable for the history of human thought. The learned brahmin, and not only in this respect, is a figure of whom India is justly proud. And when we consider how vague and inaccurate are the accounts preserved in the writings of the Christian fathers of any views except those they themselves considered to be orthodox, we see how unreasonable

[1] Above, p. 110, Chapter VII.

it would be to expect that the brahmins, whose difficulties were so much greater, should have been able to do more. What they have done they have done accurately and well. But the record they have saved for us is a partial record.

What had happened with respect to religious belief is on a par with what had happened with respect to language. From Takka-silā all the way down to Champā no one spoke Sanskrit. The living language, everywhere, was a sort of Pali. Many of the old Vedic words were retained in more easily pronounceable forms. Many new words had been formed, on analogy, from the existing stock of roots. Many other new words had been adopted from non-Aryan forms of speech. Many Aryan words, which do not happen to occur in the Vedic texts, had nevertheless survived in popular use. And meanwhile, in the schools of the priests, and there only, a knowledge of the Vedic language (which we often call Sanskrit) was kept up. But even this Sanskrit of the schools had progressed, as some would say, or had degenerated, as others would say, from the Vedic standard. And the Sanskrit in actual use in the schools was as far removed from the Vedic dialect as it is from the so-called classical Sanskrit of the post-Buddhistic poems and plays.

So with the religion. Outside the schools of the priests the curious and interesting beliefs recorded in the Rig Veda had practically little effect. The Vedic thaumaturgy and theosophy had indeed never been a popular faith, that is, as we know it. Both its theological hypotheses and its practical magic (in the ritual) show already a stage very much advanced beyond the simpler faith which they, in fact, presuppose. The gods more usually found in the older systems—the dread Mother Earth, the dryads and the dragons, the dog-star, even the moon and the sun—have been cast into the shade by the new ideas (the new gods) of the fire, the exciting drink, and the thunderstorm. And the charm of the mystery and the magic of the ritual of the sacrifice had to contend, so far as the laity were concerned, with the distaste induced by its complications and its expense.

I am aware that these views as to Vedism are at variance with opinions very widely, not to say commonly, held. Professor Max Müller insisted to the last on the primitive nature of the beliefs recorded in the Rig Veda. Those beliefs seem to us, and indeed are, so bizarre and absurd, that it is hard to accept the proposition that they give expression to an advanced stage of thought. And one is so accustomed to consider the priesthood as the great obstacle, in India, in the way of reform, that it is difficult to believe that the brahmins could ever, as a class, have championed the newer views.

But a comparison with the general course of the evolution of religious beliefs elsewhere shows that the beliefs recorded in the Rig Veda are not primitive. A consideration of the nature of those beliefs, so far as they are not found elsewhere, shows that they must have been, in the view of the men who formulated them, a kind of advance on, or reform of, the previous ideas. And at least three lines of evidence all tend to show that—certainly all the time we are here considering, and almost certainly at the time when the Rig Veda was finally closed—there were many other beliefs, commonly held among the Aryans in India, but not represented in that Veda.[1]

The first of these three lines is the history of the Atharva Veda. This invaluable old collection of charms to be used in sorcery had been actually put together long before Buddhism arose. But it was only just before that time that it had come to be acknowledged by the sacrificial priests as a Veda—inferior to their own three older ones, but still a Veda. This explains why it is that the Atharva is never mentioned as a Veda in the Buddhist canonical books.[2] They are constantly mentioning the three Vedas and the ancient lore connected with the three. They are constantly poking fun at the hocus-pocus of witchcraft and sorcery, and denying any efficiency either to it, or to the magic of the sacrifice. But in the view of the circles in which these books arose the Atharva collection had not yet become a Veda.

Yet it is quite certain that the beliefs and practices to which the Atharva Veda is devoted are as old, if not older, than those to which the three other Vedas refer; and that they were commonly held and followed by the Aryans in India. The things recorded in the Rig may seem to us as absurd as

[1] On religious ideas popular among the people, but only incidentally referred to in the Veda, and not admitted into it as part of the priestly system of belief, see Kirste in the *Vienna Oriental Journal*, 1902, pp. 63, foll.

[2] See *Dialogues of the Buddha*, i. 109.

those in the Atharva. But we cannot avoid the conclusion that the priests who made the older collection were consciously exercising a choice, that they purposely omitted to include certain phases of current belief because those phases did not appeal to them, did not suit their purposes, or did not seem to them worthy of their deities. And when we remember that what they shut out, or nearly shut out, was the lowest kind of savage superstition and sorcery, it is not easy to deny them any credit in doing so.

The second is the general view of religious beliefs, as held by the people, given to us in the Epics, and especially in the Mahā Bhārata. It is, in many respects, altogether different from the general view as given in the Vedic literature. We do not know as yet exactly which of the conceptions in the Mahā Bhārata can be taken as evidence of the seventh century B.C. The poem has certainly undergone one, if not two or even three, alterations at the hand of later priestly editors. But though the changes made in the poems are due to the priests, they were so made because the priests found that ideas not current in their schools had so much weight with the people that they (the priests) could no longer afford to neglect them. They must have recast the poem with two main objects in view—in the first place to insist on the supremacy of the brahmins, which had been so much endangered by the great popularity of the anti-priestly views of the Buddhists and others; and in the second place to show that the brahmins were in sympathy with, and had formally adopted, certain popular cults and beliefs highly esteemed by the people. In any case, there, in the poem, these cults and beliefs, absent from the Vedic literature, are found in full life and power. And though this line of evidence, if it stood alone, would be too weak to bear much weight, the most likely explanation seems to be that here also we have evidence, to some extent at least, of beliefs not included in the Vedic literature, and yet current among, and powerfully affecting, both the Aryan and the semi-Aryan peoples of India.[1]

The third line is based on the references to the religious beliefs, not of the Buddhists themselves, but of the people, recorded in the Buddhist Canon. As these have never yet been collected or analysed, and as they are in many ways both interesting and suggestive, it may be useful to point out shortly here the more important of them.

The standard passages on this question are three, the one in prose, the other two in verse, and all found in our oldest documents. The first is in the *Sīlas*,[2] and begins thus:

> "Whereas some recluses and brahmins, while living on food provided by the faithful, are tricksters, droners out of holy words for pay, diviners, exorcists, ever hungering to add gain to gain, Gotama the recluse holds aloof from such deception and patter."

There then follows a long enumeration, most

[1] Compare Professor Hopkins, *J. A. O. S.* 1899, pp. 315, 365; and *Religions of India*, chap. xiv.

[2] Translated by Rh. D. *Dialogues of the Buddha*, I. 15.

FIG. 36.—SIRIMĀ DEVATĀ.
[From the Bharahat Tope. Pl. xxiii.]

valuable to the historian, of all kinds of animistic hocus-pocus—evidently forming part of the beliefs of the people in the valley of the Ganges in the sixth century B. C., for how otherwise could such "low arts" have been the source of gain to the brahmins and others who practised them? We are told of palmistry, divination of all sorts, auguries drawn from the celestial phenomena, prognostications by interpretation of dreams, auguries drawn from marks on cloth gnawed by mice, sacrifices to Agni,—it is characteristic to find these in such company,—oblations of various sorts to gods, determining lucky sites, repeating charms, laying ghosts, snake charming, using similar arts on other beasts and birds, astrology, the power of prophecy, incantations, oracles, consulting gods through a girl possessed or by means of mirrors, worshipping the Great One, invoking Sirī (the goddess of Luck), vowing vows to gods, muttering charms to cause virility or impotence, consecrating sites, and more of the same kind. It is a queer list; and very suggestive both of the wide range of animistic superstitions, and of the proportionate importance, then and to the people at large, of those particular ones included in the Veda.

It may be noticed in passing that we have representations, of a very early date, of this Sirī, the goddess of Luck, of plenty and success, who is not mentioned in the Veda. One of these is marked in plain letters Sirimā Devatā; and like Diana of the Ephesians, she bears on her breast the signs of her productivity. The other shows the goddess seated, with two elephants pouring water over her. It is the oldest instance of the most common representasentation of this popular goddess; and figures of her, exactly in this form, can be bought to-day in the bazaars of Northern India. (Figs. 36, 48, 37.)

I am allowed, by the kindness of Mrs. Craven, to add a reproduction of a photograph of an image of this popular deity which was recently found in the south of India. It is probably of about the eleventh century, and is decisive evidence that the worship of this non-Vedic goddess prevailed also in the interval between the date of the oldest sculptures and our own time. (Fig. 38.)

That Sirī was already a popular deity in the

Buddha's time explains the fact that the priests had been compelled to acknowledge her and to invent

FIG. 37.—MODERN IMAGE OF ŚRĪ AS CONSORT VISHṆU.
[From Burgess's *Cave Temples of India*, p. 524.]

a special legend to excuse their doing so[1]; and that they incidentally mention her, once again, in

[1] Śatapatha Brāhmaṇa, xi. 4, 3.

mystic conjunction with the dread deities of the Moon, and the Sun, and Mother Earth.[1] Even these other three, though noticed in the Veda, are put far into the background compared with Indra, Agni, Soma, and Varuṇa; but it is highly probable that they really occupied a very much larger share in the minds of the people of India than these sparse notices in the Veda would tend to show. In modern mythology Sirī or Śrī is regarded as a consort of Vishṇu.

The other two passages, in verse, form whole Suttantas—the Mahā Samaya Suttanta, No. 20, in the Dīgha, now edited for the Pāli Text Society, and translated in my *Dialogues of the Buddha*, vol. ii.; and the Āṭānaṭiya Suttanta, No. 32, in the same collection. In the first of these two poems some unknown early Buddhist poet describes how all the gods of the people come to pay reverence, at Kapilavastu, to the new teacher, and to his order of mendicant recluses. In the second of them another unknown poet describes how certain of the gods come to ask him to adopt a form of words which will turn the hearts of other deities unfriendly to the new doctrine, and make them leave it and its followers in peace. And the form of words gives the names of all the gods whom it is considered desirable thus to propitiate.

These two poems form a suggestive parallel to the method followed by the brahmins of adopting, one by one, the popular faiths. It shows how similar are the motives that influence religious

[1] Taittirīya Up. 1. 4.

leaders, however diametrically opposed their views may be. And in both cases the effort had a similar result. The object was to reconcile the people to different ideas. The actual consequence was that the ideas of the people, thus admitted, as it were, by the back door, filled the whole mansion, and the ideas it was hoped they would accept were turned out into the desert, there ultimately to pass absolutely away. Nearer home, too, we may call to mind similar events.

Our two poets are naturally anxious to include in their lists all the various beliefs which had most weight with those whom they would fain persuade. The poet of the Mahā Samaya (the Great Concourse) enumerates first the spirits of the Earth and of the great Mountains. Then the Four Great Kings, the guardians of the four quarters, East and South and West and North. One of these four, Vessavaṇa Kuvera, is the god who in the second poem is the spokesman for all the rest. (Fig. 39.)

Then come the Gandharvas, heavenly musicians, supposed to preside over child-bearing and birth, and to be helpful to mortals in many ways.

Then come the Nāgas, the Siren-serpents, whose worship has been so important a factor in the folklore, superstition, and poetry of India from the earliest times down to-day. Cobras in their ordinary shape, they lived, like mermen and mermaids, beneath the waters,[1] in great luxury and wealth, more especially of gems, and sometimes, as we shall see, the name is used of the Dryads,

[1] See, for instance, Saṃyutta, vol. v. pp. 47, 63.

FIG. 38.—HINDOO GODDESS OF LUCK.

FIG. 39.—VESSAVAṆA KUVERA, KING OF THE YAKSHAS, AND REGENT OF THE NORTH.

[From the Bharahat Tope. Pl. xxii.]

FIG. 40.—CHAKAVĀKA KING OF THE NĀGAS.

[From Cunningham's *Stūpa of Bharhut.* Pl. xxi. Fig. 3.]

the tree-spirits, equally wealthy and powerful. They could at will, and often did, adopt the human form; and though terrible if angered, were kindly and mild by nature. Not mentioned either in

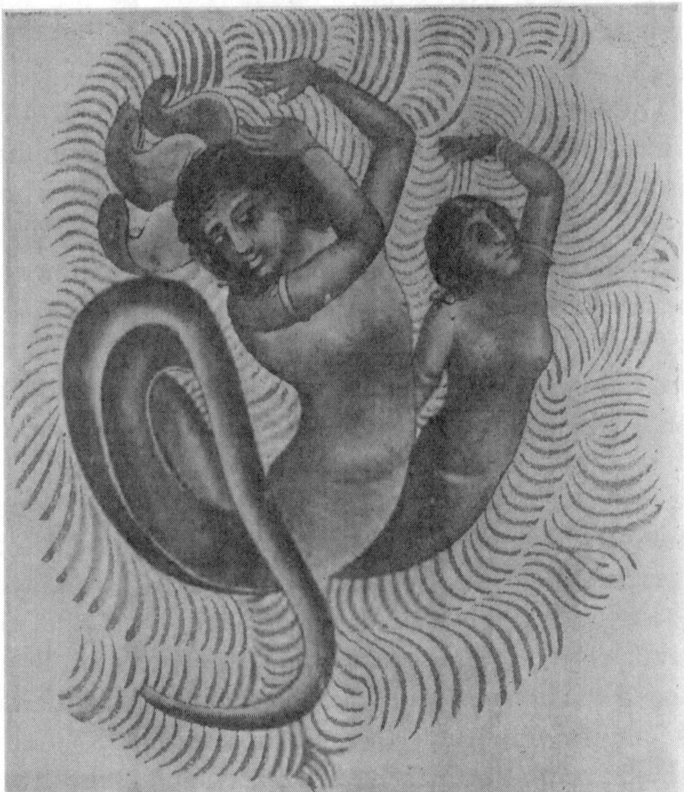

FIG. 41.—NĀGA MERMAIDS IN WATER.

[From Burgess and Grünwedel's *Buddhist Art in India.*]

the Veda or in the pre-Buddhistic Upanishads, the myth seems to be a strange jumble of beliefs, not altogether pleasant, about a strangely gifted race of actual men; combined with notions derived from previously existing theories of tree-worship, and serpent-worship, and river-worship. But the history of the idea has still to be written. These Nāgas are represented on the ancient bas-reliefs as men or women either with cobra's hoods rising from behind their heads or with serpentine forms from the waist downwards.

Then come the Garulas, or Garuḍas, the Indian counterpart of the harpy and griffin, half man, half bird, hereditary enemies of the Nāgas, on whom they feed. They were also, perhaps, originally a tribe of actual men, with an eagle or a hawk as their token on their banner.

Then come a goodly crowd of Titans, and sixty kinds of gods, of whom only about half a dozen are Vedic, the other names offering only puzzles which await the solution of future enquirers. First we have the gods of kindly nature and good character; then the souls or spirits supposed to animate and to reside in the moon and the sun (the moon is always mentioned first), in the wind, the cloud, the summer heat; then the gods of light; then a curious list of gods, personifications of various mental qualities; then the spirits in the thunder and the rain; and, lastly, the great gods who dwell in the highest heavens (that is, are the outcome of the highest speculation), like Brahmā himself, and Paramatta, and Sanaṃ Kumāra.

The list seems inclusive enough. But why does it make no mention of tree-gods? For if we take as our guide, and we could scarcely do better, Mrs. Philpot's excellent monograph on *The Sacred Tree*,

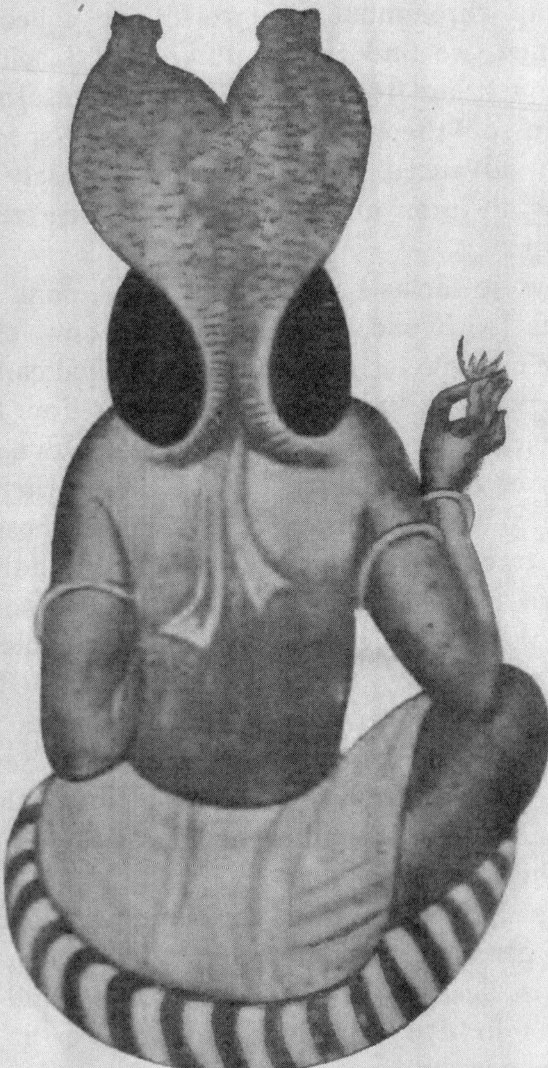

FIG. 42.—SEATED NĀGA; BACK VIEW.
[From a frescoe in Cave II at Ajanta.]

in which the most important facts as to tree-worship throughout the world are collected and classified, we find that a number of fancies about trees, varying from the most naïve results of the savage soul-theories up to philosophic speculations of an advanced kind, have been widely current among all forms of faith, and have been traced also in India.

Now, so far as I can call to mind, none of these fancies (with one interesting exception, on which see below) is referred to in the principal early books setting out the Buddhist doctrine—the Four Nikāyas, for instance, and the Sutta Nipāta. But in older and later documents several of these beliefs can be found. The conclusion is obvious. Those beliefs as to tree-worship mentioned in pre-Buddhistic literature formed part, at the time of the rise of Buddhism, of the religion of the people. They were rejected by the early Buddhists. But they continued to form part of the religion of those of the people who were uninfluenced by the new teaching. And one or two of them found their way back into one or other of the later schools of Buddhism.

Already in the Vedas themselves we have a number of passages in which trees are invoked as deities.[1] This is decisive of the attitude of mind of the Aryans in early times in India. For it was, of course, not the trees as such, but the souls or spirits supposed to dwell within them, to haunt them, that were looked upon as gods. That this notion sur-

[1] See Macdonell, *Vedic Mythology*, p. 154.

vived down to the rise of Buddhism is shown in the Upanishads. If the soul leaves the tree, the tree withers, but the soul does not die.[1] These souls may have dwelt, and may dwell again, in human bodies.[2] And long after the rise of Buddhism ideas associated with this belief are often referred to. Offerings are made to these tree-spirits,[3] even human sacrifices are offered,[4] they were consulted as oracles, and expected to give sons and wealth,[5] they injure those who injure the trees in which they dwell,[6] and they are pleased when garlands are hung upon the branches, lamps are lighted round it, and *Bali* offerings are made (that is food is thrown), at the foot of the tree.[7] The brahmin priests, too, are enjoined in their books of sacred law and custom to throw such *Bali* offerings to the tree-spirits.[8]

All the above is tree-worship—or more correctly dryad-worship—pure and simple. When we find the world-soul spoken of as a tree that has its roots in heaven,[9] that is poetry, a simile based perhaps on the mystery of growth, but still only a simile. The idea of the *Kalpa-rukkha*, the Wishing Tree, which will give one all one wants, has not as yet been traced back earlier than some centuries after the date we are considering.[10]

But Fergusson's explanation of the old monuments

[1] Chând. Up. vi. 11; see Jāt. 4. 154.
[2] Kāṭhaka Up. v. 7.
[3] *J. R. A. S.* 1901, p. 886.
[4] Jāt. 5. 472, 474, 488.
[5] Jāt. Nos. 98, 109, 307, 493.
[6] Jāt. 4. 210, 353.
[7] Jāt. 3. 23; 4. 153.
[8] Manu, iii. 88, etc.
[9] Kāṭhaka Up. vi. 1; Svet. Up., iii. 9.
[10] The earliest reference to this idea I have been able to find is the Āyāranga, p. 127 (see Jacobi, *Jaina Sutras*, 1. 197).

as being devoted to tree-worship requires altogether restating. With all his genius he was attempting the impossible when he tried to interpret the work

FIG. 43.—ELEPHANTS BEFORE THE WISDOM TREE.
[From Cunningham's *Stūpa of Bharhut.* Pl. xxx.]

of Indian artists without a knowledge of Indian literature. His mistake was really very natural. At first sight such bas-reliefs as those here figured (Figures 43 and 44) seem most certainly to show men and animals worshipping a tree, that is the spirit residing in a tree. But on looking farther we

FIG. 44.—THE WISDOM TREE OF KASSAPA, THE BUDDHA.
[From Cunningham's *Stūpa of Bharhut.* Pl. xxx.]

see that the tree has over it an inscription stating that it is "the Bodhi Tree, the tree of wisdom, of Kassapa the Exalted One." Every Buddha is supposed to have attained enlightenment under a tree. The tree differs in the accounts of each of them. Our Buddha's "Wisdom Tree," for instance, is of the kind called the Assattha or Pippal tree. Now while in all the oldest accounts of Gotama's attainment of Buddha-hood there is no mention of the tree under which he was sitting at the time,[1] yet already in a Suttanta[2] it is incidentally mentioned that this event took place under a Pippal tree; and this is often referred to in later books. In these old sculptures the Buddha himself is never represented directly, but always under a symbol. What we have here then is reverence paid to the tree, not for its own sake, and not to any soul or spirit supposed to be in it, but to the tree either as the symbol of the Master, or because (as in the particular case represented in the figures) it was under a tree of that kind that his followers believed that a venerated Teacher of old had become a Buddha. In either case it is a straining of terms, a misrepresentation or at best a misunderstanding, to talk of tree-worship. The Pippal was a sacred tree at the date of these sculptures, —sacred, that is, to the memory of the beloved Master, who had passed away; and it had acquired the epithet of "Tree of Wisdom." But the wisdom was the wisdom of the Master not of the tree or of the tree-god, and could not be obtained by eating of its fruit.

These ideas are of course post-Buddhistic. They could have arisen in a perfectly natural way simply because the tradition was that Gotama had, at that crisis in his life, sat under a Pippal tree. And it is

[1] M. 1. 22, 117, 249.

[2] D. 2. 52.

very possible that the tradition may, so soon afterwards, have been perfectly right. We know as an actual fact that thinking was much more frequent, in that beautiful climate, in the open air, than between four walls. The appreciation of the beauties of nature, so conspicuous in many of the early Buddhist poems, is an Indian, not a Buddhist trait. And it was to a prevalent Indian, not only a Buddhist, sentiment that the Buddha is represented to have appealed, when at the end of some earnest dialogue on a weighty point of ethics or philosophy, he is said to have been wont to close with the appeal: "Here are trees; think this matter out!" It is therefore by no means impossible that it *was* under a Pippal tree the Buddha clenched the essential points in his new doctrine of life. And, if so, is it not quite conceivable that his disciples should have recollected so simple and natural a fact connected with what they regarded, not only as the turning-point in his career, as his Nirvana, but as the turning-point in the history of the world?

Another hypothesis is possible — that the disciples, in all good faith, associated their Master with this particular tree because it already, before his time, had been especially sacred above all other trees. The tradition may then have been the result of this feeling. The tree was certainly held in high esteem even as early as the Vedic poems. Vessels for the mystic Soma cult were made of its wood; and so were the caskets containing the medicinal herbs used in the mystic craft of the physician of the day. The upper portion in the fire-drill — and the production of fire was held to be a mystery—was of the wood of the Pippal tree. And in one passage the tree in heaven under which the souls of the blessed recline is likened to a Pippal.[1] Whether this would be sufficient reason for the rise of the tradition may be doubtful. But such associations would certainly add to its hold on popular imagination, if it had once otherwise arisen.

It is, however, never to the Pippal tree to which the folklore quoted above attributed divine power. It happens always to be some other tree. And we know too little to be able to be quite sure that this is merely a matter of chance. The tree-deities were called Nāgas, and were able at will, like the Nāgas, to assume the human form; and in one story[2] the spirit of a banyan tree who reduced the merchants to ashes is called a Nāga-rāja, the soldiers he sends forth from his tree are Nāgas, and the tree itself is "the dwelling-place of the Nāga." This may explain why it is that the tree-gods are not specially and separately mentioned in the Mahā Samaya list of deities who are there said by the poet to have come to pay reverence to the Buddha. In any case we must add tree-worship, the worship of powerful spirits supposed to dwell in trees, to the list of those beliefs, scarcely noticed in the Vedas, that were an important part of the religion of the peoples of Northern India at the time of the rise of Buddhism.

In neither of these two lists is Indra, the great god

[1] See, on all these points, the passages quoted by Zimmer, *Altindisches Leben*, p. 58.

[2] Jātaka No. 493.

FIG. 45.—THE BUDDHA PREACHING TO NĀGAS DWELLING IN A SACRED TREE. FROM A BUDDHIST CARVING AT TAKT-I-BAHI.

[*J.R.A.S.* 1899.]

of the Veda, even mentioned. His place, as bearer of the thunderbolt, is taken by Sakka, who is in many, if not in most, respects a quite different conception. We should never forget in what degree all these gods are real. They had no real objective existence. But they were real enough as ideas in men's minds. At any given moment the gods of a nation seem eternal, unchangeable. As a matter of fact they are constantly slightly changing. No two men, thinking of the same god, even on the same day, and amid the same surroundings, have quite the same mental image; nor is the proportionate importance of that god as compared with their respective conceptions of other gods (that is, as compared with their other ideas) quite the same. Just as a man's visible frame, though no change may at any moment be perceptible, is never really the same for two consecutive moments, and the result of constant minute variations becomes clear after a lapse of time, so the idea summed up by the name of a god becomes changed by the gradual accretion of minute variations; and this change, after a lapse of time (it may be generations, it may be centuries), becomes so clear that a new name arises, and gradually, very gradually, ousts the older one. Then the older god is dead. As the Buddhist poets put it, "the flowers of the garlands he wore are withered, his robes of majesty have waxed old and faded, he falls from his high estate, and is re-born into a new life." He lives again, as we might say, in the very outcome of his former life, in the new god who, under the new name, reigns in men's hearts.

So Jupiter ousted Chronos, and Indra himself had almost ousted Trita, even in the Veda; and Indra and others had almost ousted Varuṇa. So in the period we are considering had Sakka, in his turn, almost ousted Indra. Though the epic poets afterwards did their best to re-establish Indra on the throne, they had but poor success; for his name and his fame had dwindled away. And we catch sight of him, in these records, just as he is fading dimly away on the horizon, and changing his shape into that of the successor to his dignity and power.[1]

It is the same, but in each case in different degrees, with other Vedic gods. It were tedious here to go at length into each case. Isāna, the vigorous and youthful form of the dread Śiva of the future, is already on a level with Soma and Varuṇa. And Pajāpati and Brahmā[2] will soon come to be considered as co-partners with Sakka in the lordship over all the gods.[3] The worship of Agni is scoffed at as on a par with the hocus-pocus of witchcraft and divination,[4] and it is soon to be laughed to scorn in the amusing tales of the folklore of the people.[5] Vāyu, the wind-god, never very important, is just mentioned in our list, but nowhere else in texts of that age, and will soon also be the laughing-stock of the story-teller.[6] Varuṇa is still a power, ranked with the highest,[7] but he will soon be reduced to a tree-god,[8] a Nāga king,[9] a lord of the oracle girls,[10]

[1] Jāt., 4. 8.
[2] D. I. 244; S. I. 219.
[3] Jacobi, *Jaina Sutras*, I. 198.
[4] D. I. 67.
[5] Jātakas Nos. 35 and 162.
[6] Jātaka No. 17.
[7] S. I. 219; Jāt. 5. 28, 6. 201.
[8] Jāt. 4. 8.
[9] Jāt. 6. 164, 257–329.
[10] The Vāruṇis, Jāt. 6. 586.

who, possessed by the god, will, as Pythias, prophesy smooth things. And Vishṇu, though mentioned in our poem under the name of Veṇhu, has scarcely as yet appeared above the horizon. Pajjunna is still the rain-god in the Suttantas; he is mentioned in both poems; and has retained this character even in the folklore.[1]

I know of no other Vedic gods mentioned in this literature. Dyaus, Mitra, and Sāvitri, Pūshan, the Ādityas, the Aśvins and the Maruts, Aditi and Diti and Urvaśī, and many more, are all departed. They survive only within the enclosures of the Vedic schools. The people know them no longer.

Now there is no doubt a long interval of time between the close of the Rig Veda collection of hymns and the rise of Buddhism. The Vedic anthology, small as it is, may not give, even for its own time, a complete statement of Indian belief. Some of the differences between Vedic mythology and popular religion at the time of the rise of Buddhism may therefore be due to the influence of an unrecorded past. But this can only explain a part, and probably a small part, of the difference. The old gods, that is the old ideas, when they have survived, have been so much changed; so many of them have not survived at all; so many new ones have sprung into vigorous life and wide-reaching influence, that one conclusion is inevitable. The common view that the Indians were very different from other folk in similar stages of development, that to that difference was due the stolid, not to say stupid, conserva-

[1] J. 1. 332, 4. 253; C. P. 3. 10. 7.

tism of their religious conceptions, that they were more given to superstition, less intellectual, than for instance the Greeks and Romans, must be given up. Derived partly from a too exclusive study of the priestly books, partly from reading back into the past a mistaken view of modern conditions, it cannot stand against the new evidence derived from the Jain and Buddhist literatures written, or rather composed, in independence of the priests. The real facts lead to the opposite view. They show a constant progress from Vedic times onwards. Some reasons for this will be suggested in the next chapter. But whatever the facts, and whatever the reasons for them, we are not likely to cease from hearing that parrot cry of self-complacent ignorance, "The immovable East"—the implied sop to vanity is too sweet to be neglected.

CHAPTER XIII

RELIGION—THE BRAHMIN POSITION

THESE details of the lower phases of religion in India in the sixth century B.C. have great and essential similarity with the beliefs held, not only at the same time in the other centres of civilisation,—in China, Persia, and Egypt, in Italy and Greece,—but also among the savages of then and now. But there is a further and more striking resemblance. Sir Henry Maine has said: "Nothing is more remarkable than the extreme fewness of progressive societies—the difference between them and the stationary races is one of the greatest secrets enquiry has yet to penetrate."[1]

Whatever the secret, above and beyond the influence of economic conditions, may have been, we know that civilisation, of a kind at least, extended back in time, on the four great river basins of the Nile and the Euphrates, the Ganges and the Yellow River, not merely through centuries, but through thousands of years, if reckoned from to-day. Yet in

[1] *Ancient Law*, p. 22.

each of those places—though there was a real and progressive civilisation, and ideas and customs were no doubt constantly changing and growing—there was a certain dead level, if not a complete absence of what we should call philosophic thought. The animistic hypotheses, the soul-theories, of their savage ancestors seemed sufficient, even to the progressive races, to explain all that they saw or felt. Men varied, but never dreamed of rejecting, the soul-theories. They did not even build up on the basis of them any large and general views, either of ethics, or of philosophy, or of religion. Then suddenly, and almost simultaneously, and almost certainly independently, there is evidence, about the sixth century B.C., in each of these widely separated centres of civilisation, of a leap forward in speculative thought, of a new birth in ethics, of a religion of conscience threatening to take the place of the old religion of custom and magic. In each of these countries similar causes, the same laws regulating the evolution of ideas, had taken just about the same number of centuries to evolve, out of similar conditions, a similar result. Is there a more stupendous marvel in the whole history of mankind? Does any more suggestive problem await the solution of the historian of human thought?

The solution will not be possible till we have a more accurate knowledge of the circumstances which led up, in each country, to the awakening. And in India one important factor in the preceding circumstances seems to me to have been, hitherto, too much neglected. The intense interest, from the world-history point of view, of the sixth century B.C. — the best dividing line, if there ever was any, between ancient history and modern, between the old order and the new — would be sufficient excuse, if one were needed, for a somewhat detailed consideration of this particular point.

In India, as elsewhere, the whole of the popular animistic notions mentioned in the last chapter, and no doubt others also, survived in full force. But no one man believed in them all, or even knew of them all. In that part of the priestly literature which has come down to us a certain selected portion of these beliefs is taken, as it were, under priestly patronage, has received the stamp of respectability, has been given such social rank as the priests could confer. They seldom, perhaps never, stepped outside the charmed circle of animistic magic. But what they chose was probably, on the whole, of a better kind than what they left to itself. Even so the contents of the priestly books on ritual, though a rich mine of materials for a history of magic and superstition, are unspeakably *banal*. M. Sylvain Lévi, the author of the most authoritative work on this subject, says in the introduction to his summary of the Brāhmaṇa theory of sacrifice:

> "It is difficult to imagine anything more brutal and more material than the theology of the Brāhmaṇas. Notions which usage afterwards gradually refined, and clothed with a garb of morality, take us aback by their savage realism."

Or again:

"Morality finds no place in this system. Sacrifice, which regulates the relation of man to the divinities, is a mechanical act, operating by its own spontaneous energy (par son énergie intime); and that, hidden in the bosom of nature, is only brought out by the magic art of the priest."[1]

To these writers, the sacrifice, if only rigidly carried out in each one of its details, is the source of all profit and advantage. The gods (who are quite unmoral, not immoral, though they are represented in these texts as having been guilty of falsehood, chicanery, and incest) are utterly unable to counteract the effect of such a sacrifice. Indeed they owe their own supremacy, their own position in heaven, to sacrifices they themselves had thus carried out to older gods. And it is by the same means that they continue to defeat the Asuras, that is the Titans, the rival gods, who would otherwise storm the gates of heaven.

There were no temples, and probably no images. The altars were put up anew for each sacrifice in a field or garden belonging to the sacrificer. The benefit to accrue from the sacrifice went to him, and to him alone. He therefore had to pay for the performance; for the animals to be slaughtered, for the numerous work people employed, and for the fees for the priests.

"As to the fees, the rules are precise, and the propounders of them are unblushing. The priest performs the sacrifice for the fee alone, and it must consist

[1] *Doctrine du sacrifice chez les Brāhmanas*, p. 9 (Paris, 1898).

of valuable garments, kine, horses, or gold;—when each is to be given is carefully stated. Gold is coveted most, for 'this is immortality, the seed of Agni,' and therefore peculiarly agreeable to the pious priest."[1]

It would be unnecessary to go into the interminable detail of such sacrifices. They are expounded very fully and carefully in Professor Hillebrandt's standard works on the subject.[2] The expense must have been very great, even for the less complicated; and it is probable that this had something to do with the fact that a way was discovered to obtain the desired result without sacrifice.

The nearer we get to the time of Buddhism the greater is the importance we find attached to this second method, that of *tapas*,—self-mortification, or more exactly, self-torture. The word occurs, in this its technical sense, in the latest hymns included in the Rig Veda. It is literally "burning, glow"; and had then already acquired the secondary sense of retirement into solitude in the forest, and the practise there of austerity, bodily self-mortification,—not at all with the idea of atonement or penance, but under the impression that self-torture of this kind would bring about magical results. Just as the sacrificer was supposed, by a sort of charm that his priests worked for him in the sacrifice, to compel the gods, and to attain ends he desired, so there was supposed to be a sort of charm in *tapas* by which a man could, through and by himself, attain

[1] Hopkins, *Religions of India*, 192.

[2] *Altindische neu-und vollmondsopfer*, Jena, 1879, and *Ritual-literatur*, *Vedische Opfer und Zauber*, Strasburg, 1897.

to mystic and marvellous results. The distinction seems to have been that it was rather worldly success, cattle, children, and heaven, that were attained by sacrifice; and mystic, extraordinary, superhuman faculties that were attained by *Tapas*.

Then, by a natural anthropomorphism, the gods too, in later works, were supposed—just as they had been supposed to offer sacrifice—to practise *tapas*, austerity. And it was not a mere distinction without a difference, it was a real advance in thought, when this sort of physical self-mastery, of the conquest of will over discomfort and pain, came to be placed above sacrifice. It had been by sacrifice that the gods had made the world. Now it came to be said, in different cosmological legends, that one god or another had brought forth the world by *tapas*.[1] And a Brāhmaṇa text declares:

"Heaven is established on the air, the air on the earth, the earth on the waters, the waters on truth, the truth on the mystic lore (of the sacrifice), and that on *Tapas*."[2]

It will be noticed that *tapas* is here put in the most important place, higher than sacrifice, which is, in its turn, higher than truth—a most suggestive order, as we shall see later on. We have no details in the books of this period of the particular practices in which the austerity, the self-mortification, consisted. It was no doubt of various kinds, and would tend, in course of time, to be elaborated. But we have a full statement of the stage it had

[1] Śatapatha-brāhmaṇa vi.1.1.13, and often afterwards.

[2] Aitareya Br. xi. 6. 4.

reached in the Buddha's time, as set forth by a naked ascetic in a Dialogue he had with Gotama.[1] This professor of self-torture enumerates twenty-two methods of self-mortification in respect of food, and thirteen in respect of clothing, and among these the ascetic may make his choice. And he keeps his body under in other ways:

"He is a 'plucker-out-of-hair-and-beard' (destroying by a painful process the possibility of pride in mere beauty of appearance)—or he is a 'stander-up' (rejecting the use of a seat)—or he is a 'croucher-down-on-the-heels' (moving about painfully by jumps)—or he is a 'bed-of-thorns-man' (putting thorns or iron spikes under the skin on which he sleeps)—or he sleeps on a plank, or on the bare ground, or always on the same side—or he is 'clad-in-dust' (smearing his naked body with oil and standing where dust clouds blow, he lets dust and dirt adhere to his body)."

Later on, in the epic for instance, the list grows longer, the penances harder, the self-torture more revolting. But from this time onwards, down to quite modern times, this *tapas*, self-mortification, is a permanent idea and practice in the religious life of India. As is well known it is not confined to India. Tennyson, in the monologue of St. Simeon Stylites, has given us a powerful analysis of the sort of feelings that lay at the root of this superstition in the West. But the theological views that give the tone to the Christian saint's self-revelation are very

[1] Rh. D. *Dialogues of the Buddha*, I. pp. 226–232.

different from those we find in India. The Indian way of looking at the whole conception is much more akin to the way Diogenes thought when he lived, like a dog, in his tub-kennel. The Greek word *cynic* is indeed exactly analogous to the Indian expression *kukkura-vatiko*, "one who behaves like a dog," as applied (quite courteously) to the sophist, the naked ascetic, Seniya.[1] There is no question here of penance for sin, or of an appeal to the mercy of an offended deity. It is the boast of superiority advanced by the man able, through strength of will, to keep his body under, and not only to despise comfort, but to welcome pain. By this it is not, of course, intended to imply that the Christian did not advance a similar claim. He did. But it was, in his case, overshadowed by other considerations which are absent in India.

Both in the East and the West the claim was often accepted. We hear a good deal in India of the reverence paid to the man who (to quote the words of a Buddhist poet),

> "Bescorched, befrozen, lone in fearsome woods,
> Naked, without a fire, afire within,
> Struggled in awful silence toward the goal!"[2]

Simeon, by the mere strength of popular acclaim, became a saint, even almost before he died. Diogenes, and his parallel in India, Mahāvīra, founded important schools which have left their mark on history. And ought we, after all, to be surprised that those who despise earthly comfort, and subject them-

[1] M. I. 387.

[2] M. I. 79 = Jāt. I. 390.

selves to voluntary torture, should be looked upon, with a kind of fearsome awe, as more holy, as better, than other men? There was some justice in the view. And until experience had shown the other side of the question—the attendant disadvantages, and the inadequate results of strength of will when applied to physical ends—it was inevitable that the self-mastery quite evident in such practices should appeal strongly to the minds of the people.

We find the other side put forward in India from two directions, one mainly philosophic, the other mainly ethical. The manner in which both these movements came about was perfectly natural, though it was much influenced by the custom already referred to as peculiar, at that period of the world's history, to India.[1] Students are often represented as begging, just as students did in Europe in the Middle Ages.[2] And we hear of sophists, just as we do in the history of Greek thought. But the peculiarity was that, before the rise of Buddhism, it was a prevalent habit for wandering teachers also—and not only students—to beg. Such wandering teachers, who were not necessarily ascetics except in so far as they were celibates, are always represented as being held in high esteem by the people. In the monarchies the royal family, in the clans the community, put up (as we have seen above) public halls where such Wanderers (*Paribbajakā*) could lodge, and where conversational discussions, open to everyone, were held on philosophic and religious

[1] See above, Chapter VIII.

[2] Śat. Br. xi. 3. 3. 5; and often later in the law-books.

questions.[1] The career of such a wandering teacher seems to have been open to anyone, and even to women. And the most perfect freedom, both of thought and of expression, was permitted to them —a freedom probably unequalled in the history of the world.

This curious state of things would only have been possible among people of a very fair degree both of average general intelligence and of gentle manners. And just as the Strolling Students in pre-Reformation times throughout Western Europe were both a sign of the coming change, and also helped largely to bring it about, so the conditions which made it possible for the Wanderers in Northern India to live as they did, in pursuit of what they thought to be truth, were the precursors of that movement of thought we now call Buddhism, which the Wanderers also so largely helped to bring about.

The early history of the Wanderers has yet to be written. We hear of a similar custom as already followed in one isolated case by a sacrificing priest. Uddālaka Āruṇi, of the Gotama family, of whom so many other legends have been preserved, is said to have wandered about the country offering a gold coin, as a lure for the timid, to anyone who, in a disputation on spiritual matters, could prove him wrong.[2] When defeated he becomes the pupil of his conqueror.

We may point out, in passing, that these "spiritual matters" are very characteristic of the Brāhmaṇas.

[1] Rh. D. *Dialogues of the Buddha*, I. 244; and above, p. 141.

[2] Śat. Br. xi. 4. 1.

When he is being defeated the problems put are such as this: Why are creatures born without teeth, then teeth grow, and when the creatures become old then the teeth decay? The answer of his opponent, the orthodox priest, is: The preliminary offerings of a sacrifice have no formulas of invitation, therefore creatures are born without teeth (!). The chief sacrifice has, therefore teeth grow (!). The closing acts in the sacrifice have no such formulas, therefore in old age teeth decay (!). Other explanations, equally lucid and convincing, are given for the growth and decay of the procreative power, etc. Such are the deep mysteries Uddālaka Āruṇi is scoffed at (in the priestly manual which has preserved this interesting old story) for not knowing.

This is a foreshadowing of the well-known Buddhist story of the woman sophist who wandered from village to village offering to meet all the world in argument, and when beaten in a disputation, became the pupil of her Buddhist conqueror. In the centuries between the date of these two legends the whole system had grown up. But unfortunately there is so little about it in the priestly books that it is not easy to trace its progress.

The priests, very naturally, did not like the gradually growing esteem in which a body of men (and women) were held who despised the sacrifice, the source of the priests' income and reputation. But they were quite helpless in the matter. The sacrifices the priests were ready to offer had entirely lost any significance they may have once possessed as national or tribal ceremonies. They were now merely magic rites performed for the benefit of one individual and at his expense. In the priestly books it is taken for granted that every one entitled to do so is desirous to have the sacrifices performed for him. In actual life there were probably many who gibed at the cost; and preferred, if they wanted magic, magic of other and cheaper kinds. In any case there was no central organisation of the priesthood; there were no permanent temples to their gods, and such sacred shrines as the people could frequent were the sacred trees or other objects of veneration belonging to the worship of the local gods, and quite apart from the cultus or the influence of the priests.

And the latter were divided against themselves. They vied with one another for sacrificial fees. The demand for their services was insufficient to maintain them all. Brahmins followed therefore all sorts of other occupations; and those of them not continually busied about the sacrifice were often inclined to views of life, and of religion, different from the views of those who were. We find brahmins ranking *tapas*, self-torture, above sacrifice. We find brahmins among those who reckoned insight above either, and who, whether as laymen or as Wanderers, joined the ranks of the other side. Unable therefore, whether they wanted or not, to stay the progress of newer ideas, the priests strove to turn the incoming tide into channels favorable to their Order. They formulated—though this was some time after the rise of Buddhism—the famous theory of the *Ās'ramas*, or Efforts, according to which no one could become either a Hermit or a Wanderer without having first passed many years as a student in the brahmin schools, and lived after that the life of a married householder as regulated in the brahmin law-books. It was a bold bid for supremacy. If successful it might have put a stop to the whole movement. But it remained a dead letter—probably always, certainly during the period we are here considering. It is quite true that the priestly manuals, especially those later than the Christian era, take it as a matter of course that the rule was observed. But they do not give us the actual facts of life in India. They give, and are only meant to give, what the priests thought the facts ought to be. And there is ample evidence even in the priestly literature itself of a gradual growth in the theory, of differing views about it, and of its loose hold on the people. I have elsewhere collected the evidence, which though most interesting, historically, and quite conclusive, is too long to set out here.[1]

In the second place, the priests, already before the rise of Buddhism, had (as appendices to their sacred books on the sacrifice) short treatises setting out, as the highest truth, those forms of speculation which they held most compatible with their own mysteries. Their procedure, in this respect, was exactly parallel to their treatment of gods not included in their own pantheon, but too powerful and popular to be left alone. It is quite evident, from the outcome of the whole movement, that there

[1] *Dialogues of the Buddha*, I, pp. 212–219.

must have been other ideas current besides those that the priests thus adapted and handed down in their text-books. And we have valuable evidence, in the lay literature of a later date, as to what these other ideas were, so that in this respect also, as in other matters, the priestly books have preserved an invaluable, but still only a partial, record.

The ideas they selected are, as would naturally be expected, those based on the same animistic notions as underlay their own views of the sacrifice. A soul in these texts—the pre-Buddhistic Upanishads—is supposed to exist inside each human body, and to be the sole and sufficient explanation of life and motion. In the living body, in its ordinary state, the soul dwells in a cavity in the heart.[1] It is described as being in size like a grain of barley or rice.[2] It is only in later speculation that it grows to be of the size of the thumb, and to be called therefore "the dwarf."[3] In shape it is like a man.[4] Its appearance was evidently found difficult to portray, even in simile; but it is said in different passages to be like smoke-coloured wool, like cochineal, like flame, like a white lotus, like a flash of lightning, like a light without smoke. Beliefs vary as to what it is made of. One passage says it consists of consciousness, mind, breath; eye and ears; earth, water, fire, and ether; heat and no heat; desire and no

[1] Bṛhad. iv. 3. 7, v. 6; Chānd. viii. 3. 3; Tait. i. 6. 1. Compare Kaṭha, ii. 20; iii. 1; iv. 6; vi. 17.

[2] Bṛhad. v. 6; Chānd. iii. 14. 3 (this idea is even Vedic).

[3] Kaṭha, iv. 12, 13, vi. 17; Śvet. iii. 13, v. 8.

[4] Tait, ii.; Bṛhad. i. 41; Śat. Br. xiv. 4. 2. 1.

desire; anger and no anger; law and no law—in a word, of all things.[1] We see from this that the soul was supposed to be material—the four elements of matter are there—but selected mental qualities are also in it. In another curious and deeply mystical old text the elements of matter come first, and we are told of five souls, each inside the other, each the same yet different from the one outside it, each of them in shape as a man, and made respectively of food, breath, mind, consciousness, and joy.

Certain forms of disease were supposed to be due to the fact that the soul had escaped out of the body; and charms are recorded for bringing it back.[2] In dream sleep also the "soul" is away from the body. "Therefore they say: Let no one wake a man brusquely; for that is a matter difficult to be cured for him if the soul find not its way back to him."[3]

During the dream the soul, after leaving the body, wanders at its will, builds up a world according to its fancy, creates for itself chariots and houses, lakes and rivers, manifold shapes, a gorgeous playground wherein it acts and enjoys and suffers, "either rejoicing with women, or laughing with its friends, or beholding horrible sights." Till at last, tired out,—just as a falcon after roaming hither and thither in the sky, tired, flaps its wings and is wafted to its nest,—so the soul returns from that playground of his to the body, when in deep, fast sleep it wants no

[1] Bṛhad. iv. 4. 5. See also iii. 7. 14–22.

[2] Atharva Veda, v. 29. 5; vi. 53. 2; vii. 67. Compare Ait. Ār. iii. 2. 4. 7.

[3] Bṛhad. iv. 3. 14.

more, and dreams no more.[1] It is a charming and beautiful picture.

Such dreams are premonitions of good luck or the reverse, which gave rise, in India then, as throughout the world in similar stages of culture, to many foolish fancies.

When the soul has come back to the body, which remains recumbent in dreamless sleep, the soul pervades the whole of it, down to the tips of the hair and nails, by means of seventy-two thousand arteries called Hitā (the Good). And oddly enough it is precisely then that the soul is supposed to obtain light.[2]

We are not told *how* the soul gets out of, and back into, the body. This is not surprising, for the opinions expressed as to how the soul got into its first body—whether at conception or at quickening or at birth—are contradictory. All views on this point were no doubt neither more nor less hazy then in India than they are now in the West. There are passages which suppose the soul to have existed, before birth, in some other body[3]; and other passages which suppose it to have been inserted, at the origin of things, into its first body downwards, through the suture at the top of the skull, into the heart.[4] But there is a passage which affirms that the soul was inserted upwards, through the intestines and the belly, into the head. And we find a

[1] Bṛhad. iv. 3; Chānd. viii. 12. 3.

[2] Bṛhad. ii. 1. 19, iv. 3. 20; Chānd. viii. 6. 3; Kauṣ. iv. 19.

[3] Bṛhad. iii. 2. 13; iv. 4. 6. Compare vi. 4, and Ait. Ār. ii. 3. 2.

[4] Tait. i. 6. 1; Ait. iii. 12.

curious speculation, of which there are three variants, on the transfer of the soul by generation, through the seed.

One of these is the theory that certain human souls, on going to the moon, become food to the gods there, and are thus united to the gods as a consequence of their good deeds. When the efficacy of their good deeds is exhausted, they pass from the gods to the ether, from the ether into the air, from the air into the rain, from the rain on to the earth, from the earth into plants which become food to males, and from the males they pass into females.[1]

At the death of an ordinary man the top part of the heart becomes lighted up, and the soul, guided by that light, departs from the heart into the eye, and through the eye to some other body, exalted or not, according to the deeds the man has done in that body the soul is now leaving. But the soul of the man whose cravings have ceased goes, through the suture of the skull (at the top of the head), to Brahman.[2] In each case there are many stopping-places on the way,[3] but the theories differ both about these and about other details. I have discussed these points elsewhere.[4] And a careful search would no doubt reveal passages even in other parts of the priestly literature acknowledging views which do

[1] Bṛhad. vi. 2. 16; vi. 3. 13. Comp. Kauṣ. i. 2; Ait. ii. 1–4; Ait. Ār. iii. 2. 2. 4.

[2] Bṛhad. iv. 4; Kauṣ. iii. 3; Chānd. vii. 6. 6; Tait. i. 6. 1.

[3] Bṛhad. vi. 2; Chānd. iv. 15 and v. 9.

[4] *Dialogues of the Buddha*, I. 188, 242; *Journal of the Royal Asiatic Society*, 1899, pp. 79, foll.

not happen to be referred to in the older Upanishads, but which bear the stamp of great antiquity—such passages as Mahā-bhārata, xii. 11. 704, where we are told that if, as the dying man draws up his knees, the soul goes out of him by way of the knees, then it goes to the Sādhyas.

But there is an almost entire unanimity of opinion in these Upanishads that the soul will not obtain release from rebirth either by the performance of sacrifice in this birth or by the practice of penance. It must be by a sort of theosophic or animistic insight, by the perception, the absolute knowledge and certainty, that one's own soul is identical with the Great Soul, the only permanent reality, the ultimate basis and cause of all phenomena.

The ideas had therefore just made, at the time when our history begins, a complete circle. The hypothesis of a soul—a material, but very subtle sort of homunculus within the body—had been started to explain the life and motion, sleep and death, of human beings. By analogy, logically enough, it had been extended, ever more and more widely, to explain similar phenomena in the outside world. There must be a soul in the sun. How else could one explain its majestic march across the heavens, evidently purposeful, its rising and its setting, its beauty and light and glow? If its action was somewhat mysterious, who was to limit or define the motives of the soul of so glorious a creature? There was no argument about it. It was taken for granted; and any one who doubted was simply impious. These souls in nature—gods they called them — had, of course, no existence outside the brains of the men who made them. They were logical corollaries of the human soul. And the external souls, the gods, were therefore identical in origin and nature with the souls supposed to live inside human bodies. But the very men who made these external souls, the gods, looked upon them as objective realities, quite different from their own souls. They—the gods—were always changing—that is to say, men's ideas about them were always changing, moving, being modified. The long history of Indian mythology is the history of such changes, by no means always dependent on theological reasons.[1] And with each change the objective reality of the external souls, the gods, their difference from the souls of men, seemed more clear and certain than ever.

Then came the reaction. The gods began, not in popular belief, but among thinkers, to be more and more regarded as identical one with the other until at last, just before Buddhism, the hypothesis was started of a one primeval soul, the world-soul, the Highest soul, the Paramātman, from whom all the other gods and souls had proceeded. There was a deep truth in this daring speculation. But the souls inside men were held in it to be identical with god, the only original and true reality; whereas, historically speaking, soul was the original idea, and the gods (and god) had grown out of it.

We have abundant evidence that this grand generalisation was neither due to the priests who

[1] See *American Lectures*, pp. 12–14.

adopted it, nor had its origin in the priestly schools. Precisely as regards the highest point of the generalisation, the very keystone of the arch, the priestly literature has preserved the names of the rajput laymen who thought it out and taught it to the priests. And among the priests who had the greatest share in adopting it, in procuring admission for it into their sacred books, is mentioned the very Uddālaka Āruṇi, the Gotama, whose defeat in argument on "spiritual matters" has been recorded above.

When this point had been reached, speculation on the basis of the soul theory could go no further. The only modification possible was in the ideas as to the nature and qualities of the souls, internal and external, and as to the relations between them. And to this point speculation reached, but later, and less clearly, in China also, and in Greece. But it was in India, and in India only, that the further step was taken, by Gotama the rajput and his disciples, to abandon the soul theory altogether; and to build up a new philosophy (whether right or wrong is not here the question) on other considerations in which soul or souls played no part at all.

That this thoroughgoing and far-reaching step was taken by laymen should not surprise us. To suppose that the Indians were more superstitious at that time than other folk, more under the thumb of their priests, is to misunderstand the evidence. On the contrary there was a well-marked lay feeling, a real sense of humour, a strong fund of common-sense, a wide-spread feeling, in all such matters, of courtesy and liberality. How otherwise can we explain the fact, already pointed out, of the most complete and unquestioned freedom, both of thought and expression, which the world had yet witnessed?

We shall probably be ignoring an important factor in the history of the time if we omit to notice that this state of things was due, in great part, to the very easy and simple economic conditions of those days.

CHAPTER XIV

CHANDRAGUPTA

WE have sketched in the opening chapters the political divisions of India at the time of the rise of Buddhism. We know, whether from native or foreign sources, very little of what happened during the century and a half that followed after the Buddha's death. When the curtain rises again it shows considerable changes in the picture. But the new picture is in harmony with the old; the principal figures and most of the minor ones are the same; and the changes in their position can be fairly understood in the light of their previous relations.

In the middle of the seventh century B.C., the paramount power was the great kingdom of Kosala, then at the height of its prosperity, under Pasenadi's father, the Great Kosalan (Mahākosala), whose dominions extended from the mountains to the Ganges, and from the Kosala and Rāmaganga rivers on the west to the Gandak on the east. West and south of it a number of small kingdoms maintained their independence. Eastward Kosala had already extended its suzerainty over the Sākiyas; but was stopped in its further advance by the powerful confederation of the Licchavis. South of these, again, a death-struggle was going on between the two smaller kingdoms of Magadha and Champā. This was decided in the time of the Buddha's boyhood by the final victory of Magadha. And the rising of this new star in the extreme south-east was the most interesting factor in the older picture.

The new picture, as shown to us in the Ceylon Chronicles and in the Greek accounts of India, especially in those fragments that have survived of the *Indika* of Megasthenes (300 B.C.), shows us Magadha triumphant. The free clans and the great kingdom of Kosala have been absorbed by it. One by one the kingdoms to the south and west of what had been Kosala have acknowledged its supremacy. In distant Punjab and Ujjen viceroys from Magadha administer the government. And for the first time in the history of India there is one authority from Afghanistan across the continent eastward to Bengal, and from the Himālayas down to the central Provinces.

We shall probably never know—unless the ancient sites in India shall one day, like those in Assyria and Egypt, be excavated and explored—how these great changes came actually to be brought about. But the two sets of authorities just referred to (which are quite independent one of another, and yet confirm one another in the most important matters) are conclusive evidence that the changes had actually taken place.

Taken separately, each of these authorities is

open to serious objections. The Chronicles have all the advantages, but also all the disadvantages, that belong to chronicles written by monks, whether in the East or the West. And the Greek accounts are in various ways rendered less useful than they might otherwise have been.

The work of Megasthenes has been lost. The fragments that survive in quotations by later authors have been collected by Schwanbeck, and translated in Mr. McCrindle's excellent work, *Ancient India*. Where what is evidently intended to be a quotation from the same paragraph of Megasthenes is found in more than one of the later Greek authors, the various presentations of it do not, in several cases, agree. This makes it certain that these quotations do not always give the exact words of Megasthenes, and throws considerable doubt on the correctness of those quotations which, being found in one author only, cannot be so tested. A number of these quotations contain statements that are glaringly absurd—accounts of gold-digging ants, men with ears large enough to sleep in, men without any mouths, without noses, with only one eye, with spider legs, or with fingers turning backwards. Strabo calls these stories mendacious. But they are evidence, rather, of the small amount of critical judgment possessed by Megasthenes; and also, be it said, by the other Greek writers who chose precisely these foolish puerilities as the portions of Megasthenes they thought it important to repeat. There remain a few pages which, when the mistakes have been corrected, afford a residuum of sober information, all of it interesting, and some of it not found elsewhere. Perhaps the most important is the all-too-short description of Pāṭaliputta, the capital of Magadha, at which Megasthenes resided.

"The greatest city in India is that which is called Palimbothra, in the dominions of the Prasians, where the streams of the Erannoboas [this a Greek corruption of Hiraññavatī] and the Ganges unite. . . . Megasthenes informs us that this city stretched in the inhabited quarters to an extreme length on each side of 80 stadia [nearly 10 miles], and that its breadth was fifteen stadia [nearly 2 miles], and that a ditch encompassed it all round, 600 feet in breadth and 30 cubits in depth, and that the wall was crowned with 570 towers and four-and-sixty gates. The same writer tells us this remarkable fact about India, that all the Indians are free, and that not one of them is a slave."[1]

These particulars about the size and the fortifications of Pāṭaliputta in 300 B.C. are new; and are, no doubt, also true. The number of towers allows one to every seventy-five yards, so that archers, in the towers, could cover the space intervening between any two. The number of gates would allow one to each 660 yards, which is quite a probable and convenient distance. The extent of the fortifications is indeed prodigious. Ten miles, along the river, is just the distance from the Tower of London to Hammersmith Bridge; or, if taken in a straight line, is the distance from Greenwich to Richmond; and from the river at the Chelsea Embankment to the Marble Arch is just two miles, south to north. All of

[1] Arrian, *Ind.*, ch. x.

London from the Tower to the Houses of Parliament, and from the river to the Hampstead Hills, would occupy about the same space. But, as we have seen, the native records confirm the impression that then, as now, Indian towns tended to cover a vast extent. And we may probably accept the estimate made by Megasthenes of the size of the city wherein he dwelt.

The statement about slavery is odd. The distinct and unanimous testimony of all the Indian evidence is decisive that the status of slavery was then an actual factor of Indian life, though not a very important one. When the Greek writer states, so emphatically, the contrary, one can only say that he is mistaken in the main fact, and that his evidence only shows how very little the sort of slavery then existing in India would strike a foreigner accustomed to the sort of slavery then existing in Greece.

Then Megasthenes says that the population of India was divided into seven classes as follows:

1. Philosophers.
2. Husbandmen.
3. Herdsmen.
4. Artisans.
5. Soldiers.
6. Spies.
7. Councillors.

"No one is allowed to marry out of his own class, or to exercise any calling or art except his own.[1] A

[1] Strabo, xv. 49. has in place of this last clause, "or to exchange one profession for another, or to follow more than one business. An exception is made in favour of the philosopher, who for his virtue is allowed this privilege."

soldier, for instance, cannot become a husbandman, or an artisan a philosopher." [1]

Here again Megasthenes is inaccurate. There were customs of endogamy and exogamy, and of a man following his father's trade; but not those that he specifies. He has got his classes all wrong. There were many others he does not mention; and those he does did not form real groups, either according to the marriage customs of India, or according to the habits of the people as to occupation. The true account of the matter has been given above at page 55. It is precisely in the details of such a subject that a foreigner, especially if he could not speak the language, is likely to have gone astray. With the official life, on the other hand, he would probably be better acquainted. And this is what Megasthenes says on that point:

"Of the great officers of state some have charge of the market, others of the city, others of the soldiers. Some superintend the rivers [canals ?],—measuring the land as is done in Egypt,—and inspect the sluices by which water is let out from the main canals into their branches, so that every one may have an equal supply of it.

"The same persons have charge also of the huntsmen [surely only the royal huntsmen], and are entrusted with the power of rewarding or punishing them according to their deserts.

"They collect the taxes, and superintend the occupations connected with land [that is, no doubt, look after the royal dues arising out of them], as those of woodcutters, carpenters, blacksmiths, and miners. They con-

[1] Diodorus Siculus, iii. 63.

struct roads, and at every ten stadia set up a pillar to show the byroads and distances.[1]

"Those who have charge of the city are divided into six bodies of five each. The members of the first look after everything related to the industrial arts.

"Those of the second look after the entertainment of foreigners. To these they assign lodgings; and they keep watch over their modes of life by means of those persons whom they give to them as servants. They escort them on the way when they leave the country; or, in the event of their dying, they forward their property to their relatives. They take care of them when they are sick, and, if they die, bury them.

"The third body consists of those who inquire when and how births and deaths occur, with a view not only of levying a tax, but also in order that births and deaths among high and low may not escape the cognisance of Government.

"The fourth class superintends trade and commerce. Its members have charge of weights and measures, and see that the products, in their season, are sold by public notice.[2] No one is allowed to deal in more than one kind of commodity unless he pays a double tax.

"The fifth class supervises manufactured articles, which they sell by public notice. What is new is sold separately from what is old; there is a fine for mixing the two together.

"The sixth and last class consists of those who col-

[1] Ten stadia is 2022½ yards. This is, within a few yards, the sixth part of a *yojana*, the common Indian measure of length at that time.

[2] This is very obscure. The words seem to imply either that sale was usually not by private barter, but by auction, or that sales took place through advertisement. Neither of these statements would be correct. See Chapter VI. on economic conditions.

lect the tenths of the prices of the articles sold. Fraud in the payment of this tax is punished with death."

There follows in the quotations a superficial account of the organisation of the army which is scarcely worth quoting. But the figures given are interesting: "The king [of the Palibothri] has in his pay a standing army of 60,000 foot soldiers, 30,000 cavalry, and 8000 elephants; whence may be formed some conjecture as to the vastness of his resources." Pliny, in what is evidently an echo of the same paragraph, gives the numbers as 600,000, 30,000, and 9000. But the first of these is clearly a mistake, and very probably only a copyist's error.[1] The same writer has preserved a tradition as to the numbers of the armies of other Indian kings at the same period. It is, no doubt, derived from Megasthenes, and the numbers as follows:

Kalinga,	60,000 foot,	10,000 horse,	700 elephants.
Talukta,	50,000 "	4,000 "	700 "
Andhra,	100,000 "	2,000 "	1,000 "

It will be noticed that with a curious equality in infantry, the forces of Magadha show a great superiority in cavalry, and in elephants-of-war. This is probably correct, as the unanimous testimony of the Indian records ascribes the pre-eminence in the training of horses to the districts in the extreme north and west, which then belonged to Magadha, and the pre-eminence in the training of elephants to the east, which is precisely Magadha. This use

[1] Pliny, *Hist. Nat.* vi. 21. 9–23. See the statement below.

of elephants in war, I may observe in passing, may have been an important factor in the gradual rise of Magadha to the supreme power.

It would, of course, be a very serious error to regard Chandragupta as the founder of this supremacy of Magadha. When Alexander invaded the north-west of India he was informed that the then emperor at Magadha (who must have been Dhana Nanda, the predecessor of Chandragupta) had an army of 200,000 foot, 20,000 cavalry, 2000 war-chariots, and 4000 elephants-of-war.[1] It had certainly then already absorbed Kosala, and probably also other kingdoms to the south and west of Kosala. Chandragupta added the Panjab and the provinces along the Indus down to its mouth. It was from the Panjab that he, favoured by the disorder resulting from Alexander's invasion, recruited the nucleus of the force with which he besieged and conquered Dhana Nanda. Whether the southern Indus provinces were then also under his sway we do not know, but Pliny, doubtless referring to his time, says that the Magadha empire extended right up to the river.[2] He may have subdued them afterwards, at the same time as he conquered the peninsula of Gujarat, where, as we learn from Rudra-dāman's inscription, a viceroy of his was in possession. The ancient kingdom of Avanti, with its capital Ujjeni, had probably, before his time, been already incorporated into the Empire.

Chandragupta thus found himself strong enough

[1] Diod. xvii. 93; Curtius, ix. 2; Plutarch, *Alex.* 62.

[2] *Hist. Nat.* vi. 22. 5.

to withstand even the Greeks. At the end of the fourth century B.C. Seleukos Nikator, then at the height of his power, attempted to rival Alexander by invading India. But he met with a very different foe. Alexander found a succession of small kingdoms and republics, whose mutual jealousies more than counterbalanced the striking bravery of their forces, and enabled him to attack and defeat them one by one. Seleukos found the consolidated and organised empire of Magadha, against which all his efforts were in vain. After an unsuccessful campaign he was glad to escape by ceding all his provinces west of the Indus, including Gedrosia and Arachosia (about equal to the Afghanistan of to-day), and by giving his daughter in marriage to the victorious Emperor of India in exchange for five hundred elephants-of-war.

It was then that Megasthenes was sent as ambassador to Pātaliputta. And with the princess and her suite, and the ambassador and his, not to speak of the Greek artists and artisans employed at the court, there must have been quite a considerable Greek community, about 300 B.C., at the distant city on the southern bank of the Ganges, whose foundations, as a mere fort, were being laid by the brahmin minister of the then king of Magadha, when the great Indian Teacher was starting on his last journey a few months before his death. But the Greek community cared little for these things; and, so far as we know, Megasthenes, in his account of India, has not a word about the Buddha or his system.

The deep impression made by Chandragupta's

marvellous career, in which he worked his way up from the position of a robber chief on the frontier to the mightiest throne then existing in the world, is reflected in the legendary nature of all the accounts that have reached us—Greek, Buddhist, and Hindu. He has suffered the fate of other great conquerors and rulers; and like Alexander and Charlemagne, has become the hero of popular romance.

The reader will recollect how such popular romance has woven a story about our King Alfred the Great, when a defeated refugee, and a peasant woman and her cakes. Just such an anecdote has been told of Chandragupta in the commentary on the Great Chronicle of Ceylon:

"In one of these villages a woman [by whose hearth Chandragupta had taken refuge] baked a chupatty [1] and gave it to her child. He, leaving the edges, ate only the centre, and, throwing the edges away, asked for another cake. Then she said, 'This boy's conduct is like Chandagutta's attack on the kingdom.' The boy said, 'Why, Mother, what am I doing, and what has Chandagutta done?' 'Thou, my dear,' said she, 'throwing away the outside of the cake, eatest the middle only. So Chandagutta, in his ambition to be a monarch, without beginning from the frontiers, and taking the towns in order as he passed, has invaded the heart of the country . . . and his army is surrounded and destroyed. *That* was *his* folly.'" [2]

And Chandragupta overheard, and learnt the

[1] Literally "a frying-pan-cake," (*kapalla pūva*). See Jāt. I. 345–7.
[2] Mahāvaṃsa Ṭīkā, p. 123 (Colombo edition, 1895).

lesson, and prospered. So also the future sovereign is made to owe his success, throughout the long series of adventures, defeats, and victories, of intrigues, murders, and treasons, which led him to the throne, to the constant advice and aid of a brahmin, nicknamed Chānakya, as deformed in body as he was depraved at heart (or, perhaps, we should rather say that he was, like the gods, not so much immoral as unmoral). Justin (xv. 4), on Greek authority, tells two graceful stories of the effect upon animals of the marvellous nature of the king. Once, when, as a fugitive from his foes, he lay down overtaken, not by them, but by sleep, a mighty lion came and ministered to him by licking his exhausted frame. And again, when he had collected a band of followers, and went forth once more to the attack, a wild elephant came out of the jungle, and bent low to receive Chandragupta on his back.

It is curious that in the extant priestly literature Chandragupta is completely ignored for about ten centuries. In spite of his friendship with the brahmin Chānakya, he belonged to, and indeed had the insolence to found, the hated Moriya dynasty, to which, later on, Buddhism owed so much. But the memory of him, or at least of the popular romance attached to him, must have been kept very much alive among the peoples of India. For in the eighth century of our era, a layman, the author of a famous Sanskrit drama, the Mudrā-rākshasa, takes that romance as his plot. He gives a number of details out of which Lassen already, half a century ago, tried, with the help of other traditions, to unravel the nucleus of historic fact.[1] He succeeded very well in doing so, but perhaps the most suggestive fact we may learn from the play is, that in spite of the brahmins, the memory of Chandragupta had survived, in the people's hearts, all through that long interval of priestly silence — another proof, if any were needed, that it is not very wise to trust altogether exclusively to brahmin evidence.

[1] *Indische Altherthumskunde*, 2nd Ed., pp. 205–222.

CHAPTER XV

ASOKA

CHANDRAGUPTA, aided very largely by the previous organisation of the great empire of Magadha, was able, once he had gained the mastery, not only to remain in possession for the long period of twenty-four years (about B.C. 322–298), but to hand on the empire, with enlarged territory, to his son, Bindusāra. Of him we know almost nothing. The Ceylon Chronicles merely say that he reigned for twenty-eight years, and the Greeks, who call him Amitrochates (that is, Amitra-ghāta, foe-destroyer, no doubt an official title), only tell us that Deimachos was sent to him as ambassador by Antiokhos, and Dionysios by Ptolemy Philadelphos. A few sentences from the pen of the former are still extant.

When he died, about 270 B.C., he was succeeded by his son, Asoka, then the Magadha viceroy at Ujjeni, of whom the Ceylon Chronicles and other Buddhist writings, and his own inscriptions, tell us so much. The Greeks do not mention him, and the brahmin records completely ignore him until the time when, ten or twelve centuries afterwards, all danger of his influence had passed definitely away. They then go so far as to include his name among others in a list of kings. When this was done the authors of it had no access to the Buddhist writings, and could not read the inscriptions. It follows that the tradition had been carried down, all the time, in the brahmin schools, though not one word about it had been allowed to transpire.

At the beginning of the researches by European scholars the Ceylon Chronicles were of most service. As I have said elsewhere:

"When in the thirties that most gifted and original of Indian archæologists, James Prinsep, — *clarum et venerabile nomen*, — was wearing himself out in his enthusiastic efforts to decipher the coins and inscriptions of India, whilst the very alphabets and dialects were as yet uncertain, he received constant help from George Turnour of the Ceylon Civil Service. For in Ceylon there was a history, indeed several books of history; whereas in Calcutta the native records were devoid of any reliable data to help in the identification of the new names Prinsep thought he could make out. It is not too much to say that without the help of the Ceylon books the striking identification of the King Piyadassi of the inscriptions with the King Asoka of history would never have been made. Once made, it rendered subsequent steps comparatively easy; and it gave to Prinsep and his coadjutors just that encouragement, and that element of certainty, which were needed to keep their enthusiasm alive." [1]

So Prinsep read the inscriptions. Building on the foundation that he laid, we can read them

[1] *American Lectures*, p. 46.

better now. But we are not likely to forget the genial scholar whose noble life was sacrificed in the seemingly impossible task of laying those foundations. Now that we have the contemporary records in all their simplicity, and redolent of the time, the picturesque accounts, written six centuries or more afterwards, by well-meaning members of the Buddhist Order, who were thinking the while, not of historical criticism, but of religious edification, seem of poor account. It may be human to kick down the ladder by which one has just climbed up. But we need not do so, in this case, with too great violence. We may want it again. And it jars upon the reader to hear the Chronicles called the mendacious fictions of unscrupulous monks. Such expressions are inaccurate; and they show a grave want of appreciation of the points worth considering. Just as in the case of Megasthenes, or of the early English chroniclers, so also in the case of the Ceylon chroniclers it would be unreasonable to expect that sort of historical training which is of quite recent growth even in Europe. The Ceylon Chronicles would not suffer in comparison with the best of the Chronicles, even though so considerably later in date, written in England or in France. The opinion of scholars as to the attitude to be adopted towards such works is quite unanimous. The hypothesis of deliberate lying, of conscious forgery, is generally discredited. What we find in such chronicles is not, indeed, sober history, as we should now understand the term, but neither is it pure fiction. It is good evidence of opinion as held at the time when it was written. And from the fact that such an opinion was then held we can argue back, according to the circumstances of each case, to what was probably the opinion held at some earlier date. No hard words are needed: and we may be unfeignedly grateful to these old students and writers for having preserved as much as we can gather from their imperfect records.[1]

It may be asked, perhaps, why we do not try to save the intellectual effort necessary to balance probabilities in later accounts that cannot be entirely trusted, by confining ourselves exclusively to the contemporary documents, the inscriptions? The answer is that such a method would be absurd; it would not even save trouble. The inscriptions are scanty. The text of all of them together would barely occupy a score of these pages. They give only a limited view of the set of circumstances they deal with. Royal proclamations, and official statements, are not usually regarded as telling the truth, the whole truth, and nothing but the truth. To put it mildly, there is an economy of candour in these documents, intensely interesting though they are. And they are enigmatic. It is not possible to understand them without the light thrown upon them by the later accounts. It would only add to their difficulty to reject, for instance, the identification of the Piyadassi of the inscriptions

[1] See now on these Chronicles Professor Geiger's important researches in his *Dīpavaṃsa und Mahāvaṃsa*. Erlangen, 1902.

with the Asoka of the literature, or the fact of his relationship to Chandragupta, or of his capital having been at Pāṭaliputta, or any other of the numerous side-lights to be drawn from the Chronicles. As M. Senart says:

> "I believe that the Chronicles have, in certain details, under the name of Asoka, preserved of our Piyadasi recollections sufficiently exact, not only to allow a substantial agreement (*une concordance sensible*) to appear, but even to contribute usefully to the intelligence of obscure passages in our monuments."[1]

Besides numerous passages scattered through other books (which have not yet been collected) we have four connected narratives dealing with Asoka. These are:

(1). The Asoka Avadāna, in Buddhist Sanskrit, preserved in Nepal.

(2). The Dīpavaṃsa, in Pāli, preserved in Burma.

(3). Buddaghosa's account in his commentary on the Vinaya.

(4). The Mahāvaṃsa, in Pali, preserved in Ceylon.

Of these the first was composed in the Ganges valley. The author and date are unknown; but it is probably as late as the third century of our era. It forms one of a collection of legends called the Divyāvadāna. The exact force of this title is somewhat ambiguous. *Avadāna* means a story, but as it is used exclusively of the life-story of a person distinguished in the religion, the collection corresponds to the *Vitæ Sanctorum* of the Christian Church. We

[1] *Inscription de Piyadasi*, 2. 231.

know so little, as yet, of the literature in Buddhist Sanskrit that we cannot form any clear idea of the method by which the tradition it has preserved was handed down.

It is otherwise with the other three. We know that there were two great monasteries at Anurādhapura in Ceylon, the Great Minster and the North Minster. There the canonical books were handed down, in Pali; and commentaries upon them, in Sinhalese, interspersed with mnemonic verses in Pali. In the third century of our era some one collected such of these Pali verses as referred to the history of Ceylon, piecing them together by other verses to make a consecutive narrative. He called his poem, thus constructed, the *Dīpa-vaṃsa, the Island Chronicle.* The old verses were atrocious Pali, and the new ones added are not much better. Then, as the old ones were taken, not from one commentary only, but from several, we get the same episode repeated in different verses. Added to this the work was supplanted in Ceylon by the much better-written book called the *Mahā-vamsa*, or *Great Chronicle;* and was completely lost there. The present text, which is corrupt, has been restored, in the excellent edition by Professor Oldenberg, from MSS., all of which are derived from a single copy that had been preserved in Burma.

Shortly after the Island Chronicle was composed, the celebrated Buddhaghosa, a brahmin from Behar, came over to Ceylon, and rewrote in Pali the old Sinhalese commentaries. His work supplanted the latter, which are now lost, and is the only evidence we have of the nature of the ancient tradition. He quotes, from the old Sinhalese commentary, a number of the mnemonic verses also contained in the Island Chronicle, and gives us, in Pali, the substance of the Sinhalese prose with which they had originally been accompanied.

A generation afterwards Mahānāma wrote his great work, the *Mahā-vamsa.* He was no historian, and had, besides the material used by his two predecessors, only popular legends to work on. But he was a literary artist, and his book is really an epic poem of remarkable merit, with the national idol, Dushṭa Gāmini, the conqueror of the invading hosts of the Tamils, as its hero. What he says of other kings, and of Asoka amongst them, is only by way of introduction, or of epilogue, to the main story.

I have compared historically the various versions of one episode in these and other narratives (that of Asoka and the Buddha relics),[1] and have shown how interesting are the results to be derived from that method. To retell such an episode in one's own words may be a successful literary effort, but it would be of no historical value. It would give us merely a new version, and a version that had not been believed anywhere, at any time, in India. By the historical method, a few facts of importance may yet be gathered from amidst the poetical reveries of these later authors.

So, for instance, the tradition—Indian of course in origin, but preserved in Nepal—states that Asoka's mother was the daughter of a brahmin living in

[1] *J. R. A. S.*, 1901, pp. 397–410.

FIG. 46.—DETAILS OF THE SCULPTURES ON THE GATES OF SĀNCHI TOPE.

Champā. This may well be so. We hear nothing of his youth or early training. The Ceylon books all say that at the time of his father's death he was holding the position of viceroy at Ujjeni, and that he had there married a local lady residing at Vedisa, afterwards the site of the celebrated building now known as the Sānchi Tope. They had two children, a son, Mahinda, and a daughter, Sanghamittā. But as this was really a mésalliance, the lady being only of a merchant's family, she was left behind when Asoka left Ujjeni to go to Pātaliputta and there secure the succession.

All the accounts agree that this was no easy task. His elder brother, the viceroy of Takka-silā in the Panjab, opposed him, and it was only after a severe struggle, and not without bloodshed, including the death of his brother, that Asoka made his way to the throne. The details of the struggle differ in the different stories, and there is a passing expression in one of the Edicts (all the more valuable because it is incidental) of brothers of the King being still alive well on in his reign.[1] On the whole, I am inclined to believe that the tradition of a disputed succession is founded on fact. *The Chronicles* say that Asoka was not formally anointed king till between the fourth and the fifth year after Bindusāra's death, and the language of the Edicts, which are dated, whenever they are dated, from the formal anointing, and not from the succession, would harmonise with this.

Of the events of the first few years after Asoka's

[1] *Rock Edict*, No. 5.

FIG. 47.—DETAILS OF THE SCULPTURES ON THE GATES OF SĀNCHI TOPE.

reign we have no information. In the ninth year a war broke out between Magadha and Kalinga, perhaps the then most powerful kingdom in India still independent of the empire ruled over by Asoka. Of the rights and wrongs of the dispute we cannot judge. Our sole information comes from one side only, and is an incidental reference in the thirteenth Edict, published by Asoka five years afterwards. In that document the King states that it was the remorse and pity aroused in his mind by the horrors of the conquest—the killing, death by disease, and forcible carrying away of individuals, to which non-combatants and even peaceable brahmins and recluses were exposed—that resulted in his conversion. He does not say to what. That, apparently, was supposed to be quite clear to any one. It was sufficient to say that he had come to the opinion that the only true conquest was conquest by the religion (by the Dhamma).

We are told, by the King himself, of three stages in his conversion. The Rupnath Edict is of about the same date as the last, but perhaps a little earlier, say the thirteenth year after his being formally anointed, or, as we should say, crowned—that is, in the seventeenth year after he became *de jure* the king. There he says that for two and a half years he had been a lay disciple (an *upāsaka*), but had not developed much zeal; but one year before (before the date of the Edict) he had entered the Order, and begun to show greater zeal. Then in the eighth Rock Edict he declares that in the thirteenth year after his coronation he had set out for the *Sambodhi*

FIG. 48.—REAR VIEW OF THE NORTHERN GATE OF SĀNCHI TOPE.

—that is to say, he had set out, along the Aryan Eightfold Path, towards the attainment (if not in his present life then in some future birth as a man) of the state of mind called Arahatship.[1] So in the ninth year of his reign an Upāsaka, in the eleventh year a Bhikshu, in the thirteenth, still reaching upward, he enters the Path.

This is his own account of the matter, and he gives no one else any credit for his progress. It is not by any suggestion or instruction, received either from layman or recluse, that he has adopted this course. It is his own doing throughout. The Chroniclers profess to know the name of the bhikshu who was instrumental in his conversion. I am not prepared to say, though their evidence is so much later, that there may not be some truth in their view. It is quite true that it is sound Buddhist doctrine that each man is "to be a lamp unto himself, to hold fast as a refuge to the truth [the Dhamma], to look not for refuge to any one besides himself."[2] But it is so very likely that one factor at least in the King's change of heart may have been the exhortation or conversation of one or other of the Arahats, that we may suppose both accounts to have been right. It is strange for a king, whether in India or in Europe, to devote himself strenuously to the higher life at all. It is doubly strange that, in doing so, he should select a system of belief where salvation, independent

[1] See, on this meaning of the word *sambodhi*, my *Dialogues of the Buddha*, i. 190–192.

[2] *Book of the Great Decease*, iii. 33, translated in my *Buddhist Suttas*, p. 38.

FIG. 49.—JAIN TEMPLE AT KHUJARAO.

of any belief in a soul, lay in self-conquest. No ordinary man would have so behaved; and the result must have been due mainly to his own character, his firmness of purpose, his strong individuality. But he was quite incapable of inventing the system. We know it had existed long before. And it is not probable that those who had already trained themselves in it were wholly without influence upon him.

Henceforward he devoted his great energy, and the powerful resources of his wide empire to the realisation of his new ideals. To that end all his edicts were published, all the changes he made in the administration of his empire were directed, and enormous sums were lavished in the erection of costly buildings in aid of the new faith. It is characteristic that he says not a word of these last. To his mind it was apparently the teaching that was so much the most important thing that it swallowed up every other consideration. But the unanimous testimony of all the later traditions, confirmed as it is by the actual remains discovered, leaves no doubt upon the point.

It is true that no building erected by Asoka remains intact above ground, but an inscription of his has been found at Sānchi, and it is the unanimous opinion of scholars that he built the first temple at Bodh Gayā. Sānchi, the old name of which is Chetiya Giri (the Hill with the Shrine upon it), must have been a famous place before Asoka went to Ujjeni. There are no less than eleven topes on the plateau at the top of the hill. Some of them were opened in 1822 and the rest in 1851. At the second excav-

FIG. 50.—THE GREAT BUDDHIST TOPE AT SĀNCHI BEFORE RESTORATION.

ation one of the smaller ones was found to contain part of the ashes from the funeral pyres of Sāriputta and Moggallāna, two of the Buddha's principal disciples. The village Vedisa, where Asoka made the acquaintance of his first wife, lies close by, and the tops of other hills in the neighbourhood are also crowned with stūpas.

The person in whose honour the largest tope of all was built has not been discovered, as the relic box within it could not be found. But a large number of inscriptions in characters of the Asoka period have been found on the pillars and railing surrounding it. And General Cunningham was of opinion that, while this tope itself, like the other topes on the plateau, was older and the gateways younger than Asoka's time, the Buddhist railing round it belonged to his reign. But it is by no means impossible that the gateways also should be ascribed to Asoka. And, in any case, the remains at Sānchi may be fairly used to give us an idea of the kind of building that was likely to be put up by Asoka's command, and has played so great a part in the history of Buddhist India. The whole site is now a desolate ruin; and no attempt has yet been made to give, in drawing, a restoration of how it must have appeared in the days of its early beauty. But the annexed illustrations show the present appearance of the principal tope, and some of the details of the surrounding sculptures. And a portion of the railing round Bharahat is added for the sake of comparison.

At Bodh Gayā, on the other hand, though it is

FIG. 51.—SĀNCHI TOPE. A GENERAL VIEW FROM THE SOUTH.

known that Asoka built the original temple, it has been so often changed, and added to, that only a few fragments of railing, and probably the very remarkable *sinhāsana*, or throne, remain of the work done in his time. The present building has been restored, as a national monument, by order of the English Government. It will be noticed how different it is in outline from the ancient form, as shown in the illustration of the Sānchi Tope. This is due to a difference of ideal. The ancient tope was an enlarged and glorified circular burial mound. The later ones imitate an ordinary dwelling-hut, the outline of which was determined by the natural bend of two bamboos, planted apart in the ground, and drawn together at the top. This shape is characteristic of all the mediæval temples in India, and an illustration of the Jain temple at Khujarao is annexed, as one of the best examples of this style. But to return to Asoka's own doings.

The Edicts hitherto discovered are thirty-four in number. We know of others seen in the seventh century, and we know, approximately, the sites on which they were seen,—such, for instance, as those at Sāvatthi and Rāmagāma,—and there must be others besides. Further discoveries, therefore, may be confidently anticipated. Of those now known two are merely commemorative proclamations recording visits paid by Asoka — one to the stūpa erected over the funeral urn of Konāgamana the Buddha, and one to the birthplace of Gotama the Buddha. Three others are merely short dedications of certain caves to the use of the Ājīvakas, a body

FIG. 52.—EASTERN GATE OF SĀNCHI TOPE.

of ascetic recluses often mentioned in the Buddhist canonical books. The remainder are so many tracts, short proclamations on stone, published with the view of propagating the Dhamma, or of explaining the methods adopted by the Emperor to that end.

The word "Dhamma" has given, and will always give, great trouble to the translators. It connotes, or involves, so much. Etymologically it is identical with the Latin word *forma;* and the way in which it came to be used as it was in India, in Asoka's time, is well illustrated by the history of our own colloquialism "good form." Dhamma has been rendered Law. But it never has any one of the various senses attached to the word "law" in English. It means rather, when used in this connection, that which it is "good form" to do in accord with established custom. So it never means exactly religion, but rather, when used in that connection, what it behoves a man of right feeling to do—or, on the other hand, what a man of sense will naturally hold. It lies quite apart from all questions either of ritual or of theology.[1]

On such Dhamma the brahmins, as such, did not then even pose as authorities. But it was the main subject of thought and discussion among the Wanderers, and to them the people looked up as teachers of the Dhamma. And while, on the one hand, the Dhamma was common property to them all, was Indian rather than Buddhist, yet, on the other hand,

[1] Dhammas, in the plural, meant phenomena, or forms of consciousness considered as such. See Mrs. Rhys-Davids's *Buddhist Psychology*, pp. xxxii.–xl.

FIG. 53.—REAR VIEW OF THE EASTERN GATE OF SĀNCHI TOPE.

the people we now call Buddhists (they did not call themselves so) were concerned so exclusively with the Dhamma, apart from ritual or theology, that their doctrine was called the Dhamma. It fell, naturally, for them into three divisions, quite distinct one from the other,—the theory of what it was right (good form) for the layman (the *upāsaka*) to do and to be, of what it was right for the Wanderer (the *Pabbajita*) to do and to be; and, thirdly, what the men or women, whether laity or Wanderers, who had entered the Path to Arahatship, should do, and be, and know. On each of these three points their views, amidst much that was identical with those generally held, contained also, in many details, things peculiar to themselves alone. Now the Dhamma promulgated by Asoka was the first, only, of these three divisions. It was the Dhamma for laymen, as generally held in India, but in the form, and with the modifications, adopted by the Buddhists.

The curious thing about this Dhamma, as a description of the whole duty of man, of the good layman, is—especially when we consider its date—its extraordinary simplicity. This is, historically, so very interesting, that it will be worth while to set it out in full.

ASOKA'S DHAMMA.

Rock Edict, No. 1.

1. No animal may be slaughtered for sacrifice.
2. Tribal feasts in high places are not to be celebrated.

Rock Edict, No. 3.	3. Docility to parents is good. 4. Liberality to friends, acquaintances and relatives, and to brahmins and recluses is good. 5. Not to injure living beings is good. 6. Economy in expenditure, and avoiding disputes, is good.
Rock Edict, No. 7.	7. Self-mastery 8. Purity of heart 9. Gratitude 10. Fidelity are always possible and excellent even for the man who is too poor to be able to give largely.
Rock Edicts, Nos. 9 and 11.	11. People perform rites or ceremonies for luck on occasion of sickness, weddings, childbirth, or on starting on a journey—corrupt and worthless ceremonies. Now there is a lucky ceremony that may be performed,—not worthless like those, but full of fruit,—the lucky ceremony of the Dhamma. And therein is included right conduct towards slaves and servants, honour towards teachers, self-restraint towards living things, liberality to brahmins and recluses. These things, and others such as these, are the lucky ceremony

Rock Edicts, Nos. 9 and 11.

according to the Dhamma. Therefore should one—whether father or son or brother or master—interfere and say: "So is right. Thus should the ceremony be done to lasting profit. People say liberality is good. But no gift, no aid, is so good as giving to others the gift of the Dhamma, as aiding others to gain the Dhamma."

Rock Edict, No. 12.

12. Toleration. Honour should be paid to all, laymen and recluses alike, belonging to other sects. No one one should disparage other sects to exalt his own. Self-restraint in words is the right thing. And let a man seek rather after the growth in his own sect of the essence of the matter.

Pillar Edict, No. 2.

13. The Dhamma is good. But what is the Dhamma? The having but little, in one's own mind, of the Intoxications [1]; doing many benefits to others; compassion; liberality; truth; purity.

[1] This is a technical term of the Buddhist system of self-training. They were originally threefold,—the mental intoxication arising from lusts, that arising from the craving after a future life, and that arising from ignorance. Then a fourth was added—the intoxication of mind arising from dogmas, or speculative metaphysics. The Arahat has none at all of these. Asoka's good layman is to have "but little."—See Rhys-Davids, *Dialogues of the Buddha*, vol. i., p. 92.

Pillar Edict, No. 3.

14. Man sees but his good deeds, saying: "This good act have I done." Man sees not at all his evil deeds, saying: "That bad act have I done, that act is corruption." Such self-examination is hard. Yet must a man watch over himself, saying: "Such and such acts lead to corruption,—such as brutality, cruelty, anger, and pride. I will zealously see to it that I slander not out of envy. That will be to my advantage in this world, to my advantage, verily, in the world to come."

That is all. There is not a word about God or the soul, not a word about Buddha or Buddhism. The appeal is made, in apparent confidence that the statements are self-evident, to all the subjects of the empire. Under what conditions would such a state of things have been possible? Had there been then anything new or strange in this view of life (which now seems so strange to a European reader) there would have been phrases in the Edicts striving to meet the natural objection that must certainly have arisen. There is nothing of the kind. It follows that the doctrine, as an ideal, must have been already widely accepted, though men did not always act up to it. It is exactly as if, in a country already Christian, the king should issue proclamations calling on the people, in this point or in that, to act up to the recognised ideal of the Christian life. Asoka, precisely as in the parallel case of Constantine, embraced a cause so far successful that it seemed on the verge of victory. And it is not at all unlikely that reasons of state may have had their share in influencing Asoka, just as they certainly did in the case of Constantine.[1]

It was not only within the boundaries of his own empire that Asoka tried to spread the Dhamma. In the thirteenth Edict, in about 255 B.C., addressed to his sons and grandsons, after declaring that he himself found pleasure rather in conquests by the Dhamma than in conquests by the sword, he says that he had already made such conquests in the realms of the kings of Syria, Egypt, Macedonia, Epirus, and Kyrene, among the Cholas and Pāndyas in South India, in Ceylon, and among a number of peoples dwelling in the borders of his empire.

> "Everywhere" he adds, "men conform to the instructions of the King as regards the Dhamma; and even where the emissaries of the King go not, there, when they have heard of the King's Dhamma, the folk conform themselves, and will conform themselves, to the duties of the Dhamma, that dyke against . . . [here the context is lost].

It is difficult to say how much of this is mere royal rhodomontade. It is quite likely that the Greek kings are only thrown in by way of makeweight, as it were; and that no emissaries had been actually sent there at all. Even had they been sent,

[1] See Professor Hardy's *Asoka : Ein-Charakter-Bild*, etc., p. 30.

there is little reason to believe that the Greek self-complacency would have been much disturbed. Asoka's estimate of the results obtained is better evidence of his own vanity than it is of Greek docility. We may imagine the Greek amusement at the absurd idea of a "barbarian" teaching them their duty; but we can scarcely imagine them discarding their gods and their superstitions at the bidding of an alien king.

Here, fortunately, the Chronicles come to our assistance. In a curt record they give us the names of missionaries sent out by Tissa, the son of Moggali (the author of the Kathā Vatthu, and the president of the 3rd Council held in Asoka's reign and under his patronage).[1] They were sent to Kashmir, to Gandhāra, to the Himālaya (Nepal or Tibet), to the border lands on the Indus, to the coast of Burma, to South India and Ceylon. Each party consisted of a leader and four assistants. Of the five missionaries to the Himālaya region three are named as Majjhima, Kassapa-gotta, and Dundubhissara.

Now when Cunningham opened the Topes (brick burial mounds) at and near Sānchi he discovered under them several of the funeral urns containing ashes from the funeral pyres of the distinguished persons in whose honour the Topes had been built. One of the urns has inscribed round the outside of it, in letters of the 3rd Century, B.C., the simple legend: "Of the good man, Kassapa-gotta, the teacher of all the Himālaya region." Round the

[1] Dīpavaṃsa, chap. viii.; Mahāvaṃsa, chap. xii.

inside of the urn is the legend: "Of the good man, Majjhima." In another Tope close by at Sonāri two urns bear the separate inscriptions: "Of the good man, Kassapa-gotta, son of Koti,[1] teacher of all the Himālaya region," and: "Of the good man Majjhima, the son of Kodini."[2] In the same Tope was a third urn with the inscription: "Of the good man Gotiputta, of the Himālaya, successor of Dundubhissara."[3]

Many of the Topes had been opened, in search of treasure, and the urns in them ruthlessly destroyed, before the archæologists examined them; so the evidence is incomplete. Even as it stands the evidence of the old characters on those preserved to us will be estimated in different ways by different minds. With these, and similar facts before them, some still consider the literature as a 'tissue of mendacious fictions; others still consider that the Buddha is only a sun myth, and his disciples merely stars. I must humbly confess myself unable to follow speculations so bold. The Ceylon scholars knew, of course, nothing of these long-buried inscriptions; and could not have read or understood them, even had they had access to them. What we have to explain is how they came, centuries afterwards, to record precisely the same names in precisely the same connection. It is only the wildest

[1] Cunningham's *Bhilsa Topes*, pp. 287, 316.

[2] This is his mother's, not his father's, name.

[3] The rare and curious form "Ḍundubhissara" is a nickname, and may be rendered "Trumpet-voiced," though the *dundubhi* is not a trumpet.

credulity that could ascribe this to chance. And, dull as it may seem, I see no better explanation than the very simple one that these men really went as missionary teachers to the Himālaya region, and that the fact that they had done so was handed

FIG. 54.—DETAILS FROM EASTERN GATE OF SĀNCHI TOPE.

down, in unbroken tradition, till the Chroniclers put it down for us.

The Chronicles thus not only confirm but also supplement Asoka's information about the missions. And when we find that they ascribe the sending out of the missionaries, not to Asoka, but to the leaders of the Order, and that they make no mention of any such missions to the Greek kingdoms in the distant

West, it is at least probable that the view they take is more accurate, in these respects, than the official proclamation.

So Asoka mentions a mission to Ceylon. But it is *his* mission. No credit is given to any one except himself. He merely says it was successful, and gives no details. As we might expect, the Chroniclers of the island give names and details, which they work up into a picturesque and edifying legend. Its central incident is the transplanting to Ceylon of a branch of the tree at Bodh Gayā under which the Buddha had achieved enlightenment.

Now this event is portrayed on two curious bas-reliefs on the Eastern Gateway at Sānchi, which must be nearly as old as the event itself. In the middle of the lower picture is the Bodhi Tree, as it stood at Gayā, with Asoka's chapel rising half-way up the tree.[1] A procession with musicians is on both sides of it. To the right a royal person, perhaps Asoka, is getting down from his horse by the aid of a dwarf. In the upper picture there is a small Bodhi tree in a pot, and again a great procession, with to the left a city, perhaps Anurādhapura, perhaps Tamralipti, to which the young tree was taken before it went to Ceylon. The decorations on either side of the lower bas-relief are peacocks, symbolical of Asoka's family, the Moriyas (the Peacocks); and lions, symbolical of Ceylon, or of the royal family of Ceylon (that is, of Simhala, the Lion island).

[1] It is so represented also in the Bharahat bas-relief, which bears an inscription saying it is the Bodhi Tree. See Cunningham, plates xii. and xxx.

Opinions may differ as to the meaning of some of the details, but there can be no doubt as to the main subject.[1]

It was a great event, an impressive state ceremony, and a fitting climax to that one of the missionary efforts of Asoka's reign which was most pregnant of

FIG. 55.—DETAILS FROM EASTERN GATE OF SĀNCHI TOPE.

results. For there, in that beautiful land, the province most fruitful of any in India or its confines in continuous and successful literary work and effort, there have never been wanting, from that day to this, the requisite number of earnest scholars and

[1] Dr. Grünwedel was, I believe, the first to point this out. See his *Buddhist Art in India*, translated by Dr. Burgess, pp. 69–72.

students to keep alive, and hand down to their successors, and to us, that invaluable literature which has taught us much of the history of religion, not only in Ceylon, but also in India itself.

In the seventh Pillar Edict, dated in the twenty-eighth year (that is, in the thirty-second year after Bindusāra's death, say about 248 B.C.), Asoka sums up all the other measures he had taken for the propagation of what he calls *his* Dhamma. They are as follows:

1. The appointment of functionaries in charge of districts and provinces to instruct the people.

2. The putting up of pillars of the Dhamma (that is, pillars with the Edicts inscribed on them), and the appointment of special ministers at the court to superintend the propagation of the Dhamma.

3. The planting of trees for shade, and the digging of wells, at short intervals, along the roads.

4. The appointment of special ministers to superintend charities to both householders and Wanderers, and to regulate the affairs of the Order,[1] and of other sects having jurisdiction apart from the ordinary magistrates.

5. The appointment of these and other officers to superintend the distribution of the charities of the Queen and their children.

He claims by these means to have had great success in promoting the Dhamma (as set out above, pp. 294–297), and adds that such positive regulations as he has made are of small account compared with

[1] It is noteworthy that he does not say which. *The* Order would be taken, in his opinion, by everybody to mean the Buddhist Order.

the change of disposition which he has been able to bring about; and that, above all, his own example will lead people to adopt his teachings.

Any one who knows Indian feeling will be amazed at the boldness of this program. That the king should appoint Lord High Almoners or Charity Commissioners to look after his own gifts would offend none. That these officials should be required to look into the manner in which the great people at the court disbursed their charities and report if they went wrong (wrong, that is, from the king's point of view), would be unpopular enough in any case, but doubly so when his point of view was what it was. That the king should settle disputes, when brought before him or his court, between members of the various Orders, was right enough. That he should arrogate to himself to look after their private concerns was quite another matter. That he should hold a certain set of opinions, and be bent on propagating them, was comfortable to those that held the same. That he should ignore every one else, even on his own side, and give out that he was the teacher, and that the Dhamma was his Dhamma, would be accepted, of course; but with a shrug, suggestive that much allowance must be made for the self-complacency of kings.

That he failed was no wonder. The set of opinions he favoured with his patronage was enfeebled and corrupted by his favour. With all his evident desire to do the very best possible things, and always to be open to the appeals of the subjects he looked upon as his children, he left his empire in such a condition that it soon disintegrated and crumbled away. He made the boast (vain boast) that the brahmins, who claimed to be gods upon the earth, had, by his efforts, ceased to be so regarded, and he himself committed the irreparable blunder of imagining himself to be a *deus ex machinâ*, able and ready to put all things and all men straight.

Yet, in spite of all, he surely remains one of the most striking and interesting personalities in the history of the world. There is a personal touch in the Edicts which cannot be ignored. The language must be his own. No minister would have dared to put such confessions and such professions into the mouth of so masterful a master. The language is rugged, uncouth, involved, full of repetitions, reminding us often of the mannerisms of the speeches of Cromwell. And the preoccupation with himself, his opinions, his example, his good deeds, amounts almost to megalomania. But how sane the grasp of things most difficult to grasp! How simple, how true, how tolerant, his view of conduct and of life! How free from all the superstitions that dominated so many minds, then as now, in East and West alike! It was not his own view, it is true, quite as much as he makes out. But he had made it his own, and was keen to bring others to know it. To realise what this means, one may consider how many of the Greek princes in all the vast domains which had once formed the empire of Alexander were intellectually capable of rising to the same height. Unless it be maintained that the general average of intelligence in such things was higher then in India than in Greece it seems difficult to avoid the conclusion that Asoka must have been a man of quite exceptional natural ability. The style of his Edicts, on the other hand, is scarcely compatible with much intellectual culture or training. His early years were apparently otherwise occupied. But his long reign is a a sign of physical vigour; and of his strong will and moral earnestness, even to the point of self-control, there can be no question. Those who think Indian affairs should be looked at through the spectacles of mediæval brahmins can never forgive him for having made light of the priests, and the gods, and the superstitious ceremonies of the day. But the gospel he preached was as applicable to the India of that day as it would be to India now. That he was wanting in the most efficient sort of practical statesmanship seems to have been chiefly due to the glamour of his high position, of a majesty that was, indeed (and we should never forget this), so very splendid that it was great enough to blind the eyes of most. The culture of a Marcus Aurelius or an Akbar might have saved him from this. But even as it was, it is, among European rulers, with Marcus Aurelius for some things, with Cromwell for others, that he deserves to be compared. That is no slight praise, and had Asoka been greater than he was he would not have attempted the impossible. We should have had no Edicts. And we should probably know little of the personality of the most remarkable, the most imposing, figure among the native princes of India.

CHAPTER XVI

KANISHKA

FROM the death of Asoka onwards to the time of the Guptas, the history of India is, at present, in a state of the utmost confusion and darkness. The Jain and Buddhist literature of this period is still, almost entirely, buried in manuscript. From time to time a ray of light, now in one part of what had been the great Magadha empire, now in another, illumines the darkness. The labours of numismatists and epigraphists have been directed to the reconstruction, from such isolated data as the the coins and inscriptions give us, of a continuous chronology and of a connected history. The progress of this work, especially in the past few years, has been great. But the field is so vast, the data are so sporadic, doubt as to the eras used is so persistent an obstacle, that the difficulty of this reconstruction is immense.

One or two of the ancient sites have been partially excavated; but archæological exploration has been almost confined, as yet, in India, to what can be found on the surface. There was a widely diffused and continuous literary activity throughout the whole of this (now, to us) dark period; and much of it is still extant. But only one portion of it, that portion preserved in the brahmin schools of theosophy and the sacrifices, has been as yet, adequately explored. And this portion—partly because it has been mostly recast at a later date, partly because the priests, very naturally, tended to ignore the events of a period when they were not yet in the ascendant—has yielded but little result. No attempt has, therefore, been made to describe the social or economic condition of the people, or to trace the gradual change of opinion, according to the varying local influences, within this period. And even as regards the bare lists of kings and names of battles, the loss or gain of this or that town or province by this or that combatant, there is at present only little evidence, and a very imperfect consensus of opinion as to the meaning even of that little. It will be sufficient, under these circumstances, if we confine ourselves here to a rapid outline of the salient facts.

During the whole period there was no really paramount power in India. One or other of the many smaller kingdoms into which it was divided attained, at one time or another, considerable extension of boundary, and held for a generation or two a position superior to the rest. But no one of them attained at any time to so much as a quarter of the size of the old empire of Magadha.

It is very suggestive that of Magadha itself we hear almost nothing for more than five centuries after the death of Asoka. This is, indeed, scarcely surprising. For while, in the western parts of India, the coins have preserved the names of the kings, in Magadha the people continued to use the coinage bearing only the private mark or marks of the individual or guild that issued them. None of the ancient sites there—Sāvatthi or Vesāli or Mithila, Pāṭaliputta or Rājagaha—have been excavated. And, thirdly, the literature of Magadha in this period, mostly Jain or later Buddhist, lies also still buried in MSS. But as early as 150 B.C. we have one short note in the Elephant Cave inscription of Kharavela, King of Kalinga, who claims to have twice invaded Magadha successfully, having advanced the second time as far north as the Ganges. As he also gives us to infer that his father and grandfather had preceded him on the throne, Kalinga must, in that case, have become independent of Magadha very soon after the death of Asoka. It is unfortunate that the name of the then King of Magadha is not mentioned in this inscription. We may fairly conclude, at all events provisionally, from the fact that no neighbouring king claims to have conquered them, that both Magadha and Kalinga retained their independence from the time of Asoka down to that of Kanishka. Magadha, however, must have lost all its outlying provinces, and consisted, usually, only of the ancient kingdoms of Magadha and Champa, together with the eastern portion of Kosala.

South of Kalinga was the important and powerful kingdom of the Andhras, with its chief capital at Dhanakaṭaka or Amarāvati, at the mouth of the Krishṇa. We know little of its history in early times (after the death of Asoka), but later on, though it was never able to conquer the other Dravidian states in the south of India, it pushed its conquests to the north, and conquered a large province in the Dekkan. There in Patiṭṭhāna, the subordinate Andhra capital, ruled a viceroy who was often at war with the sovereigns of Avanti and Gujarat.

The south of the peninsula was occupied with the three kingdoms of the Cholas, the Keralas, and the Pāṇḍyas. All the ancient traditions of these peoples have been lost. But it is evident from the few references to them in the second Rock Edict of Asoka, and in the Chronicles of Ceylon, that they had attained, at and shortly after Asoka's time, to a civilisation not incomparable with that of the Aryan settlements. The conquest of Ceylon by the Chola Tamils under their prince Elāra, and the victorious combat afterwards waged against him by the Sinhalese national hero, Dushṭa Gāmini, form the main episode in the Great Chronicle. This must have been about the beginning of the second century B.C. Twice afterwards, in the middle and at the end of the same century, the Chola Tamils, under Bhalluka and Bāhiya respectively, issued from their capital, Madhura, overran the north of Ceylon, and remained for some years in possession of Anurādhapura, the capital of the island. It is true that they were each time driven back again out of the island. But this shows us at least an amount of military organisation which may make it easier to understand how the Andhras found it easier to push forward to the north-west than to attempt the conquest of the south of the peninsula.

When they established themselves in the Dekkan, probably shortly after the Christian era, the Andhras found opposed to them in the north and north-west viceroys (called Satraps) of a Scythian overlord. There had probably been distinct viceroys, one ruling from Ujjen over Avanti, the other ruling from Giri-nagara over the Kāthiawād and Katch. But early in the second century A.D. they had declared themselves independent of their overlord, and had then, by a process we are not yet able to follow, become amalgamated into a powerful kingdom extending about six hundred miles from east to west and more than three hundred miles from north to south. The reigning king, usually resident, it is supposed, at Giri-nagara, was called the Great Satrap. The crown prince bore the title of Satrap. And as their coins have been found in large numbers, and give the names and titles both of the reigning satrap and his father, and also a date, it is possible to reconstruct the line of this dynasty with unusual precision. The names, also, of most of the Andhra kings are known to us, but there is a difference of opinion as to the order in which they should be arranged. We thus have the dry bones of the skeleton of the history of one kingdom, and many of the bones of the history of the adjacent kingdom, for a long period after the commencement of the Christian era.

For the more than two centuries between Asoka

and that time we are still almost in the dark. Only a few hints have survived, and those in Chinese sources, as to how or when the Sakas or Scythians had come into possession of these provinces. These hints enable us to conjecture that immediately after the death of Asoka the provinces to the extreme north-west of the empire of Maghada (those provinces which Seleukos had ceded to Chandragupta) asserted their independence; and that they did this not as a whole, but in small divisions, under the leadership of local magnates, mostly of Greek extraction. In the course of internecine conflicts these smaller states had been gradually amalgamated into one or two, or perhaps three, Greek kingdoms, when, in about 160 B.C., the Sse or Sakas, just then expelled from Sogdiana by the Yueh-ti, appeared upon the scene. After a long-continued series of campaigns, with varying fortune, against the possessors of the country, they forced their way through, in about 120, into India proper. Their route was probably southward through Sind. But, in any case, in the course of the following years they established outposts, under the rule of officers called Kshatrapas (the Persian word "satraps") at Mathura, Ujjeni, and Giri-nagara, the overlord remaining behind in Seistan, which means simply, "the land of the Sse," or Sakas.

Meanwhile the five tribes of the Yueh-ti, themselves pressed on from behind by other nomad tribes, followed close on the heels of the Sakas, and, in about 120 B.C., became the rulers of Baktria. About a century afterwards, one of the five tribes, the Kushanas, became the predominant partner in the confederation. This added very greatly to the power of the organisation; and it was probably the pressure they were able to exert on the Saka overlord that gave opportunity to the Saka satraps in the south to make themselves independent of their suzerain in Seistan. Soon afterwards the Kushanas, also, in their turn, pushed forward into India, but by a northern route, taking possession of the Panjab, and then ousting the Saka satrap from Mathura. The capital of the whole of this wide dominion, from Baktria, or even west of Baktria down to the Doab, became Takka-silā, the ancient rock fortress of the Takka tribe, the Taxila of the Greeks. Mathura, however, remained the subordinate capital. And it is chiefly in the course of the systematic excavations carried out there that the numerous inscriptions have been found, giving the names and the dates of Kushan kings. With the help of these, and of the coins, the dynastic list has now been drawn up with comparative certainty; but there is the greatest diversity of opinion as to the era to which the dates ought to be referred.

It is strange that the third line of evidence, that of the Indian literature, has not been hitherto taken in aid towards the decision of this question. It supplies at least one consideration of the first importance that should not have been overlooked. By the unanimous testimony of the best authorities we yet have (pending the publication of the Buddhist Sanskrit texts themselves) on the later forms of Buddhism, that is to say, the Tibetan and Chinese historiographers, Aśvaghosha, the author of the *Buddha Carita*, lived in the time of the most famous of the Kushan kings, Kanishka. This work is a poem in pure Sanskrit, and in elegant style, on the life of the Buddha. It is addressed therefore, of course, not to brahmins as such, but to the laity. Now at what period in the history of Indian literature could such a poem have been composed, taking into consideration the facts as to the history of the language set out above in Chapter IX.?[1] The oldest inscription in pure Sanskrit is of the middle of the second century A.D. Even if Aśvaghosha's poem be the very earliest literary work written in regular Sanskrit for the use of the laity (and that is not at all impossible), it can scarcely be dated earlier. It is therefore improbable, if the authorities just referred to can be relied on, that the era used in the Kushana inscriptions can be fixed at any date so early as to be incompatible with the evidence as to the history of language, drawn from hundreds of inscriptions of equal genuineness.[2] On the other hand, if Kanishka be much earlier it is impossible that the poem can have been written at his court; but the evidence is such that we should,

[1] These facts have now been admirably collected and criticised in Professor Franke's *Pali and Sanscrit* (1902); a work, which, I regret to say, reached me too late to be utilised in Chapter IX.

[2] All the authorities on this question of the Kushan era are mentioned in the valuable article by Mr. Vincent Smith in the *Journal of the Royal Asiatic Society* for 1903. He dates Kanishka from 125 to 153 A.D. Mr. J. F. Fleet will also discuss the question in an article to be immediately published in the same *Journal*.

provisionally, accept this till the authorities on which it rests shall have been proved to be mistaken. In either case the date of the poem must be approximately the last half of the second century A.D. And just as the first public proclamation addressed, in regular Sanskrit, to the public, was written at the court of a foreign king, the Scythian satrap at Giri-nagara, so it would be consistent with all our other information if one of the first, if not the first, literary work addressed, in regular Sanskrit, to the laity, should have been written at the court of a foreign king, the Tartar sovereign of the Kushan realm.

The above argument is further confirmed by the fact that at a Council of the Buddhist Order, held under the patronage of Kanishka, three works were composed in Sanskrit as official commentaries on the ancient canonical books. These three Sanskrit works are extant in our European libraries, and it is most deplorable that these important documents have not yet been published. But even without having them, in full, before us, we can safely draw the conclusion that Kanishka cannot have reigned before the time when it had become recognised that the right language to use on such an occasion was, not Pāli, but Sanskrit, and this would be equally true though the Sanskrit of these works should turn out, when we can consult them, to be less elegant than that written by Aśvaghosha.[1]

This introduction of the use of Sanskrit as the *lingua franca* is a turning-point in the mental

[1] See, on this Council, my *Milinda*, vol. ii., pp. xv., xvi.

history of the Indian peoples. The causes that preceded it, the changes in the intellectual standpoint that went with it, the results that followed on both, are each of them of vital importance. The main cause has been supposed to be the study, in the brahmin schools, of the Vedic forms no longer familiar, the evolution in this manner of a grammatical system, and then the gradual application of this system to the vernacular speech, until at last any form not in accordance with the system became considered as vulgar, and fell into disuse. A subsidiary cause, which also deserves consideration, is the influence of the intercourse with foreigners, and especially with the socially powerful Greeks, Scythians, and Tartars. The teaching of grammar, and the spread of ideas of learned diction among the more educated people, would be greatly strengthened by the necessity of explaining linguistic forms to people of this sort. Who so likely to have been asked to do this as those who were known to have already devoted attention to the subject, and had a well-earned reputation, that is, the brahmins? And why, otherwise, should it be precisely these border districts on the extreme north-west frontier (not looked upon in other matters as the home of orthodox teaching) that were the home of the most developed and most authoritative grammatical teaching, and the place of residence of the most distinguished grammarians?

Hand in hand with the gradual adoption, and at last with the almost exclusive use, of the brahmin literary language, must have come a gradual increase in the deference and respect paid to the acknowledged masters of that tongue. There were other reasons, of course; and there was action and reaction in all these matters. But the result is very striking. Three-fourths or more of the persons named, and the objects of donation specified, in all the inscriptions throughout India, from Asoka's time to Kanishka's,[1] are Buddhist, and the majority of the remainder are Jain. From that time onwards the brahmins, the gods they patronised, the sacrifices they carried out, receive ever-increasing notice till the position of things is exactly reversed, and in the fifth century A.D. three-fourths are brahmin, and the majority of the rest are Jain. This is the clearest evidence of a strange revulsion of feeling. What had been the predominant national faith has become the faith of a minority. India, which can fairly, down to the time of Kanishka, be called "Buddhist India," ceases to be so. And the process goes on, slowly indeed but continually, until there is not a Buddhist left in the land where Buddhism arose.

How slow the process was is shown by the accounts of the state of things when the Chinese pilgrims travelled in India. Fa Hian, in the early years of the fourth century A.D., finds Buddhism nearly everywhere in decay. He unfortunately gives no figures. But Yuan Chwang, in the seventh century, has done so. These I have examined in detail,[2] and the result shows still, at that time, in India,

[1] 3rd century B.C. to 2nd century A.D.

[2] *Journal of the Royal Asiatic Society*, 1891, pp. 418–421.

nearly two hundred thousand of the Buddhist Order, of whom three-fourths still adhered to the older forms of the faith, and one-fourth were Mahāyānist. Brahmin accounts attribute the final stages in the movement to a furious persecution brought about at the instigation of the great brahmin apostle, Kumārila Bhaṭṭa, in the first half of the eighth century. This view, having received the support of the distinguished European scholars, Wilson and Colebrooke,[1] has naturally been widely repeated until we find the Rev. W. T. Wilkins saying:

> "The disciples of Buddha were so ruthlessly persecuted that all were either slain, exiled, or made to change their faith. There is scarcely a case on record where a religious persecution was so successfully carried out as that by which Buddhism was driven out of India."[2]

I do not believe a word of it. In the *Journal of the Pali Text Society* for 1896, I have discussed the question in detail, and have come to the conclusion, entirely endorsed by the late Professor Bühler,[3] that the misconception has arisen from an erroneous inference drawn from expressions of vague boasting, of ambiguous import, and doubtful authority. We must seek elsewhere for the causes of the decline of the Buddhist faith; and they will be found, I think, partly in the changes that took place in the faith itself, partly in the changes that took place in the

[1] Wilson, *Sanskrit Dictionary*, p. xix.; Colebrooke, *Essays*, vol. i., p. 323.

[2] *Daily Life and Work in India* (London, 1888), p. 110.

[3] *J. P. T. S.*, 1896, pp. 108–110.

intellectual standard of the people. And in both respects the influence of the foreign tribes that invaded India from the north-west can scarcely be exaggerated.

Just as when the Goths and Vandals invaded the Roman Empire in Europe—and it is surprising that an historical parallel so close, and so full of suggestive analogues, has not been pointed out before—they did indeed give up their paganism and adopted the dominant Christian faith; but in adopting it they contributed largely to the process of change (some would call it decay) that had already set in; so also in India the Scythians and the Kushan Tartars, after they had conquered all the Western provinces, gave up their paganism, and adopted the dominant Buddhist faith of their new subjects. But in adopting it they contributed largely, by the necessary result of their own mental condition, to the process of change (some would call it decay) that had already set in.

Gibbon has shown us, in his great masterpiece, how interesting and instructive the story of such a decline and fall can be made. And it is not unreasonable to hope that, when the authorities, especially the Buddhist Sanskrit texts, shall have been made accessible, and the sites shall have been explored, the materials will be available from which some historian of the future will be able to piece together a story, equally interesting and equally instructive, of the decline and fall of Buddhism in India.

APPENDIX TO CHAPTER VI.

THE MOST ANCIENT COINS OF INDIA.

Mr. Rapson, of the British Museum, has been kind enough to prepare the plates for Figs. 24 and 25, and to draw up the following key, giving explanations of each of the coins.

FIG. 24.

1. Æ; Taxila: Single-die Coin.
   In incuse, l., pile of balls; r., *chaitya*: beneath, wavy line and uncertain designs (? vine-branches).
2. AR; Punch-marked Coin, showing on both sides various countermarked symbols.
3. Æ; Taxila: Double-die Coin.
   Obv. Elephant to r.; above, *chaitya*.
   Rev. in incuse, Maneless Lion to l.; above, *svastika*; in front, *chaitya*.
4. Æ; Vaṭasvaka.
   Chaitya: l., *Vaṭasvaka* in Brāhmī characters; r., standing figures worshipping; beneath, pile of balls.
5. Æ; Kāḍa: Cast Coin.
   Obv. and *Rev.* similar: *Kāḍasa* in Brāhmī characters; above, Snake.
6. Æ; Mathurā.
   Upātikyā in Brāhmī characters; above, *svastika*.
7. Æ; Ujjain.
   Obv. Humped Bull to r.; above, 'Ujjain' symbol.
   Rev. *Ujeni(ya)* in Brāhmī characters; above, a Hand.

8. Æ; Uddehika.

Obv. Humped Bull to r.; above, Tree within railing represented horizontally.

Rev. *Udehaki* in Brāhmī characters; above, three symbols. [J. R. A. S., 1900, p. 98, Pl. 1.]

9. Æ; Tripuri.

In incuse, *Tripuri* in Brāhmī characters; beneath, two symbols. [J. R. A. S., 1894, p. 554, Pl. 15.]

10. Æ; Kulūta, Vīrayaśasa.

Obv. *Chaitya* surmounted by three symbols; r., *Ra;* l., *ña,* in Kharoṣṭhē characters.

Rev. Wheel surrounded by circle of dots; inscr. in Brāhmī characters. *Rājña Kolūtasya Vīrayaśasya.*

[*cf.* Cunningham, *Coins of Ancient India*, p. 70, Pl. IV., 14, and J. R. A. S., 1900, pp. 415, 429.]

11. Ꝛ; Kuṇinda, Amoghabhūti.

Obv. Deer to r., facing female figure; above, symbol; below, *chaitya.* Inscription in Brāhmī characters. *Raña Kuṇiṃdasa Amoghabhūtisa Mahārājasa.*

Rev. Various symbols; Inscr. as on *obv.*, but in Kharoṣṭhē characters.

12. Æ; Ayodhyā: Cast Coin.

Obv. Fish to l.; above, *svastika.*

Rev. Steelyard; above, crescent.

13. Æ; Ayodhyā, Sūryamitra.

Obv. Peacock to r., facing Palm-tree.

Rev. in incuse, Humped Bull to l.; *Suyyamitrasa* in Brāhmī characters.

14. Æ; Kosāmbē, Bahasatimita.

Obv. Humped Bull to r., facing *chaitya;* above, 'Ujjain' symbol.

Rev. Tree within railing; on either side, symbols; *Bahasatimitasa* in Brāhmī characters.

FIG. 25.

1. Eran Coin. Dhanapālasa in very ancient Brāhmī letters written from right to left. Described in Cunningham's *Coins of Ancient India*, Pl. XI., No. 18. Now in the British Museum.
2. Eran Coin. *Obv.* Horse to l.; above, Ujjen symbol. *Rev.* r. and l., Tree within railing. Eraka in Brāhmī letters. Now in Mr. L. White King's collection.

INDEX

A

Aboriginal tribes in India, 43, 44, 54, 55
Ādityas, the gods, 236
Āgama, later term for Nikāya, 168
Agni, 216, 219, 235, 242
Ajātasattu, king of Magadha, 3, 12–16, 89
Ājīvakas, an order of ascetics, 143, 290
Akbar, 307
Ākhyānas (Akkhānas), 183, 185
Aldermen of the guilds, 96, 97
Alexander, his Indian coin, 100; his invasion of India, 267, 268
Alphabets, 116–118, 124, 131
Alwis, James, 28
Ambaṭṭha's visit to the Sākiyas, 19
Amitra-ghāta, 272
Ancient history and modern, the dividing line between, 240
Andhra dynasty, 310–312
Angas, name of a tribe, 23; name of Jain books, 164
Animism, 210–230
Añjana, the Buddha's grandfather, 18
Añjana Wood, near Sāketa, 39
Anurādhapura, 69, 70, 75, 85, 201, 277, 311
Āpastamba, date of, 32
Arachosia, 268
Archæology in India, 41, 132
Architecture in old times, 63 foll.
Ārdha-Māgadhi, 154
Armies, size of, in India, 266
Aryan, immigration, routes of, 31; settlements in the South, 156
Āsavas (Intoxications) 296
Asceticism, *see* Tapas
Asoka, not mentioned in the Buddhist canon, 174, nor by the Greeks, 272; Indian accounts of, 276; his treatment of the Buddha-relics, 278; his marriage, 279; his coronation, 280; his conquest of Kalinga, 282; his conversion, 282–284; his buildings, 286–290; his Edicts, 290–299; his missions, 298–300; his sending the Bo Tree to Ceylon, 302–304; other measures to propagate his Dhamma, 304; his failures, 305; his character, 306
Asoka Avadāna, 276
Āśramas, the four, brahmin theory of, 249, 250
Assakas, an ancient tribe, 27, 203
Assattha tree, 230, 234
Assyria, 113
Asuras, *see* Titans
Aśvaghosha, poet, 315
Aśvins, 236
Āṭānaṭiya Suttanta, 219
Atharva Veda, 166, 213, 252

Attha Sālinī, revised in Ceylon, 175
Authors, none known before Asoka, 179, 180
Avanti, one of the four great kingdoms, 3, 4, 27, 28; incorporated into Magadha, 267; probable home of Pāli, 153, 154
Avesta, 181
Ayojjhā, 34, 39

B

Babylon, 104, 113, 115, 116
Bacon's Essays, 166
Baktria, 313
Bali offerings, 227
Banyan Deer Jātaka, 190–194, 198
Barbers, guild of, 94
Barrows, round, the origin of stūpas, 80
Barter, traffic by, 100
Basket makers, 54, 96
Baths, hot-air, 74; open-air, 75
Baveru (Babylon), 104
Behar, 42
Benares, conquest of, by Kosala, 25; size of, 34
Bengal, ignored in old records, 29
Bhaddiya, consul of the Sākiyas, 19
Bhandarkar, Professor, 32, 150, 177
Bharahat Tope, 10, 82, 198, 209, 288
Bharhut, *see* Bharahat
Bharukaccha, first mention of, 31; trade at, 38; sea vogages from, 96, 104, 116
Bimbisāra, king of Magadha, 3; builds Rājagaha, 37
Bindusāra, king of Magadha, 272, 304
Blacksmiths, 264
Boats, 94, 103
Bodh Gayā, 288, 302
Bodhi, prince of the Vacchas, 7
Bodhi, the sacred tree, 229
Bodhisatva, progress of the idea, 177
Books and MSS., 110
Bower MS., 124, 128
Brahmā, the god, 235
Brahma-Vihāras, 197
Brāhmaṇas, language of, 147; morality of, 240, 247
Brāhmī Lipī, later name of the Asoka alphabet, 117
Brahmin, spelling of the word, 2; their social rank, 54; trades they followed, 57; could marry a Kshatriya, 59; were considered low-born as compared with Kshatriyas, 60; their theories as to learning, 118; claimed to be divinities, 118; as grammarians, 149, 317; their influence in Buddhist times, 150, 159; their struggle against the rajputs, iii, 158; the debt we owe to the learned, 210; their divisions, 249
Bricks used for writing on, 121–124
Buddha Carita, 315
Buddha Vaṃsa, age of, 176
Buddhaghosa, 201, 277
Buddhist Literature, down to Asoka, chronological table of, 188
Bühler, Professor, 43, 113, 126, 202, 319
Burgess, James, 31
Burma, 94, 104
Burnouf, 171
Butchers, 93

C

Caravans, 98
Cariyā Piṭaka, 176, 196
Carpenters, 264
Carts, 93, 98
√Caste, 56, 59, 62
Cattle, customs as to village, 45, 46

Cetis, an ancient tribe, 26, 29
Ceylon Chronicles, 261, 274–277
Ceylon, ignored in the old records, 29; date of first Aryan settlement in, 33, 104; history of language in, 155; were the Pali books forged there? 170 foll.; scholarship in, 304
Chambā, 32
Champā, 23, 35, 104, 260
Chānakya, 270
Chandragupta, emperor of India, 259–271
Charms, 5
Childers, Professor, 201
Cholas, 298, 311
Chunam work in ancient buildings, 69, 82
Cities, very few in number, 50; architecture of, 61 foll.; great size of, 35, 263
Clans, in ancient India, 17–22
Climate, influence of, 42, 43
Coins, 100 foll., 106; the oldest Sanskrit, 136
Colours, the four, 53, 62
Commensality and connubium, 52, 57, 58
Common lands, 45-48
Constantine, 298
Copper plates, 122–125
Cowell, Professor, 189
Credit, instruments of, 101
Cromwell, 306, 307
Cutch, *see* Kacch

D

Dagabas, 80
Dakkhināpatha, 30
Dancing and music, 186
Dantapura, settlement at, 31
Dasaratha, Asoka's grandson, 143
Dead, curious customs as to disposal of the, 78–82
Dekkan, 30, 311, 312
Delhi, 27
Deussen, Professor, 190
Devadaha, the Buddha's ancestor, 18
Devadatta, the Buddha's cousin, 13, 193
Dhamma, meaning of, 292; sketch of Asoka's, 294–297
Dhamma-kathika, 167
Dhana Nanda, king of Magadha, 267
Dialogues of the Buddha, date of, 107
Diana, the goddess, 217
Diogenes, 245
Dīpavaṃsa, 276, 277
Disease due to escape of the soul, 252
Divyāvadāna, a book of legends, 10
D'Oldenburg, Professor Serge, 209
Drama, use of the, 184–186
Dravidian, names of imports into the West, 116; tribes, civilisation of, 53, 56; dialects, charged with Sanskrit, 156; kingdoms, 311
Dreams, 252, 253
Drugs, 98
Dundubhissara, 299, 300
Dushṭa Gāmini, king of Ceylon, 278, 311
Dvāraka, capital of Kambojā, 28
Dyaus, 236
Dyers, 93

E

Earth, the mother, 47, 219
East, the immovable, 237
Economic conditions, 87 foll., 258
Eights, the name of a book of lyrics, 178
Elephant, legend of the decoy, 5; their use in war, 266–268
Elu, the Prakrit of Ceylon, 155
Endogamy and exogamy, 52
Epics, growth of, 179–183, 206
Eran coins, 115

F

Family rights, 47
Famines, 49, 50
Fausböll, Professor, 189, 200, 204
Feer, M. Léon, 194
Fergusson, James, 227
Fick, Dr., 62, 87, 202
Fields, custom as to cultivation of, 46; not salable, 47
Fire-drill, 231
Fishing, only in rivers, not in the sea, 93
Fleet, Mr. J. F., 31
Folk-lore, 208
Forests, large expanse of, 20, 21; *see* Mahā-vana
Fortifications of Pāṭaliputta, 262
Forts in ancient times, 38, 63
Franke, Professor Otto, 315
Freedom of thought in ancient India, 247, 258
Frescoes, 96

G

Gaggarā, queen of Anga, 35
Gambling halls, public, provided by the king, 71, 72
Games, 108
Gandak, river, 259
Gandhārā, the country, 28
Gandharvas, 220
Garuḍas, harpies or griffins, 224
Gavelkind, custom of, 47
Gedrosia, ceded to Magadha, 268
Geiger, Professor, vi, 275
Geldner, Professor, 181
Giribbaja, old capital of Magadha, 37, 38
Giri-nagara (Girnar), in the Kathiawad, 134, 312
Gods, origin of, 255
Godhāvari river, 27, 30, 156
Gold plates used for writing, 124
Golden Age, in India, 187
Gonaddha, in Avanti, 103
Gosinga Vihāra, MS. from, 122, 124, 128, 173
Grammar, studied in the North-West, 203
Grierson, Mr., 32
Grimblot, 185
Grünwedel, Dr., 303
Guilds of work people, the eighteen, 90 foll. 96
Gupta dynasty, 150, 308

H

Hardy, Professor E., 298
Hardy, Spence, 30
Hermits, 140; distinct from Wanderers, 143
Hillebrandt, Professor, 242
Himālayas, 29; dialects of, 32; as boundary, 260; missionaries sent to, 299–301
Hiranya-keśin, date of, 32
History, how treated in brahmin records, 157
Hoernle, Dr., 126
Hopkins, Professor, 87, 152
Hume's "Essay," 166
Hunting and hunters, 44, 93

I

Images, none in ancient times, 241
Indika of Megasthenes, 260 foll.
Indra, the god, 232–235
Inscriptions in India, were first in Pāli, 130; gradual growth of use of Sanskrit in, 131–139; specimen of an Asoka, 135; donations recorded in, 151
Interest on loans, 101
Intermarriages in ancient India, 59
Internal evidence as to the age of literary records, 165
Intoxication, god of, *see* Soma; ethical, 296
Irish legends, 181
Irrigation, 46, 86, 264

Isisinga legend, 201
I-Tsing's travels, 35
Ivory, 94; ivory-workers, 93, 98

J

Jacobi, Professor, 31, 163, 164, 183, 185, 227, 235
Jain records, 12, 163, 318
Jain temple at Khujarao, 285, 290
Jains, founder of, 41; early name of, 143
Janaka, king of Videha, 26
Jātaka Book, discussion of history of, 189–208; summary of results, 207, 208
Jetavana, 99
Jewellers, 93
Jhānas, 197
Jumna, the river, 27
Jupiter, 235

K

Kacch, Gulf of, 28, 32, 38
Kahāpaṇa, square copper coin, 100-102
Kāḷāsoka, king of Magadha, makes Pāṭaliputta the capital, 37
Kalinga, earliest settlement in, 31
Kalpa-rukkha, the Wishing Tree, 227
Kambojā, the country, 28
Kammāssa-dhamma, in the Kuru country, 27
Kampilla, capital of the Kurus, 27, 35
Kāñcipura, 156
Kanishka, 315–320
Kanoj, capital of the Kurus, 27
Kapilavastu, the old town and the new, 18, 103
Kāsi, township of, matter of dispute between Kosala and Magadha, 3; the Kāsis as one of the sixteen great tribes, 24
Kassapa, the Buddha, 229
Kassapa-gotta, a Buddhist missionary, 299, 300
Kathā Vatthu, the book, age of, 167, 176; author of, 299
Kennedy, Mr., 115
Kerala, 311
Kharavela, king of Kalinga, 310
Kharoṣṭrī alphabet, 124
Khotan, MS. from, 124
Kolarian tribes, 53, 56
Konāgamana, the Buddha, 290
Kosala, one of the four great Kingdoms, 3; importance of, in the Buddha's time, 25; its influence on language, 147; the language of, its place in history, 153; the Rāmāyaṇa arose in, 183; centre of Buddhist literary activity, 183
Kosambi, city on the Jumna, 3, 36, 103
Kshatriyas, 53; working as artisans, 54, 55; not always Aryan by race, 56; when made outcaste, 58; disputed the claim of the brahmins to social supremacy, 61
Kumārila, iv, 156
Kurus, ancient tribe, 27
Kushanas, 314 foll.
Kusinārā, the Mallian town, 26, 37, 103
Kuvera, the god, 220

L

Land tenure, 46 foll.
Language, outline of history of, in India, 153, 211
Learning, its nutriment, 111
Leather-workers, 54, 92
Lena dialect, 154
Lettering, an ancient game, 108
Lévi, Professor, 124, 240
Licchavis, the clan, 26, 40; their public hall for religious and philosophical discussion, 141; their political power, 25, 260
Linga, worship of, 166

Literature, pre-Buddhistic, 120 foll.; Pāli, 161 foll.
Luck, goddess of, *see* Sirī; Asoka's view of, 295
Lüders, Dr., 201

M

McCrindle, his *Ancient India*, 261
Macchas, an ancient tribe, 27
Macdonell, Professor, 226
Madda, the country, 29, 39
Madhurā, on the Jumna, 36; in South India, 311
Magadha, one of the four great kingdoms, 3; one of the sixteen main tribes, 24; its struggle with Champā, 260; in Alexander's time, 267; after Asoka's death, 309 310
Mahā-bhārata, iii, 183, 184, 190, 214, 255
Mahā Kaccāna, lived at Madhurā, 36
Mahā Kosala, king of Kosala, 8, 10
Mahā-nāma, 278
Mahā-samaya Suttanta, 219
Mahā-seṭṭhi, 97
Mahā-sudassana Jātaka, 195–197
Mahā-vaṃsa, 276–278
Mahā-vana, the Great Wood, 20, 21, 41, 142
Mahā-vastu, 173
Mahāyāna, 177, 319
Māhissati, 103
Mahosadha, his underground dwelling, 66
Maine, Sir Henry, 238
Mallas, their Mote Hall, 19; their territory, 26; their power, 29
Mallikā, queen at Sāvatthi, her hall for public debates, 141
Marcus Aurelius, 307
Markets, 100, 101
Maruts, wind gods, 236
Maung-gon, gold plates from, 124, 126
Medicine, ancient, 231
Megasthenes, 49, 50, 260–268, 274
Mesa inscription, 113
Mesopotamia, its influence on India, 70
Metal-work, 90
Middle Country, the so-called, 172
Milanda, the king, 39
Milinda, the book, 37, 38, 167, 173
Millionaires, 102
Miners, 264
Mithilā, capital of Videha, 37
Mitra, a god, 236
Moggallāna, 288
Moon, as a god, 219
Mora-nivāpa, 142
Mortgage, not allowed, 46
Mote Halls, in the old republics, 19; in heaven, 66
Mother Earth, 47, 219, 220
Mountains, Spirit of the, 220

N

Nāgas, siren-serpents, 220–224, 233, 235
Nālandā, in Magadha, 103
Nikāyas, the five, 168; differ in doctrine, 173; age of, 176; importance of, 187; tree-worship in, 226
Nirvana, under the tree, 231
Northern and Southern Buddhism, discussion of the phrase, 171–173

O

Occupation, facility of change of, 56, 57
Octroi duties, 98
Oldenberg, Professor, 181
Ophir, perhaps - Sovīra, 38
Order, the Buddhist, 304, 316
Orissa, 29
Ossian, 181

P

Painting, 96
Paithana, *see* Patiṭṭhāna
Pajāpati, the god, 235
Pajjota, king of Avant, 3 foll.
Pāli, its relation to Sanskrit, 120–153; the Pāli literature, 161 foll.
—— Text Society, 163
Pañca-nekāyika, 168
Pañchālas, ancient tribes, 27, 203
Pāṇḍyas, 298, 311
Pāṇini, 144, 203
Pañjab, 260, 267
Paramatta, the god, 224, 256
Pārāmitās, the ten, a late doctrine, 177
Parantapa, king at Kosambi, 7
Pārasāriya, a brahmin teacher, 144
Pārāyana, sixteen lyrics, 178
Pasenadi, king of Kosala, 3, 8–11, 19
Pāṭaliputta, capital of Magadha, 203; its size and fortifications, 262
Pātimokkha, rules of the order, learnt by heart, 111
Patiṭṭhāna, 30, 103, 311
Pāvā, a capital of the Mallas, 26
Payāga, 30
Peasantry, social position of, 51
Peppé, Mr., his discovery of the Sākiya Tope, 84, 130, 131
Peṭakin, one who knows a Piṭaka, 167
Peta Vallhu, the book, age of, 176
Phallus-worship, 165
Philpot, Mrs., 224
Piṇḍola, a recluse, 7
Pingalaka, a king, 176
Pippal tree, 230, 234
Pischel, Professor, 148, 154
Piyadassi, name of Asoka, 273–276
Police, 21, 98, 108
Population in ancient India, 18, 33
Potters, 54, 55, 92
Prakrit, meaning of the term, and date of, 154
Prices of commodities, 101
Prinsep, his first readings of the Asoka inscriptions, 273
Progressive societies, 238, 239
Pukkusāti, king of Gandhārā, 28

R

Rainy season, 112
Rāja, meaning of the word on old documents, 19
Rājagaha, capital of Magadha, 36, 37
Rājasthān, dialects of, 32
Rājasūya sacrifices, 203
Rāma-gāma, 290
Rāma-gangā river, 259
Rāmāyaṇa, geography of, 31, 34; place of origin of, 183
Rapson, Mr., 136
Republics, in ancient India, 1, 2; organisation of, 17 foll.; their Mote Halls, 18; consuls in the, 19; list of names of, 22
Rhys-Davids, Mrs., on economic conditions, 87; on the Attha Sālinī, 175; on the meaning of Dhamma, 292
Riddles of Sakka, an old Suttanta, 180
Rig Veda, 30, 46, 213, 223, 226, 232, 236, 242
Roruka, later Roruva, capital of Sovīra, 38
Rudradāman's inscription, 28, 134, 267

S

Sacrifice, brahmin theory of, 240–242; lay view, of 248, 249; Asoka's view of, 296
Sāgala, capital of the Maddas, 38
Sailors, 94
Sakas, 312 foll.
Sāketa, town in Kosala, 39, 103

Sākiyas, the clan, 17 foll.; Viḍūḍabha's campaign against, 11; pride of, 11; the Sākiya tope, 17, 90, 100, 130, 133; subject to Kosala, 259
Sakka, the god, the riddles he asked, 180; takes the place of Indra, 234
Samajja, 185
Sāmaratī, queen of the Vacchas, 7
Sambodhi, 282
Sanaṃ Kumāra, the god, 224
Sānchi Tope, 198, 288
Sanitary arrangements, 78
Sankara, 156, 187
Sanskrit, Indian use of the term, 154; its relation to Pali, 128–139; date of the use of, in India, 134–136, 315, 316; compared to Latin, 136, 137; was it a spoken language? 148, 149, 154; its alphabets, 155; of the schools, 211
Sāriputta, 169, 288
Satraps, 312–314
Sāvatthi, in Nepal, capital of Kosala, 25, 40, 103, 290
Scrollwork, along buildings, 77
Seleukos Nikator, 268
Self-torture, *see* Tapas
Semitic alphabets, 114
Senart, on caste, 62; on the Gosinga anthology, 124; on the Asoka inscriptions, 132; on the post-Asoka inscriptions, 152; on the Jātaka verses, 205; on the Ceylon chronicles, 276
Seniya, an ascetic, 245
Setavya, in Kosala, 103
Seven-storied buildings, 70
Sigālovada Suttanta, 185
Sīlas, a tract, 107, 215
Singhalese, the so-called canon of the, 171; commentaries, 201, 207
Sirī, the goddess of luck, 217
Sisunāga, king of Magadha, makes Vesāli the capital, 37
Sirva, the god, 166
Sivi, the country, 28
Slaves in ancient India, origin, position, and numbers of, 55, 263
Smith, Mr. Vincent, 315
Social grades in ancient India, 52–62
√Soma, the intoxicating drink, as god, 219, 231, 235
Soṇa, the river, 24
Sophists, 246, 248
Soul-theories, souls in trees, 227; size and shape of the soul, 251; absent in disease and sleep, 252
South India, not mentioned in the Buddhist canon, 29–32, 174
Sovīra, the country, 29, 38, 104; the port, 116
Spelling, in Indian inscriptions, compared with English, 132–135
Spiritual matters, 247, 257
Stars, beliefs about, 6
Stonework, 66, 90
Strabo, 260 foll.
Stylites, St. Simeon, 244
Suddhodana, the Buddha's father, 19
Sūdras, their position among the Colours, 54; fate of learned, 118
Suicide, 109
Sumanā, princess in Kosala, 10
Sun-god, 197, 219, 255
Suppāraka, the seaport, 31, 38, 116
Surā, intoxicating drink, 204
Sūrasenas, ancient tribe, 27
Sutta, as name of book or chapter, 168, 169
Sutta Nipāta, growth of, 177–180; tree-worship in, 226
Suttantas, treatises so-called, 8; learning them by heart, 110; cut off at the root, 111; forgotten, 112; afterwards called Suttas, 169
Suttantika, one who knows a Suttanta, 168

T

Tagara, the town, 31
Tagara-sikhin, 31
Takka-silā (Takshila), seat of learning in N. W. India, 8, 28, 203; copper plates from, 124; capital of the Kushanas, 314
Tamil words in use in the West, 116
Tāmralipti, seaport, 103
Tanks, for bathing, 74, 75; for irrigation, 86
Tapas, self-torture, growth of doctrine of, 242 foll.
Teaching, etiquette of, 5; brahmin views about, 249
Temples, none, in ancient times, 241
Tilaura Kot, site of Kapilavastu, 18
Tirhut, 32, 41
Tissa, son of Moggali, 299
Titans, 224, 241
Toleration, 296
Topes, *see* Dagabas
Trade routes, 102–104
Trades, 89 foll.
Tree-worship, 224–233
Tribal migration in India, 32
Tribes, the sixteen chief, in pre-Buddhistic times, 23 foll.
Trita, the god, 235
Truth lower than sacrifice, 243
Turbans, 94, 97
Turkestan, MSS. discovered in, 128

U

Uddālaka Āruṇi, his defeat in argument, 247; his influence on pantheistic thought, 257
Udena, king of Kosambi, 3 foll., 7
Udyāna, the country, 29
United Provinces, 42
Ujjeni, capital of Avanti, 3, 40, 103; Magadha viceroys at, 260, 272
Upanishads, 162, 187, 223, 226, 250, 255
Upāsaka, 282, 294
Ūrvaśī, 236.

V

Vacchas, *see* Vaṃsas
Vaikhānasa Sūtra, 144
Vaiśyas, their social rank, 54
Vājapeya sacrifices, 203
Vajirā, daughter of Pasenadi, married to Ajātasattu, 4
Vajjians, their powerful confederation, 25, 26, 40
Vālmīki, 31
Vaṃsas, or Vatsas, 3, 27
Varuṇa, the god, 219, 235
Vāsula-dattā, legend of, 4 foll.
Vāyu, wind-god, 235
Vedānta, 163, 168
Vedic language, 153; divinities, 155, 158; hymns, interpretation of, 162
Vedisa, in Avanti, 103, 288
Vegetable diet, result of, 42
Vekhanassa, follower of Vikhanas, 142, 144
Vesāli, 29, 40
Vessaṣ, 54, 55
Vessavana, the god, *see* Kuvera
Videha, as kingdom and republic, 26, 37
Viḍūḍabha, king of Kosala, 4, 11, 12
Vikhanas, a teacher, 144
Village, customs, 45 foll.; head men, 49
Vimāna Vatthu, 176
Vindhya Hills, 29
Vishṇu, 219, 236

W

Wanderers, the, their discussion halls, 141; names of corporate bodies among, 143–146; freedom of thought among, 247, 258; their Dhamma, 294

Weavers, 54, 57, 90
Weber, Professor, 113, 114
Wickramasinha, Mr., 115
Windisch, Professor, 180
Winternitz, Professor, 190
Wisdom-tree, 230
Woodwork, 66, 90, 264
Writers, astrade, 108
Writing, history of, 107–127

Y

√Yoga Sūtras, 197
Yueh-ti, 313 foll.

Z

Zimmer, Professor, 87, 232

WORKS BY

T. W. RHYS DAVIDS, LL.D., PH.D., F.B.A.

I. American Lectures on the History of Religions. *First Series.* Buddhism. (8vo, pp. xiv + 230; New York and London—G. P. Putnam's Sons, 1896.) $1.50.

"Now, in spite of ourselves, we cannot choose but hear what we ought to have known for at least half a century, the true story of Buddhism as it is."—*Saturday Review.*

"A luminous and fascinating introduction to a profoundly interesting subject. Apart, however, from its leading purpose, the book is an eloquent plea for the use of the historic method in the study of religions."—*The Nation.*

"If all books about Buddhism, or about other religions, were as thoughtful and sober as this one, the scoffer would have less occupation."—*Tribune* (New York).

II. Dialogues of the Buddha. *Vol. I.* (8vo, pp. xxiv + 330; London—Oxford University Press, 1899.)

"Prof. Rhys Davids has produced a book which no future historian of Indian thought can pass over."—*Athenæum.*

"Very timely, therefore, is the appearance in English form of such ancient and authoritative texts of Buddhism as are these Dialogues of the Dīgha Nikāya, and withal from so masterly a hand as that of Prof. Rhys Davids."—PROF. LANMAN in the *Journal of the Royal Asiatic Society.*

"These dialogues—some of which are dramatic enough to recall the contrpversies of St. Patrick with the old pagan Oisin—will open a new world to the Western reader."—*Speaker.*

"No better translator could have been selected than the Secretary of the Royal Asiatic Society, who is admittedly the best Pāli scholar in England. . . . It will be seen that we have here not only the earliest traditional record of the viva voce teaching of the Buddha, but also a vivid commentary on the manners and customs of his time. Mr. Rhys Davids's introductions to the several Suttas and his footnotes leave little to be desired."—*Saturday Review.*

"The notes throughout are a mine of information; and the whole work is well worthy of the reputation of the learned translator."—*Asiatic Quarterly Review.*

III. Buddhism: being a Sketch of the Life and Teachings of Gotama the Buddha. With a Map. (Small 8vo; London—Society for Promoting Christian Knowledge. 1878.) *Fifteenth Thousand.* 2*s.* 6*d.*

"We do not know of any other work from which so fair and complete an account can be obtained of that wonderful religion which has so much in common with Christianity, and has numbered more adherents than any other religion in the world."—*Academy.*

"Altogether higher stands the little work of Mr. Rhys Davids, . . . written in an agreeable style, and with great knowledge of the facts, . . . which we should wish to see in the hands of all students of religious history, and hope to see translated into our own language."—*Theologisch Tijdschrift.*

"Difficult to speak in too high terms of this admirable little book."—*Theological Review.*

"Undoubtedly the best introduction to the history of Buddhism at present existing."—*Ceylon Observer.*

IV. Buddhist Birth Stories, or Jātaka Tales; the Oldest Collection of Folk-lore Extant. (8vo; London—Trübner. Vol. I. 1880.) 18*s*.

"Among the various contributions to the comparative study of folk-lore, Mr. Rhys Davids's translation of the Jātakas must take a foremost place."—*Saturday Review.*

"These tales are probably the nearest representatives of the original Aryan stories from which sprang the folk-lore of Europe as well as of India, and from which the Semitic nations also borrowed much. The Introduction contains a most interesting disquisition on the migrations of those fables, tracing their reappearance in the various groups of folk-lore legends known as 'Æsop's Fables,' 'The Hitopadesa,' 'The Kalilag and Damnag Series,' and even 'The Arabian Nights.' Among other old friends we meet with a version of the Judgment of Solomon, which proves after all to be an Aryan, and not a Semitic tale."—*Times.*

"No more competent exponent of Buddhism could be found than Mr. Rhys Davids. These Birth Stories, of which he has now given us the first instalment, will be of the greatest interest and importance to students."—*St. James's Gazette.*

"The translation could not have fallen into better hands. And what is no small merit, when we consider the involved style of Buddhist writings, it is easy to read, though at the same time it is faithful throughout."—*Revue de l' Histoire des Religions.*

"The English version, while strictly literal, is thoroughly idiomatic. It is not too much to say that no Pāli scholar could have been found more competent for the work than he to whom it has been entrusted. He has thoroughly entered into the spirit of his original, and his renderings, even of the most difficult passages, are always most accurate and felicitous. In a valuable and interesting introduction, the translator traces the course of transmigration of the Buddhist stories and fables from East to West—by many and various courses, Hindu, Persian, Arabic, Syriac, Greek—through the Kalilag and Damnag literature down to the so-called fables of Æsop."—*Contemporary Review.*

V. The Hibbert Lectures, 1881; being Lectures on the Origin and Growth of Religion as illustrated by some points in the History of Indian Buddhism. (8vo; London—Williams & Norgate, 1881.) *Second Edition.*

"Cannot be too highly praised for learned research and lucidity of expression."—*Spectator.*

"It is a subject with which Mr. Rhys Davids is singularly well qualified to deal: from his probably unequalled knowledge of the Pāli literature, which is the fountain-head of Buddhism; the wide intellectual cultivation whereby he is able to bring out of his treasures things new and old for comparison, for illustration, for embellishment; his firm grasp of scientific principles; and the breadth of his sympathies, at once keen and discriminating. And the manner in which he has executed his task is such as to satisfy the high expectations raised by these qualifications. In conclusion, let us add—what, indeed, will have been evident from our extracts—that he is a master of clear, vigorous, and graceful English."—*St. James's Gazette.*

"No one has expounded the doctrines of Buddhism as we know them here, in such a trustworthy and scholarly manner."—*Ceylon Times.*

"Singularly bright and graceful, incisive in criticism, easy and flexible, familiar yet dignified in style, full of suggestive matter suggestively presented, and everywhere lighted up with a fine moral enthusiasm for the higher ideals and nobler personalities of the faith described. When Mr. Rhys Davids is most the critical scholar, he never forgets that he is handling a religion; when he is most earnest as the interpreter of a religion, he never ceases to be critical and scholarly."—PRINCIPAL FAIRBAIRN in the *Academy.*

"For what I have said about Indian Philosophy I am particularly indebted to the luminous exposition of primitive Buddhism and its relations to earliest Hindu thought, which is given by Professor Rhys Davids in his remarkable 'Hibbert Lectures' for 1881, and 'Buddhism,' 1890. The only apology I can offer for the freedom with which I have borrowed from him in these notes is my desire to leave no doubt as to my indebtedness."—PROFESSOR HUXLEY in the "Romanes Lecture," 1893.

"Mr. Rhys Davids has sought to throw light on religion generally. The exposition clearly indicates the fountains of emotion and thought whence the system issued; and the process of after crystallization is also put before the reader in clear and impressive outlines. The author's reflections on the story take the form of suggestions for comparative study. . . . So Buddhism may help the understanding of Christian origins as the Vedas illustrate classical mythology. The inculcation of such methods and principles give the book its greatest value, and it will be esteemed as a discipline even more than as a source of information."—*Mind.*

The Story of the Nations.

In the story form the current of each National life is distinctly indicated, and its picturesque and noteworthy periods and episodes are presented for the reader in their philosophical relation to each other as well as to universal history.

It is the plan of the writers of the different volumes to enter into the real life of the peoples, and to bring them before the reader as they actually lived, labored, and struggled—as they studied and wrote, and as they amused themselves. In carrying out this plan, the myths, with which the history of all lands begins, will not be overlooked, though these will be carefully distinguished from the actual history, so far as the labors of the accepted historical authorities have resulted in definite conclusions.

The subjects of the different volumes have been planned to cover connecting and, as far as possible, consecutive epochs or periods, so that the set when completed will present in a comprehensive narrative the chief events in the great Story of the Nations; but it is, of course, not always practicable to issue the several volumes in their chronological order.

Nos. 1–61, each	$1.50
Half leather	1.75
Nos. 62 and following Nos., each (by mail,	1.50
net	1.35
Half leather (by mail, $1.75) ....net	1.60

For list of volumes see next page.

THE STORY OF THE NATIONS.

GREECE. Prof. Jas. A. Harrison.
ROME. Arthur Gilman.
THE JEWS. Prof. James K. Hosmer.
CHALDEA. Z. A. Ragozin.
GERMANY. S. Baring-Gould.
NORWAY. Hjalmar H. Boyesen.
SPAIN. Rev. E. E. and Susan Hale.
HUNGARY. Prof. A. Vámbéry.
CARTHAGE. Prof. Alfred J. Church.
THE SARACENS. Arthur Gilman.
THE MOORS IN SPAIN. Stanley Lane-Poole.
THE NORMANS. Sarah Orne Jewett.
PERSIA. S. G. W. Benjamin.
ANCIENT EGYPT. Prof. Geo. Rawlinson.
ALEXANDER'S EMPIRE. Prof. J. P. Mahaffy.
ASSYRIA. Z. A. Ragozin.
THE GOTHS. Henry Bradley.
IRELAND. Hon. Emily Lawless.
TURKEY. Stanley Lane-Poole.
MEDIA, BABYLON, AND PERSIA. Z. A. Ragozin.
MEDIÆVAL FRANCE. Prof. Gustave Masson.
HOLLAND. Prof. J. Thorold Rogers.
MEXICO. Susan Hale.
PHŒNICIA. George Rawlinson.
THE HANSA TOWNS. Helen Zimmern.
EARLY BRITAIN. Prof. Alfred J. Church.
THE BARBARY CORSAIRS. Stanley Lane-Poole.
RUSSIA. W. R. Morfill.
THE JEWS UNDER ROME. W. D. Morrison.
SCOTLAND. John Mackintosh.
SWITZERLAND. R. Stead and Mrs. A. Hug.
PORTUGAL. H. Morse-Stephens.
THE BYZANTINE EMPIRE. C. W. C. Oman.
SICILY. E. A. Freeman.
THE TUSCAN REPUBLICS. Bella Duffy.
POLAND. W. R. Morfill.
PARTHIA. Geo. Rawlinson.
JAPAN. David Murray.
THE CHRISTIAN RECOVERY OF SPAIN. H. E. Watts.
AUSTRALASIA. Greville Tregarthen.
SOUTHERN AFRICA. Geo. M. Theal.
VENICE. Alethea Wiel.
THE CRUSADES. T. S. Archer and C. L. Kingsford.
VEDIC INDIA. Z. A. Ragozin.
BOHEMIA. C. E. Maurice.
CANADA. J. G. Bourinot.
THE BALKAN STATES. William Miller.
BRITISH RULE IN INDIA. R. W. Frazer.
MODERN FRANCE. André Le Bon.
THE BRITISH EMPIRE. Alfred T. Story. Two vols.
THE FRANKS. Lewis Sergeant.
THE WEST INDIES. Amos K. Fiske.
THE PEOPLE OF ENGLAND. Justin McCarthy, M.P. Two vols.
AUSTRIA. Sidney Whitman.
CHINA. Robt. K. Douglass.
MODERN SPAIN. Major Martin A. S. Hume.
MODERN ITALY. Pietro Orsi.
THE THIRTEEN COLONIES. Helen A. Smith. Two vols.
WALES AND CORNWALL. Owen M. Edwards. Net $1.35.
MEDIÆVAL ROME. Wm. Miller.
THE PAPAL MONARCHY. Wm. Barry.
MEDIÆVAL INDIA. Stanley Lane-Poole.
BUDDHIST INDIA. T. W. Rhys-Davids.